United States Foreign Policy
in the Interwar Period,
1918–1941

Praeger Studies of Foreign Policies of the Great Powers

Italian Foreign Policy in the Interwar Period: 1918–1940
H. James Burgwyn

United States Foreign Policy in the Interwar Period, 1918–1941

The Golden Age of American Diplomatic and Military Complacency

BENJAMIN D. RHODES

Praeger Studies of Foreign Policies of the Great Powers
B.J.C. McKercher and Keith Neilson, Series Editors

Westport, Connecticut
London

Library of Congress Cataloging-in-Publication Data

Rhodes, Benjamin D.
    United States foreign policy in the interwar period, 1918–1941 : the golden age of
American diplomatic and military complacency / Benjamin D. Rhodes.
        p. cm.—(Praeger studies of foreign policies of the great powers, ISSN 1090–8226)
    Includes bibliographical references and index.
    ISBN 0–275–94825–0 (alk. paper)
    1. United States—Foreign relations—20th century.   2. Statesmen–United
States—History—20th century.   3. United States—History, Military—20th century.
4. United States—Foreign relations—20th century—Historiography.   I. Title.
II.   Praeger studies of foreign policies of the great powers.
E744 .R49 2001
327.73—dc21   00–069862

British Library Cataloguing in Publication Data is available.

Library of Congress Catalog Card Number: 00–069862
ISBN: 0–275–94825–0
ISSN: 1090–8226

First published in 2001

Praeger Publishers, 88 Post Road West, Westport, CT 06881
An imprint of Greenwood Publishing Group, Inc.
www.praeger.com

Printed in the United States of America

The paper used in this book complies with the
Permanent Paper Standard issued by the National
Information Standards Organization (Z39.48–1984).

10 9 8 7 6 5 4 3 2 1

Contents

United States Foreign Policy in the Interwar Period: A Historiographical Overview

Veterans of the college classroom have often observed that the very mention of the term "historiography" can cause undergraduate minds to wander and eyes to glaze over. The effect can be especially great when the discussion centers on the historiography of American foreign policy during the interwar period, and for good reason: namely, that the wandering of minds and the closing of eyes is not out of character with the indecisive, directionless, and often shortsighted course of American foreign policy from 1918 to 1941. It was not an era of imaginative, purposeful public diplomacy; on the contrary, the main themes of the era were national introversion, a sullen reaction toward political but not economic or cultural isolation, and general confusion. Historians and students of history like to write and study about bold and dynamic leaders—about winners, not losers. But, in their stewardship of foreign policy, the presidents and secretaries of states of the interwar era were more often losers than winners in that they focused on domestic matters and assigned foreign policy a low priority. Stuck in a historical cycle that was hostile to an extroverted foreign policy, they typically opted for a low-risk strategy of avoiding controversial actions. At critical turning points they often chose to do nothing rather than risk decisive action.

The few triumphs of American diplomacy in the interwar period can be counted on the fingers of one hand: the limitation of battleships—which were practically obsolete—at the Washington Conference of 1921; the Good Neighbor Policy; the signing of an international pact renouncing war, which later proved absurdly unworkable; and the New Deal's belated efforts to encourage and assist Britain on the eve of World War II. Far more numerous were the missed chances of American diplomacy: the failure to join either the League of Nations or the World Court; the failure to maintain amicable Anglo-American, Franco-American, or Soviet-American relations;

and the failure to find workable solutions to such problems as disarmament, war debts, reparations, neutrality, or collective security. American secretaries of state of the interwar era—men who were all products of the legal profession—repeatedly demonstrated an impulse to lecture the rest of the world on the purity of American morals and the need to abide by the rule of law.

For all their lack of foresight, American policy makers of the interwar era could have plausibly denied they had lost sight of basic national interests. Since, according to the conventional wisdom of the day, World War I had been a deviation from a normal pattern of international affairs, America could safely return to traditional policies. The defeat of the Central Powers in the World War effectively eliminated any threat to the western hemisphere. And who in 1918 could have predicted the Great Depression or the rise of fascism in Italy, Germany, and Japan? Even the menace of Bolshevism seemed to diminish following the death of Lenin in 1924. Viewed from a day in which gasoline and diesel vehicles were in their infancy and airplanes could not yet cross the oceans, the very concept of intercontinental ballistic missiles equipped with thermonuclear weapons would have struck readers as an H.G. Wells fantasy. Based on the readily available facts, it seemed reasonable for the United States to mind its own political and military business and avoid binding obligations. Only in retrospect were Americans of the interwar era living in a dream world.

The study of the history of American foreign relations (or diplomatic history, to use an older term) was late in becoming established. It was not until the interwar period that United States diplomatic history emerged as a separate field largely due to the pioneering efforts of such scholars as Samuel Flagg Bemis, Julius W. Pratt, Arthur P. Whitaker, and Thomas A. Bailey. Viewed from a nineteenth-century perspective the lack of attention paid to foreign relations was natural enough since the United States prior to the 1890s was still a minor power economically, politically, and militarily. What appeared historically significant was the winning of independence and the preservation of the union, not struggles over neutral rights and expansion into a largely vacant continent at the expense of Indians and Mexicans. The emergence of the United States as a world power gave the study of foreign relations renewed importance. Interest in the field was stimulated as well by the decisive interventions of the United States in the two world wars. In between those two outbursts of dynamic world involvement lay the dismal interwar period of political, although not cultural or economic, isolation. The crucial but ultimately unanswerable historical question concerning the interwar period is whether the nation's mood of political and military withdrawal represented a normal historical pattern or a deviant historical pattern.

The logical starting point for bibliographical information about American diplomacy is Richard Dean Burns, editor, *Guide to American Foreign Relations since 1700* (Santa Barbara, 1983), which was definitive at the time of its publication, but is badly in need of being brought up to date in general and for the interwar period in particular. For an exhaustive survey of the nuances of recent contributions to the field of interwar American diplomatic history, see Brian McKercher, "Reaching for the Brass Ring: The Recent Historiography of Interwar American Foreign Relations," *Diplomatic History* 15 (Fall, 1991), 565–98. As an analytical concept, the term "interwar period" has, strangely enough, rarely been used by historians. A favorite method of organization has been to present the era from the Peace Conference to the New Deal as a unit; representative examples are Harold U. Faulkner, *From Versailles to the New Deal: A Chronicle of the Harding-Coolidge-Hoover Era* (New Haven, 1950); Allan Nevins, *The United States in a Chaotic World: A Chronicle of International Affairs, 1918–1933* (New Haven, 1950); and Warren Cohen, *Empire Without Tears: America's Foreign Relations, 1921–1933* (New York, 1987). A similar treatment has been to consider the foreign policy of the New Deal as a compact unit. Typical examples are Allan Nevins, *The New Deal and World Affairs: A Chronicle of International Affairs, 1933–1945* (New Haven, 1950); and Robert Dallek, *Franklin D. Roosevelt and American Foreign Policy, 1932–1945* (New York, 1979). Another logical approach has been to cover the era 1921–1933 as a unit as in L. Ethan Ellis, *Republican Foreign Policy, 1921–1933* (New Brunswick, 1968). A further organizational refinement is Selig Adler's survey, *The Uncertain Giant, 1921–1941: American Foreign Policy Between the Wars* (New York, 1965), and especially his *The Isolationist Impulse: Its Twentieth Century Reaction* (New York, 1957), which emphasizes the interwar period while exploring the roots and effects of isolationism from the colonial era to the Eisenhower administration. Another skillful and well-researched survey is Akira Iriye, *The Globalizing of America, 1913–1945* (New York, 1993). The most comprehensive survey of American interwar foreign policy—one which shows that the United States was usually not at the center of world events—is Arnold Offner, *The Origins of the Second World War: American Foreign Policy and World Politics, 1917–1941* (New York, 1975). The author's narrative actually begins four years earlier than the date listed in the title.

The foregoing citations, in common with most works about the interwar period, emphasize specific American foreign policies (e.g., in relation to the League of Nations, the World Court, disarmament, war debts, the neutrality acts, friction with Nazi Germany and the Japanese Empire), as well as the personalities of the various secretaries of state and members of the foreign service. In contrast to the orthodox historical treatment of the interwar period, a revisionist school appeared during the 1950s and 1960s that questioned the basic assumptions and conclusions of previous writers. Instead of portraying the United States as withdrawing from world affairs during the interwar period, revisionist authors saw a nation seeking world stability through vigorous economic expansion in terms of developing markets and investments, in conceiving plans for salvaging German reparations, and in intervening militarily in Russia and Central America. Behind the scenes American foreign policy was shaped by an elite of government officials and representatives of the private sector whose goal was a world governed by the principles of the "open door," as interpreted by the United States. Structural factors are typically presented as being of greater importance than the individual choices of statesmen in directing the nation's drive for economic opportunity and "hegemony." Led by William Appleman Williams, the work of the "Wisconsin School" has concentrated on the last decades of the twentieth century and the period of the Cold War. Possibly revisionist scholarship has given less emphasis to the interwar era than other periods because American administrations, Democratic and Republican, often followed policies (such as maintaining a high tariff and collecting war debts) that were in direct conflict with economic expansion. Another paradox of the period was that American administrations insisted on supporting China instead of Japan even though the Japanese market for American goods was three times that of China's. A frequent complaint of conventional historians has been that revisionist scholarship is often vague in relating specific events and individuals to the overall revisionist interpretation. To critics the revisionist view is too narrow and too often written in an affected and opaque style, while defenders of the faith regard the conventional approach as hopelessly old fashioned and unsophisticated. Practically without exception students of history either love the revisionist interpretation or hate it. The classic revisionist statement was William A. Williams, "The Legend of Isolationism in the 1920's," *Science and Society* 18 (1954), which has been widely reprinted. See also William A. Williams, *The Tragedy of American Diplomacy* (New York, 1972); Carl P. Parrini, *Heir to Empire: United States Economic Diplomacy, 1916–1923* (Pittsburgh, 1969); David S. Fogelsong, *America's Secret War Against Bolshevism: U.S. Intervention in the Russian Civil War, 1917–1920* (Chapel Hill, 1995); Leo J. Bacino, *Reconstructing Russia: U.S. Policy in Revolutionary Russia, 1917–1922* (Kent, Ohio, 1999); Lloyd C. Gardner, *Economic Aspects of New Deal Diplomacy* (Madison, 1964) and *A Covenant with Power: America and World Order from Wilson to Reagan* (New York, 1984). Milder examples of the genre are Frank Castigliola, *Awkward Dominion: American Political, Economic, and Cultural Relations with Europe, 1919–1933* (Ithaca, 1984); Michael J. Hogan, *Informal Entente: The Private Structure of Cooperation in Anglo-American Economic Diplomacy, 1918–1929* (Columbia, 1977); and Joan Hoff Wilson, *American Business and Foreign Policy, 1920–1933* (Lexington, 1973). The concept that the United States entered World War II out of concern for the future of American business and the maintenance of foreign markets is described in Patrick J. Hearden, *Roosevelt Confronts Hitler: America's Entry into World War II* (DeKalb, 1987).

The peacemaking diplomacy of Woodrow Wilson has generated an enormous literature. An excellent starting point is Thomas A. Bailey's two-volume account of Wilson's "supreme act of infanticide," *Woodrow Wilson and the Lost Peace* (New York, 1944) and *Woodrow Wilson and the Great Betrayal* (New York, 1945). Wilson's mistakes and misconceptions are thoughtfully explored in John Milton Cooper, *The Warrior and the Priest* (Cambridge, 1983); Robert H. Ferrell, *Woodrow Wilson and World War I* (New York, 1989); Daniel M. Smith, *The Great Departure: The United States and World War I, 1914–1920* (New York, 1965); and Arthur Walworth, *Wilson and His Peacemakers* (New York, 1966). Specialized aspects of Wilson's peacemaking are covered in Lawrence E. Gelfand, *The Inquiry: American Preparations for Peace, 1917–1919* (New Haven, 1963); Ralph Stone, *The Irreconcilables: The Fight Against the League of Nations* (Lexington, 1970); William C. Widenor, *Henry Cabot Lodge and the Search for an American Foreign Policy* (Berkeley, 1980); and Thomas J. Knock, *To End All Wars: Woodrow Wilson and the Quest for a New World Order* (New York, 1992). Lloyd E. Ambrosius, *Woodrow Wilson and the American Diplomatic Tradition: The Treaty Fight in Perspective* (New York, 1987) explains the president's failure in terms of his inability to appreciate that the modern world was too complex to accept ideas unilaterally championed by Wilson.

The Wilsonian response to Bolshevism is critically explored in George F. Kennan, *Russia Leaves the War* (Princeton, 1956) and *The Decision to Intervene* (Princeton, 1958); John Thompson, *Russia, Bolshevism, and the Versailles Peace* (Princeton, 1967); Peter C. Filene, *Americans and the Soviet Experiment, 1917–1933* (Cambridge, 1967); Benjamin D. Rhodes, *The Anglo-American Winter War with Russia, 1918–1919: A Diplomatic and Military Tragicomedy* (Westport, 1988); Betty Miller Unterberger, *America's Siberian Expedition* (Durham, 1956) and *The United States, Revolutionary Russia, and the Rise of Czechoslovakia* (Chapel Hill, 1989). The diplomacy of Wilson's third secretary of state is surveyed in Daniel M. Smith, *Aftermath of War: Bainbridge Colby and Wilsonian Diplomacy, 1920–1921* (Philadelphia, 1970).

An excellent introduction to the foreign and domestic policies of the 1920s is the generally friendly account of Robert K. Murray, *The Harding Era: Warren G. Harding and His Administration* (Minneapolis, 1969). See also John D. Hicks, *Republican Ascendancy, 1921–1933* (New York, 1960); and Eugene P. Trani and David L. Wilson, *The Presidency of Warren G. Harding* (Lawrence, 1977). For the Washington Conference the standard surveys are Thomas H. Buckley, *The United States and the Washington Conference, 1921–1922* (Knoxville, 1970); and Roger Dingman, *Power in the Pacific: The Origins of Naval Arms Limitation* (Chicago, 1972). Charles Evans Hughes is praised for his foresight in Merlo J. Pusey, *Charles Evans*

Hughes, 2 vols. (New York, 1951), and criticized for a glaring lack of fore-sight in Betty Glad, *Charles Evans Hughes and the Illusions of Innocence* (Urbana, 1966). The role of Frank B. Kellogg is presented critically in L. Ethan Ellis, *Frank B. Kellogg and American Foreign Relations, 1925–1929* (New Brunswick, 1961); Kellogg is largely rehabilitated in Robert H. Ferrell, *Frank B. Kellogg and Henry L. Stimson* (New York, 1963), a volume in the definitive series "The American Secretaries of State and Their Diplomacy." Calvin Coolidge and foreign affairs is covered briefly in Claude M. Fuess, *Calvin Coolidge: The Man from Vermont* (Westport, 1976, reprint of 1939 edition); in detail in Donald R. McCoy, *Calvin Coolidge: The Quiet President* (New York, 1967); and in Robert H. Ferrell, *The Presidency of Calvin Coolidge* (Lawrence, 1998).

Most specialized studies of foreign policy in the 1920s are user-friendly and are empirical rather than ideological. For economic diplomacy, see: Bruce Kent, *The Spoils of War: The Politics, Economics, and Diplomacy of Reparations, 1918–1932* (Oxford, 1989); Melvyn P. Leffler, *The Elusive Quest: America's Pursuit of European Stability and French Security, 1919–1933* (Chapel Hill, 1979); Stephen A. Schuker, *The End of French Predominance in Europe: The Financial Crisis of 1924 and the Adoption of the Dawes Plan* (Chapel Hill, 1976); and Marc Trachtenberg, *Reparation in World Politics: France and European Economic Diplomacy, 1916–1923* (New York, 1980). For American policy toward Latin America, see Kenneth J. Grieb, *The Latin American Policy of Warren G. Harding* (Fort Worth, 1977); William Kamman, *A Search for Stability: United States Diplomacy toward Nicaragua, 1925–1933* (Notre Dame, Indiana, 1968); Walter LaFeber, *Inevitable Revolutions: The United States in Central America* (New York, 1993); Lester D. Langley, *The United States and the Caribbean, 1900–1970* (Athens, 1980); and Ivan Musicant, *The Banana Wars: A History of United States Military Intervention in Latin America from the Spanish-American War to the Invasion of Panama* (New York, 1990). For American policy toward the Soviet Union, see Robert J. Maddox, *William E. Borah and American Foreign Policy* (Baton Rouge, 1969); James K. Libbey, *Alexander Gumberg and Soviet-American Relations, 1917–1933* (Lexington, 1977); Benjamin D. Rhodes, *James P. Goodrich: Indiana's "Governor Strangelove": A Republican's Infatuation with Soviet Russia* (Selinsgrove, Pennsylvania, 1996); Benjamin Weissman, *Herbert Hoover and Famine Relief to the Soviet Union, 1921–1923* (Stanford, 1974); and Joan Hoff Wilson, *Ideology and Economics: United States Relations with the Soviet Union, 1918–1933* (Columbia, 1974). For the Pact of Paris the standard monograph is Robert H. Ferrell, *Peace in Their Time: The Origins of the Kellogg-Briand Pact* (New Haven, 1952). The peace movement is surveyed by Charles Chatfield, *For Peace and Justice* (Knoxville, 1971), and Charles De Benedetti, *Origins of the Modern American Peace Movement* (Millwood, New York, 1978). New insights explaining the failure of the 1927 Geneva Conference are contained in B.J.C. McKercher, *The Second Baldwin Government and the United States, 1924–1929: Attitudes and Diplomacy* (New York, 1984).

The collapse of the Great Depression placed President Herbert Hoover and Secretary of State Henry L. Stimson in the unenviable position of trying to salvage as much as possible of the system of debts, disarmament, and peace established by their Republican predecessors. Still the best overall survey is Robert H. Ferrell, *American Diplomacy in the Great Depression: Hoover-Stimson Foreign Policy, 1929–1933* (New Haven, 1957). The role of Henry L. Stimson is critically reviewed in Richard N. Current, *Secretary Stimson: A Study in Statecraft* (New Brunswick, 1954), and praised in Elting Morison, *Turmoil and Tradition: The Life and Times of Henry L. Stimson* (Boston, 1960). Hoover's role in launching the Good Neighbor Policy is favorably reviewed in Alexander DeConde, *Herbert Hoover's Latin American Policy* (Stanford, 1951). The Hoover-Stimson balancing act in the field of disarmament is capably discussed in Raymond G. O'Connor, *Perilous Equilibrium: The United States and the London Naval Conference of 1930* (Lawrence, 1962). For the collapse of war debts and reparations see Edward W. Bennett, *Germany and the Diplomacy of the Financial Crisis, 1931* (Cambridge, 1962); Patricia Clavin, *The Failure of Economic Diplomacy: Britain, Germany, France and the United States, 1931–1936* (New York, 1997); Louis P. Lochner, *Herbert Hoover and Germany* (New York, 1960); and Manfred Jonas, *The United States and Germany: A Diplomatic History* (Ithaca, 1984). The moralistic response of Hoover and Stimson to the Manchurian Crisis has been universally criticized as ineffective, although critics assiduously avoid the question of what options were practical given the debacle of the Great Depression. Representative studies on the subject are Sara R. Smith, *The Manchurian Crisis, 1931–1932: A Tragedy in International Relations,* (New York, 1948); Akira Iriye, *After Imperialism: The Search for a New Order in the Far East, 1921–1931* (Cambridge, 1965); Christopher Thorne, *The Limits of Foreign Policy: The West, the League, and the Far Eastern Crisis of 1931–1932* (London, 1972); Armin Rappaport, *Henry L. Stimson and Japan* (Chicago, 1973); Justus D. Doenecke, *When the Wicked Rise* (Lewisburg, Pennsylvania, 1984); Takehiko Yoshihashi, *Conspiracy at Mukden: The Rise of the Japanese Military* (New Haven, 1963); Michael Barnhart, *Japan Prepares for Total War* (Ithaca, 1987); and Walter LaFeber, *The Clash: A History of U.S.-Japan Relations* (New York, 1997).

In contrast to the energetic domestic policy of the New Deal, Roosevelt's foreign policy prior to 1937 often consisted of a series of hastily improvised responses to individual problems. The Good Neighbor Policy was one of the few New Deal foreign policies with a long-range focus. Understandably writers have been more attracted to the more dynamic years after 1937, and correspondingly the list of works emphasizing early New Deal diplomacy is a slim one. There are two major overviews: Robert Dallek, *Franklin D. Roosevelt and American Foreign Policy, 1932–1945* (New York, 1979); and Frederick W. Marks III, *Wind Over Sand: The Diplomacy of Franklin Roosevelt* (Athens, 1988). Both works are based on extensive research, but they reach opposite conclusions. Dallek presents Roosevelt as intensely involved in all aspects of the foreign policy making process, as a master politician who saw the need to build a consensus before taking bold steps, and as a leader who was occasionally devious in explaining his policies because he feared political reprisals from isolationists of both parties. That latter characteristic, Dallek concedes, set an unfortunate precedent for devious actions by subsequent presidents on behalf of causes that were not so vital to America's national interest as Roosevelt's opposition to European and Far Eastern fascism. Marks, on the other hand, portrays Roosevelt as an ineffective and clumsy dilettante who did little to fight isolationism and who often made promises that were impossible to keep. He finds that Roosevelt's Good Neighbor Policy, despite its success in America, signally failed to win the respect of Latin Americans. Worst of all was Roosevelt's ambiguous and contradictory Far Eastern policy that left Japan confused and convinced that America intended to drive Japan into a corner. Marks does not question Roosevelt's patriotism but his effectiveness. Perhaps the next logical step for future students of New Deal foreign policy is an interpretation somewhere between Dallek and Marks.

Detailed and generally favorable accounts of early New Deal foreign policy can be found in Frank Freidel, *Franklin D. Roosevelt: Launching the New Deal* (Boston, 1973); William E. Leuchtenburg, *Franklin D. Roosevelt and the New Deal, 1932–1940* (New York, 1963); and Arthur M. Schlesinger, Jr., *The Coming of the New Deal* (Boston, 1959). Roosevelt's feud with the isolationists, which explains much of his early foreign policy timidity, has been explored by Wayne Cole in a series of well-researched and clearly written studies: *Roosevelt and the Isolationists* (Lincoln, 1983); *Gerald P. Nye and American Foreign Relations* (Minneapolis, 1962); and *Charles A. Lindbergh and the Battle Against American Intervention in World War II* (New York, 1974). See also Manfred Jonas, *Isolationism in America, 1935–1941* (Ithaca, 1966). Roosevelt's Good Neighbor policy is covered in detail by Irwin F. Gellman, *Good Neighbor Diplomacy: United States Policies in Latin America, 1933–1945* (Baltimore, 1979); *Roosevelt and Batista: Good Neighbor Diplomacy in Cuba, 1933–1945* (Albuquerque, 1973); Lester D. Langley, *The United States and the Caribbean, 1900–1970* (Athens, 1980); Donald Dozer, *Are We Good Neighbors? Three Decades of Inter-American Relations* (Gainesville, 1959); Bryce Wood, *The Making of the Good Neighbor Policy* (New York, 1961); E. David Cronon, *Josephus Daniels in Mexico* (Madison, 1960); Frederick B. Pike, *FDR's Good Neighbor Policy: Sixty Years of Generally Gentle Chaos* (Austin, 1995); and Eric Paul Roorda, *The Dictator Next Door: The Good Neigh-*

bor Policy and the Trujillo Regime in the Dominican Republic, 1930–1945 (Durham, 1998).

The inner workings of Roosevelt's State Department are explored by Martin Weil, *A Pretty Good Club: The Founding Fathers of the U.S. Foreign Service* (New York, 1978); and Irwin Gellman, *Secret Affairs: Franklin Roosevelt, Cordell Hull, and Sumner Welles* (Baltimore, 1995). Many of the participants in the making of New Deal foreign policy have written autobiographies or have been the subject of biographies: Cordell Hull, *The Memoirs of Cordell Hull*, 2 vols. (New York, 1948) wearies readers by reproducing practically every memorandum contained in Hull's voluminous papers and by projecting an image of self-righteousness; Raymond Moley, *After Seven Years* (New York, 1939) defends and rationalizes his brief performance as assistant secretary of state; Julius W. Pratt, *Cordell Hull, 1933–1944* (New York, 1964) generally praises Hull, but finds his moral preaching tiresome; the role of Ambassador to Japan Joseph C. Grew is favorably portrayed in Waldo Heinrichs, *American Ambassador: Joseph C. Grew and the Development of the American Diplomatic Tradition* (Boston, 1966); Roosevelt's outspoken Ambassador to Germany is assessed in Robert Dallek, *Democrat and Diplomat: The Life of William E. Dodd* (New York, 1968); the checkered career of the longtime chairman of the Senate Foreign Relations Committee is the subject of Betty Glad, *Key Pittman: The Tragedy of a Senate Insider* (New York, 1986); and the pivotal role of Harry Hopkins is documented in the classic biography by Robert E. Sherwood, *Roosevelt and Hopkins: An Intimate History* (New York, 1948).

The American response to the initial phase of the fascist challenge in Europe is surveyed in Brice Harris, *The United States and the Italo-Ethiopian War* (Stanford, 1964); David F. Schmitz, *The United States and Fascist Italy, 1922–1940* (Chapel Hill, 1988); Richard Traina, *American Diplomacy and the Spanish Civil War* (Bloomington, 1968); Arnold A. Offner, *American Appeasement: United States Foreign Policy and Germany, 1933–1938* (Cambridge, 1969); James V. Compton, *The Swastika and the Eagle: Hitler, the United States and the Origins of World War II* (Boston, 1967); and Robert A. Divine, *The Illusion of Neutrality: Franklin D. Roosevelt and the Struggle over the Arms Embargo* (Chicago, 1962). Roosevelt's decision to recognize the Soviet Union and his subsequent disillusionment are well covered in Edward M. Bennett, *Recognition of Russia: An American Foreign Policy Dilemma* (Waltham, Massachusetts, 1970) and *Franklin D. Roosevelt and the Search for Security: American-Soviet Relations, 1933–1939* (Wilmington, Delaware, 1985); Thomas R. Maddux, *Years of Estrangement: American Relations with the Soviet Union* (Gainesville, 1980); and Hugh De Santis, *The Diplomacy of Silence: The American Foreign Service, the Soviet Union, and the Cold War, 1933–1947* (Chicago, 1980).

With the exception of Marks, most recent students of New Deal foreign policy have concurred with Dallek's assessment of Roosevelt as an astute and statesmanlike leader. Examples include Waldo Heinrichs, *Threshold of War: Franklin D. Roosevelt and American Entry into World War II* (New York, 1988), a massively researched work; Warren F. Kimball, *The Juggler: Franklin Roosevelt as Wartime Statesman* (Princeton, 1991); and Doris Kearns Goodwin, *No Ordinary Times; Franklin and Eleanor Roosevelt: The Home Front in World War II* (New York, 1994). The complexities of Anglo-American relations and the Roosevelt-Churchill collaboration are laid out in David Reynolds, *The Creation of the Anglo-American Alliance, 1937–1941: A Study in Competitive Cooperation* (Chapel Hill, 1981) and *Lord Lothian and Anglo-American Relations, 1939–1940* (Philadelphia, 1983); B.J.C. McKercher, *Transition of Power: Britain's Loss of Global Preeminence to the United States, 1930–1945* (New York, 1999); James R. Leutze, *Bargaining for Supremacy: Anglo-American Naval Collaboration, 1937–1941* (Chapel Hill, 1971); Theodore A. Wilson, *The First Summit: Roosevelt and Churchill at Placentia Bay, 1941* (Lawrence, 1991); and William R. Rock, *Chamberlain and Roosevelt: British Foreign Policy and the United States, 1937–1941* (Columbus, 1988).

American diplomacy and the Far Eastern crisis is typically approached by studying United States policy toward China and Japan, either together or in combination with the Pearl Harbor attack. Outstanding studies on China policy are: Dorothy Borg, *The United States and the Far Eastern Crisis of 1933–1938: From the Manchurian Incident through the Initial Stage of the Undeclared Sino-Japanese War* (Cambridge, 1964); Russell D. Buhite, *Nelson T. Johnson and American Policy Toward China* (East Lansing, 1968); Akira Iriye, *The Origins of the Second World War in Asia and the Pacific* (London, 1978); and Michael Schaller, *The U.S. Crusade in China* (New York, 1979). That the deterioration of United States–Japanese relations was the product of complex, cross-cultural forces is the theme of Dorothy Borg and Shumpei Okamoto, editors, *Pearl Harbor as History: Japanese-American Relations, 1931–1941* (New York, 1973). One of the factors contributing to the collision course in the Pacific was the naval race, which is convincingly documented in Stephen Pelz, *Race to Pearl Harbor: The Failure of the Second London Naval Conference and the Onset of World War II* (Cambridge, 1974). The competence of American and Japanese negotiators was seriously questioned by Robert J.C. Butow, *The John Doe Associates: Backdoor Diplomacy for Peace, 1941* (Stanford, 1974). For the fascinating story of a would-be peacemaker, see Sandra C. Taylor, *Advocate of Understanding: Sidney Gulick and the Search for Peace with Japan* (Kent, 1984). Jonathan G. Utley, *Going to War with Japan, 1937–1941* (Knoxville, 1985) is highly critical of Cordell Hull, contending that the secretary of state exhibited symptoms of "burnout" and did not seriously pursue a *modus vivendi* in November 1941.

Despite the best efforts of professional historians, the Pearl Harbor conspiracy thesis, originally identified with Charles A. Beard, refuses to die—

at least on a popular level. Beard initiated the debate when he published *President Roosevelt and the Coming of the War, 1941: A Study in Appearances and Realities* (New Haven, 1948), accusing Roosevelt of deliberately deceiving the American people about his goals and objectives. Instead of leading America into war, he mendaciously evaded the Constitution and paved the way for a future dictatorship. Better researched and cleverly written was Charles C. Tansill, *Back Door to War: The Roosevelt Foreign Policy, 1933–1941* (Chicago, 1952), charging Roosevelt with inviting a Japanese attack after Hitler failed to respond to American provocations in the Atlantic. Even more explicit was Robert A. Theobald, *The Final Secret of Pearl Harbor* (New York, 1954), who claimed that Roosevelt deliberately sacrificed the Pacific Fleet to unify public opinion and destroy isolationism. The assault of the conspiracy writers produced a frenzied counteroffensive by conventional historians who viewed the conspiracy thesis as based on innuendo, circumstantial evidence, and distortions of the facts. Among the best known of the conventional writers are William L. Langer and S. Everett Gleason, *The Challenge to Isolation: The World Crisis of 1937–1940* (New York, 1952) and *The Undeclared War, 1940–1941* (New York, 1953); Herbert Feis, *The Road to Pearl Harbor: The Coming of the War between the United States and Japan* (Princeton, 1950); Roberta Wohlstetter, *Pearl Harbor: Warning and Decision* (Stanford, 1962); and Gordon Prange, *At Dawn We Slept: The Untold Story of Pearl Harbor* (New York, 1981) and *Pearl Harbor: The Verdict of History* (New York, 1986). All find the conspiracy thesis as lacking even a shred of solid evidence and assign the blame for the conflict upon the Nazi and Japanese leaders; they place much of the responsibility for the Pearl Harbor attack upon the complacent military commanders. In effect, say conventional historians, the conspiracy theorists are asking the public to believe that the United States government, which has difficulty delivering the mail and keeping Social Security payments in order, can permanently and effectively suppress all evidence of an elaborate and treasonous scheme. Conceivably, future conspiracy buffs will argue that the lack of evidence only proves how clever and diabolical the evil plotters were.

If there is one thing that all commentators can agree on about United States foreign policy during the interwar period, it is that it was a time when a great many well-intentioned policies went awry. Although there is always room for revisionism, it is difficult to imagine a portrayal of American diplomacy from 1918 to 1941 as a bright, shining example of what should be done in the future.

CHAPTER 2

Wilson and Democratic Peacemaking: A Tragic Beginning to the Interwar Era

Until 7:55 A.M. (Hawaii time) on December 7, 1941, the most important date to Americans of the interwar generation was November 11, 1918. Armistice Day promptly became an emotional national day of remembrance, and in recognition of Germany's capitulation American school children were often instructed to face the east while observing a solemn moment of silence. The humiliation of Germany was savored all the more because American and British propaganda had successfully portrayed Germany as evil incarnate. The signing of the armistice meant that the forces of righteousness and democracy had triumphed over rapacious Huns and the "Beast of Berlin."

America's participation in the "World War," as contemporaries called it, marked a dramatic departure in the nation's traditional foreign policy role. Prior to the conflict the United States had enjoyed a platonic political relationship with Europe. In effect, Europe was held at arm's length as America expanded across a largely vacant continent at the expense of Indian tribes, Mexico, and Spain. America's sense of security was reinforced by the geographical isolation of the western hemisphere and by the primitive state of nineteenth-century military technology. Not even Britain, the arch foe of America, was able to annex territory during the ill-advised War of 1812, and it was Britain that blinked in crises with the United States over Maine, Oregon, and Civil War disputes over commerce raiders constructed by Britain for the Confederacy. Then, quite unexpectedly, at the turn of the century, hatred of Britain faded substantially as the United States and Britain discovered common interests; "hands across the sea" replaced "the ancient grudge."

The Anglo-American rapprochement coincided with America's transition from a minor power to almost a major power. When World War I broke out, the population of the United States numbered about 100 million, more than triple the population during the Civil War era. In terms of industry America had not just matched Europe but surpassed the Old World by every measure of productivity, especially steel tonnage. Only militarily was the United States less than a major power. To be sure, the "new navy" of the 1880s and 1890s had easily vanquished weak Spain in the "splendid little war" of April–August 1898. Typically, American naval planners in 1917 were well enough prepared to fight the last war—a battleship conflict in the Caribbean—but the navy was woefully short of destroyers with which to conduct anti-submarine warfare. Apart from the meaningless dispatch of eight battleships to the North Sea, the American naval contribution to the Allied cause was limited to the development of new mining technology and participation in the development of the convoy system for escorting shipping through danger zones. As had been the case when the Spanish-American War broke out in 1898, the United States Army found itself in an embarrassing situation. In every respect—organization, strategy, training, equipment, and numbers—the Americans were behind the times. Inferior to the armed forces of even Portugal, the United States Army ranked just seventeenth among world armies. The German General Staff thought so little of America's military prowess that it embarked on unrestricted submarine warfare, not caring that it would certainly bring the United States into the conflict on the Allied side.

Loans were the most immediate contribution the United States could make to the common war effort. And the Allies, recalled Treasury Secretary William G. McAdoo, were "at their wits end for money."[1] Private bankers, according to one of J.P. Morgan's partners, had "scraped the bottom of the box.... You people in the Treasury must now bear the whole burden."[2] McAdoo's response was a brilliant improvisation: the Liberty Loan program. Through funds raised by selling bonds to the American people, McAdoo was able to loan twenty foreign governments $10.3 billion, an immense sum for the time. More than ninety percent of this sum was loaned to Britain, France, and Italy. In his war message, to applause, President Woodrow Wilson endorsed extending "the most liberal financial credits" to nations at war with Germany.[3] Tactfully, Wilson chose not to mention that, in view of America's colossal lack of preparation, financial assistance was the only alternative available.

To the surprise of everyone, especially the German General Staff, the United States played a decisive role in the struggle. Practically overnight an American Expeditionary Force—two million men strong—was drafted, trained, and shipped to France. Whether the first doughboys to land actually said, "Lafayette, we are here," is apocryphal, but those forty-two American divisions doomed the German war effort. The large scale American deployment in the spring and summer of 1918 probably saved Paris from German capture and contributed to slumping German morale. Strangely the victorious Allied coalition was organized on an informal basis.

In keeping with America's tradition of aloofness, the nation had eschewed formal alliances (with the exception of the Franco-American Alliance of 1778). Technically France and Britain were only associates of the United States in the war, not allies. When Germany, nearing collapse on November 11, 1918, was forced to request an armistice, the United States was indisputably an international power of the first rank. From a geopolitical perspective the United States was well positioned to fill the power vacuum left by the collapse of the great European empires in Germany, Austria-Hungary, and Russia. For the United States the real question of the interwar era was whether the nation would continue its wartime role of international participation or revert to its former tradition of platonic nonentanglement.

The provincial innocence of America in general was also shared by the Democrat who occupied the White House when the United States intervened on the Allied side in April 1917. The son of a Presbyterian minister from Staunton, Virginia, Wilson was precocious (once he overcame a disability that retarded his learning to read), politically and professionally ambitious, gifted as a writer, and infinitely complex mentally. He was one of the best educated of American presidents, possessing a bachelor's degree from Princeton University, legal training at the University of Virginia (although he never completed his law degree), and a Ph.D. from Johns Hopkins University. Prior to his election as governor of New Jersey in 1910, Wilson achieved brilliant success as a scholar and teacher at Princeton University. His climb up the academic ladder culminated in his selection as Princeton's president in 1902. In his turbulent eight years in that position, Wilson strove mightily to build his alma mater into the foremost American institution of higher learning. In the process Wilson stepped on toes and fought bitter, long-drawn-out battles over such seemingly trivial issues as the abolition of Princeton's eating clubs and the location of a new graduate school building. In both cases he displayed headstrong determination, a stubborn disinclination to compromise, and an occasional loss of poise. Whether Wilson's somewhat puzzling tenure as president of Princeton University was a product of his personality or his neurological health is a subject upon which there is no agreement among scholars.

In 1912 Wilson, a decided underdog and outsider, had the good fortune to win the Democratic nomination for president. He was also unbelievably lucky that the Republican split between William Howard Taft and Theodore Roosevelt occurred when it did; it was a rupture which made possible Wilson's victory in the electoral college, even though he did not win the popular vote. As a university president and state governor, Wilson had had little previous exposure to foreign policy. Thus it was the irony of fate, as he himself had remarked prior to his inauguration, that he had to deal chiefly with foreign affairs. Essentially he approached foreign policy as a moralistic defender of democracy and Christian values, but he was not a pacifist. Prior to joining the Allied coalition against Germany, Wilson had demonstrated his missionary impulse by approving military interventions in Mexico, Haiti, and the Dominican Republic. In the summer of 1918 he had also agreed to participate in the weak Allied intervention in Russia, theoretically limiting the American role to that of noncombatants. His reluctant decision to join the Russian intervention had less to do with moral considerations than with checking German expansion and cooperating with other members of the Allied coalition. To portray Wilson as an uncompromising idealist who thought only in terms of morals and never took account of practical considerations would be misleading. Often in his political career he had compromised, and during the two and a half years of American neutrality he was often receptive to realistic arguments phrased in moral terminology. One of the most critical foreign policy questions of the interwar period was whether Wilson, who had already decided to attend the Paris Peace Conference, would approach the postwar world as the practical, flexible statesman who had skillfully maneuvered through Congress a sweeping program of progressive reform, or follow the rigid, headstrong pattern associated with his presidency of Princeton University.

Wilson should have been well equipped to direct American postwar foreign policy. In his celebrated Fourteen Points address (January 8, 1918), he had singlehandedly conceived and enunciated the Allied peace program. The most important of Wilson's points were: (1) open covenants of peace, openly arrived at; (2) absolute freedom of the seas; (3) the removal of economic barriers; (4) the reduction of armaments to the lowest point consistent with domestic safety; (5) self-determination of nations, a principle Wilson wished to apply to colonial claims and to the territories of Russia, Belgium, France, Italy, Austria-Hungary, Rumania, Serbia, Montenegro, the Ottoman Empire, and Poland; and (6) a general association of nations "for the purpose of affording mutual guarantees of political independence and territorial integrity to great and small states alike."[4] The idealistic Fourteen Points represented Wilson's missionary conception of America's proper role in the world. The goals he outlined were primarily moral, rather than concrete, expressions of national interest (except for such specific objectives as the evacuation of Russia, Rumania, Serbia, and Montenegro; independence for Poland; and the return of Alsace-Lorraine to France). Conceived by one man, the Fourteen Points amounted to a revolution in America's political relations with the rest of the world. No longer would international relations be regulated by the old-fashioned balance of power, but by a league of nations. The most precarious aspect of Wilson's program was that its success depended upon the political fortunes and health of its author.

In conducting foreign policy Wilson often acted as his own secretary of state as he bypassed William Jennings Bryan, the first occupant of that post. Bryan proved well intentioned but out of his depth as the premier member of the cabinet. After Bryan's resignation in the summer of 1915 during the *Lusitania* crisis, in which 1,198 persons died, Wilson chose as Bryan's successor the State Department's number two man, Robert Lansing. Once again Wilson proved less than a good judge of men, since Lansing, a realist in the tradition of Admiral Alfred Thayer Mahan, was philosophically out of step with the missionary approach of the president. Trained as an international lawyer, and married to the daughter of a former secretary of state, Lansing reached the height of his influence during the years of American neutrality. As an expert on international law, Lansing was in his element during the neutrality period. Like Wilson, Lansing was strongly pro-Allied and he steered Wilson toward endorsing neutrality policies that tilted toward the Allies. Lansing's view, which he confided to his diary, was that America's ideals, security, and basic national interests could not tolerate a decisive German victory. Lansing's influence was on the wane at the time of the Armistice as he was increasingly out of sympathy with Wilson's soaring idealism.

Wilson's closest foreign policy adviser and confidant was the enigmatic and wealthy Colonel Edward M. House of Texas. The two men first met in 1911 and immediately became close personal friends. House, who had many contacts in the Democratic Party, helped make Wilson acceptable to the Bryan wing of the party. Wilson consulted him on all important policies and appointments and twice sent House to Europe on futile mediation missions. Those who worked closely with the intense chief executive found it notoriously difficult to keep in his good graces. Colonel House, however, succeeded brilliantly in establishing himself as Wilson's second personality by concealing disputes and offering tactful, indirect suggestions. Wilson was apparently unaware of the manipulative tendencies of his seemingly disinterested adviser. His second wife, Edith, whom the widowed president married in 1915, justifiably distrusted the honorary Texas colonel. At the time of the Armistice, House's influence with Wilson was slowly diminishing as the president more and more assumed personal, solitary direction of the peace process.

The war ended so suddenly in 1918 that many important decisions had to be improvised. One example was the Armistice agreement, which required the better part of a month to complete. In the process the Allies reluctantly accepted the Fourteen Points, although Britain filed a reservation concerning freedom of the seas, and France insisted that Germany must pay reparations for the reconstruction of the devastated regions. With these exceptions, the Germans, who agreed to evacuate Allied territory and surrender huge amounts of equipment and ammunition, were promised a peace treaty based on Wilson's program. Such a peace would have been difficult to achieve had the conference been held on Mt. Olympus; Paris, the location accepted by Wilson, was far too partisan a location. Only the Constitution and not Wilson could be blamed for the timing of the national mid-term elections on November 6, 1918. Responding to the pleas of congressional Democrats, Wilson called on the American people to return a Democratic majority to both houses. Conceivably he could have been less forthright in his appeal, but he could hardly have sat on his hands without badly damaging his status as head of the Democratic Party. In twentieth-century American politics, the party out of power normally gained seats during midterm elections. That the Republicans narrowly gained control of both houses of Congress should not have been a great surprise under the circumstances. Had Wilson been luckier, and the conflict prolonged another month or so, the election result might have been far different. Wilson would then have presented a peace treaty to a Senate organized by his party rather than one dominated by its new majority leader, Senator Henry Cabot Lodge of Massachusetts.

Even before the election Wilson told his cabinet that he intended to attend the Peace Conference in person. The mission Wilson was about to undertake was as formidable as any faced by any American leader in all of United States diplomatic history. Unlike McKinley in 1898, Wilson was not dictating terms to a defeated opponent. Rather in 1919 Wilson's task was to negotiate with a coalition of jealous powers with the ultimate objective of presenting a final treaty to the Central Powers. Only in theory did the Allies support Wilson's Fourteen Points. Furthermore, the defeat of the common enemy removed much of the reason for the very existence of the uneasy Allied coalition in the first place. And, in a series of secret treaties, the Allies had agreed to divide much of the territory of the Central Powers, especially in the Adriatic region, the Alps, and the Pacific islands owned by Germany. (Wilson probably stretched the truth when he later told the Senate Foreign Relations Committee that he had no knowledge of the secret treaties before arriving at Paris.) Somehow Wilson was to produce on the basis of the Fourteen Points a treaty that was acceptable to the rapacious Allies and the emerging nationalities of Europe, and then convince a Senate controlled by the Republican Party to give its advice and consent to a document establishing a vaguely defined league of nations. The wonder is not that Wilson failed to achieve his objectives, but that he came as close as he did.

Military history is replete with examples of wars that were lost because of overconfidence, arrogance, and conceit. Wilson's campaign on behalf of the Fourteen Points was hampered by similar miscalculations. His decision to go to Paris was made without consultation with either Democrats or Republicans and left Wilson open to the charge that he had a "messiah complex." Illinois Senator Lawrence Y. Sherman was so outraged that he introduced a ridiculous resolution that would have stripped Wilson of his power as president once he left the North American continent and transferred all presidential authority to the vice president. Wilson's selection of a five-man delegation headed by himself was likewise a solitary decision.

Besides Wilson, the American commissioners were Secretary of State Lansing, Colonel House, General Tasker Bliss, and Henry White. Only White, a retired career diplomat, belonged to the Republican Party. Lansing had long since lost Wilson's confidence, and House was about to suffer the same fate. Bliss had served as the American representative on the Supreme War Council in Paris, earning Wilson's admiration as "a real thinking man who takes the pains to think straight."[5] Afterward it was a common criticism of Wilson that he should have named a stronger delegation and, in particular, should have selected some representatives of the opposition. In a sense, the strength of the delegation or lack thereof was irrelevant since Wilson intended to undertake much of the negotiation himself. Since the forthcoming peace treaty required the advice and consent of two-thirds of the Senate, Wilson's almost arrogant neglect of that body is inexplicable. Perhaps no major Republicans would have agreed to accompany Wilson to Paris, but he did not even give them an opportunity to turn him down.

In the days immediately before his departure Wilson lost other opportunities for ingratiating himself with the Senate. On December 2, 1918, Wilson delivered his State of the Union message before a joint session of Congress, but made only a few passing references to the Senate and foreign policy. Afterward critics, not unreasonably, said Wilson had given neither a convincing nor a candid explanation as to why his trip was necessary. Wilson's explanation that he was going to defend the Fourteen Points and to ensure that American soldiers had not died in vain struck such senators as Hiram Johnson of California and James A. Reed as egotistical posturing. Presumably Wilson, prior to sailing, could have sought to flatter senatorial egos by soliciting senators' advice, or by possibly holding forth the lure of federal projects or appointments. Never one to pander to the opposition, Wilson probably would have regarded such conduct as unworthy of the presidency and as the worst form of ambulance chasing. Still, his failure to reach out to the Republicans meant that he went abroad without having a clear political strategy for securing Senate approval of the peace treaty.

When Wilson sailed for Europe on December 4, 1918, on board the former German liner *George Washington*, he was embarking upon the most daunting mission ever undertaken by an American president. He aimed at nothing less than altering, personally and permanently, the course of world history. He would commit the United States to an internationalist foreign policy through membership in a league of nations drawn to his specifications, then include the league in a peace treaty based on the Fourteen Points, so as to make it as awkward as possible for the Senate to reject it. For such an ambitious program Wilson was surprisingly short of strategy and specific preparation. Presumably Wilson could have used the voyage to study the recommendations of the American academic experts known as the Inquiry.

With Wilson's approval, Colonel House had assembled at a New York City office building owned by the National Geographical Society a prestigious group of scholars who were to do research on problems relating to the forthcoming peace settlement. Twenty-three members of the group were taken to Paris, including such luminaries as George Louis Beer, Stanley K. Hornbeck, Sidney Mezes, Charles Seymour, and James T. Shotwell. Meeting with Wilson on board the *George Washington*, the members found Wilson to be alternately witty, charming, and arrogantly self-righteous. But at the same time Wilson preferred to lecture rather than to listen. Once in Paris the experts and the American commissioners found they had little of substance to do since Wilson, playing a solitary and secretive role, intended to make all major decisions himself. For the American delegation the Paris Peace Conference was a continuous puzzle because only the president and Colonel House knew what was going on. However, the early arrival of the American delegation on December 13 meant that Wilson had sufficient time for state tours of Britain, France, and Italy. But the tours were physically wearing on a man who was not robust and consumed time that might have been used in preparing intellectually and emotionally for the conference.

Not until January 12 did the conference hold its opening session. At first the gathering of twenty-seven nations groped along, entrusting the initial decisions to a Council of Ten (consisting of two representatives each from the United States, Britain, Japan, France, and Italy) and the Commission on the League of Nations. For the camera the victorious leaders appeared playful, collegial, and relaxed. And it is true that initially there were fewer personality conflicts and power clashes than later. Obsessively and with outward success Wilson threw his energies into achieving his life's goal of creating a league of nations and integrating it into the peace treaty. Wilson amiably shared authorship of the Covenant of the League of Nations with Jan Christian Smuts of the Union of South Africa and Britain's Lord Robert Cecil. Probably the work would not have gone so smoothly had British Prime Minister David Lloyd George and French Premier Georges Clemenceau participated. But Lloyd George, a crafty political opportunist and expert debater, and Clemenceau (whose anti-Americanism was derived in part from a failed marriage to a young student of French from Wisconsin) declined to serve on the drafting commission.

The least controversial features of the Covenant were: an assembly, a council dominated by five permanent members, and a secretariat to provide administration. Article X was, in Wilson's opinion, "the heart" of the document. It read simply: "The members of the League undertake to respect and preserve as against external aggression the territorial and existing political independence of all members of the League."[6] Apparently blinded by a combination of self-righteousness and stubbornness, Wilson did not consult with his fellow commissioners, House excepted, regarding the wording of Article X. No president has ever made a greater error in judgment. By insisting on a league dedicated to enforcing peace through collective security he was committing the nation to a fundamental shift in the direction of its foreign policy. Was it really necessary to spell out such details in the Covenant? Wilson contended it was and thereby handed his opponents a golden opportunity to discredit him. Inexplicably Wilson had played into the hands of his Republican opponents at home.

How much wiser Wilson would have been to have listened to the counsel of Secretary of State Robert Lansing. Instead the single-minded president shunned Lansing's suggestions and often kept him in ignorance of the most basic information. First of all, Lansing favored the sensible strategy of preparing in advance of the negotiations an American draft treaty to provide guidance and structure for the American delegation. Insultingly Wilson rebuffed Lansing, who was trained as an international lawyer, with the cutting remark that "he did not intend to have lawyers drafting the treaty of peace."[7] In regard to the wording of the League Covenant, Lansing was also more perceptive than the president. In Lansing's opinion the mutual territorial guarantee was unworkable, and worse than that, was likely to arouse the fierce ire of Republican nationalists and isolationists. As he recorded, "It is simply loaded with dynamite and he must not go through with it."[8] Instead, Lansing would take the safer route of having each state disclaim any intention of violating the territorial or political integrity of others. As Lansing was already out of favor with Wilson, his ideas were rejected out of hand. In frustration the secretary of state surreptitiously, but deliberately, let it be known that he disapproved of Article X. Since he could not loyally support Wilson, Lansing should have gracefully made his exit from the administration even if it meant advertising the dissention within the government.

During the initial stage of the Peace Conference, the disillusioned secretary of state had further reason to question Wilson's judgment. To resolve the fate of the colonial empire of the vanquished, Wilson proposed a seemingly brilliant solution: the mandate system. The original idea was to apportion the colonies of Germany and the Ottoman Empire among neutral nations. In the name of civilization the recipients would embark upon a humane mission of regenerating backward peoples. In practice Wilson was forced to compromise with Japan and Great Britain, who had divided all of Germany's Pacific Ocean possessions in a secret treaty signed in 1917. In the final disposition the neutrals were excluded and the mandates were awarded to the Allies. Thus the German possessions in Africa (Cameroon, German Southwest Africa, and German East Africa) were awarded respectively to France, the Union of South Africa, and Great Britain. The German possessions in the Pacific south of the equator were awarded to Australia and New Zealand, and those to the north of the equator went to Japan. No one at the time could have foreseen that giving Japan mandates over the Caroline, Marshall, and Mariana Islands would have had highly adverse military consequences in the next world conflict. At least the mandate system put a moralistic gloss upon the division of the German Empire. Because the mandates were awarded in close conformity to the secret treaties, it became difficult for Wilson in the next phase of the conference to oppose giving Japan the former German rights in China's Shantung province.

By February 15, as Wilson began his return to America aboard the *George Washington*, he had taken several major strides toward accomplishing his objectives. The Allies, because they needed Wilson's signature on the final document, had agreed to include the League of Nations in the peace treaty. "A living thing is born," Wilson announced.[9] The acceptance by the Allies of the mandate principle represented at least a cosmetic victory for Wilson. Amidst the progress at the peace table, Wilson was often his own worst enemy in that he consistently neglected public relations. From the perspective of the press the promise of "open covenants of peace, openly arrived at," the first of the Fourteen Points, was a farce. Reporters were excluded from all but meaningless plenary sessions, forced to rely on sanitized official communiques, rumors, and occasional leaks. Had the president cultivated reporters by holding regular press briefings, he could have painlessly laid the groundwork for mobilizing public opinion in the United States. Wilson, who had never enjoyed much rapport with reporters, held only a few press conferences and thereby missed an opportunity for enlisting the press on his behalf.

Meanwhile, at home Wilson's critics took advantage of his absence to lambast the president and his League. In particular Wilson was attacked by the group of sixteen senators known as "the irreconcilables." Composed of fourteen Republicans and two Democrats, the irreconcilables found fault with anything connected to the Peace Conference and the League of Nations, from Wilson's partisan appeal to the voters prior to the congressional elections, to his decision to attend the conference in person. The most energetic of the group were senators William E. Borah of Idaho, Hiram Johnson of California, Philander Knox of Pennsylvania, and James A. Reed of Missouri, the latter being one of the two Democratic diehard opponents of the League. Initially the irreconcilables criticized Wilson mainly for ignoring the advice given by Washington in his Farewell Address to avoid permanent foreign alliances and for allegedly ignoring the Monroe Doctrine. After the completion of the Covenant on February 14, Wilson's opponents concentrated their fury upon specific articles in Wilson's handiwork. Besides attacking the territorial guarantee in Article X, the irreconcilables criticized as sinister the admission to the League of Britain and its dominions, which would then be able to outvote the United States six to one. Borah and Reed charged that America would be dominated by a league controlled by the British Empire.

When Wilson landed in Boston on February 23 for a two-week stay, he made an impressive effort to approach the Senate without letting his anger show. He even consented to be grilled in the East Room of the White House by members of the House and Senate foreign affairs committees. The irreconcilable Senator Frank Brandegee of Connecticut, Wilson's most persistent questioner, afterward compared the president to the "mad hatter" in Lewis Carroll's *Alice in Wonderland.* Wilson, forgetting his resolve to be conciliatory, may have provoked such an outburst by letting slip recriminations of his own. "Any man who resists the present tides that run through the world," the president unwisely remarked, "will find himself thrown upon a shore so high and barren it will seem as if he had been separated from his human kind forever." Equally tactless was Wilson's characterization of his Republican opponents as "blind and little, provincial people."[10] His Senate opponents vindictively struck back with a filibuster that prevented needed appropriation bills from passing, thus requiring a special session. And as the Senate adjourned, Senator Henry Cabot Lodge of Massachusetts seriously embarrassed Wilson by reading into the record the Republican Round Robin, a statement signed by thirty-nine Republican senators opposing the League of Nations "in the form now proposed."[11] Artfully, Lodge maneuvered to prevent a roll call vote on his sense of the Senate resolution because he knew he was unlikely to win the support of a majority of the Senate. Lodge's clever strategy dealt Wilson a serious psychological blow as only thirty-three votes were needed to block Wilson's desires. If Lodge's purpose was to provoke Wilson, he succeeded brilliantly. Wilson defiantly held steadfast to his original strategy of placing the Covenant in the treaty so as to make rejection of the entire package necessary to keep the United States from becoming a member of the League. "When that treaty comes back gentlemen on this side will find the Covenant not only in it," he declared at New York just before returning to Paris, "but so many threads of the treaty tied to the Covenant that you cannot dissect the Covenant from the treaty without destroying the whole vital structure."[12]

On his return to Paris the president found waiting for him even more recriminations and partisanship than he had experienced at home. His personal relationship with colleagues on the Council of Four and with Colonel House now sharply deteriorated. House, who had been left in charge during Wilson's absence, was blamed for having made unnecessary concessions to the French. Clemenceau and Lloyd George could hardly conceal their scorn when Wilson spoke on behalf of an idealistic new world order. The disillusioned British delegate John Maynard Keynes, in his memoir of the conference, described Wilson as a bewildered Presbyterian who was "bamboozled" by the leaders of Europe. And, he unfairly added: "Never could a man have stepped into the parlour a more perfect and predestined victim to the finished accomplishments of the Prime Minister."[13] Since Keynes was a close associate and admirer of Lloyd George, it is likely that these were also the views of the prime minister.

For his part Wilson had a genuine grievance against the government of Lloyd George. In the summer of 1918, against his better judgment, Wilson had agreed to send American troops to North Russia under British command, primarily to block German occupation of the Archangel region. Wilson intended the 5,800 Americans to be used as noncombatants, and he was incensed when British commanders employed the 339th Infantry in offensive operations against the Bolsheviks hundreds of miles from the port of Archangel. In mid-March Wilson named Brigadier General Wilds P. Richardson, an officer with Alaskan experience, to head the dispirited Americans. Interviewing Richardson at Paris, Wilson was emphatic in denouncing the misuse of the 339th Infantry by the British, and he stated that he wanted the evacuation of all Americans as soon as the spring thaw made navigation possible.

The president's relations with Clemenceau likewise remained tenuous. Wilson would have to have been deaf, blind, and dumb had he failed to notice the premier's derogatory mimicking of his idealism. Inevitably Wilson learned of rude remarks by Clemenceau to the effect that Lloyd George merely regarded himself as Napoleon while Wilson "considered himself to be Jesus Christ."[14] Herbert Hoover, who was present at Paris as head of the American Relief Administration, recalled Clemenceau's bluntness and bitterness: "He treated the 'New Order' and the Fourteen Points as a joke on history. His essential creed was that force always triumphed over abstract justice. . . . He never did understand Mr. Wilson. I don't think he tried to."[15] With Vittorio Orlando, the premier of Italy, Wilson's relationship was far more cordial until Italy claimed the Adriatic port of Fiume (present day Rijeka), which logically belonged to the new nation of Yugoslavia. Wilson responded by releasing to the press an appeal to Italy to respect self-determination. Italian public opinion cheered Orlando and vilified Wilson; Gabriele D'Annunzio called Wilson a "croatianized Quaker."[16] Orlando made the Council of Four a Council of Three by leaving the conference, although he eventually returned to take title to Trieste and the Tyrol.

Fundamental financial disputes contributed to Allied distrust at Paris. One irritant was the Allied determination to extract from Germany the maximum in reparations. Lead by France the Allies demanded that Germany pay the entire cost of the conflict. The opposing American position held that the German indemnity should be confined to actual war damages and that the final figure should be based upon Germany's capacity to pay. Eventually the entire issue was handed to a Reparations Commission which in 1921, without the participation of the United States, fixed the German indemnity at the astronomical sum of $33 billion—far beyond the ability and the willingness of Germany to pay.

Closely linked to the reparations controversy was the simmering issue of "war debts" owed to the United States by the Allies. In 1917 loans were the only immediate contribution the United States could make to the common cause. On short notice Treasury Secretary William G. McAdoo conceived a brilliant solution: the loans to America's allies would be provided from liberty bonds sold to the American public. Except for the initial advances, which were short-term obligations renewed at maturity, the loans were made payable on demand. Because these were loans between friends, it was understood that the United States would not suddenly demand payment. A permanent, mutually agreeable settlement would be negotiated in the calm atmosphere of the postwar world. Altogether twenty foreign governments borrowed $10.3 billion, although over ninety percent of the total was owed by Britain, France, and Italy. Improvised as a stopgap long before the precedents of Lend-Lease, the Marshall Plan, and foreign aid, the Allied war debts to the United States became one of the most divisive disputes of the interwar era. Europeans became convinced the United States was an unscrupulous creditor (and said the initials U.S. stood for "Uncle Shylock"); American isolationists cited Europe's lack of gratitude as the justification for avoiding European commitments.

Officially the American loans to the Allies were not on the agenda at Paris. But unofficially the subject came up repeatedly, a phenomenon that had a way of repeating itself at many other conferences of the interwar era. Shortly before the opening of the conference Colonel House recorded in his diary: "There is every evidence that the Allies have a growing intention not to repay us the money we have loaned them. One hears the argument, both in France and England, that we ought to pay our full share of the Allies' war debt; that we ought to have come in sooner, and that their fight was our fight."[17] Likewise Thomas W. Lamont, a prominent New York financier who served as an economic adviser to the American delegation, recalled: "The question in one form or another constantly arose. It was always 'stepped on' by the American delegates. There was no commitment, expressed or inferred, near or remote, moral or otherwise, as to the handling of the Allied indebtedness to the United States Government."[18] Back in Washington, Secretary of the Treasury Carter Glass expressed "grave concern" that Wilson or the American delegates might unwisely make debt concessions without his knowledge or approval.[19] To the relief of Glass, Wilson categorically replied: "There can be no proper basis for a discussion of foreign loans in connection with the Peace Conference."[20] And to Assistant Secretary of the Treasury Norman H. Davis, Wilson wrote: "I agree entirely with the Secretary of the Treasury that questions relating to our foreign loans should be discussed and settled in the Capital of the United

States."[21] Thus the Wilson administration laid down a policy that was followed by every president, Democratic or Republican, of the interwar era: the loans were a subject that could be discussed properly only in Washington, that repayment had no relation to any reparations that might or might not be paid by Germany, and that the loans were a debt of honor to the American taxpayer.

Health concerns added to Wilson's frustration. On April 3, 1919, the president was felled by what most observers then and now believe was the influenza virus then making the rounds of Europe. It was a particularly virulent microbe that often proved fatal even to young people in good health. Wilson's physician, Dr. Cary Grayson, was justifiably concerned when Wilson developed a fever of 103 degrees; after all, the patient was sixty-two years old and suffering from high blood pressure and hardening of the arteries. As Wilson joined Clemenceau on the sick list (the French premier was recovering from an assassin's bullet in his lung), the conference marked time. Angered by French demands for the annexation of the Saar, the feverish Wilson appeared to have suffered an attack of nerves when he threatened to send for the *George Washington* and go home. As a tactical maneuver, however, Wilson's threat worked almost to perfection, as it caused the French to retreat on the Saar; they agreed that for fifteen years France would have the Saar's coal while at the end of the period a plebiscite would determine whether France or Germany would acquire the region permanently. (In 1935 the region voted overwhelmingly to return to Germany.) To bolster French security the Rhineland was permanently demilitarized (a provision which Germany flamboyantly defied in 1936). Alsace-Lorraine, annexed by Germany after the Franco-Prussian War, was returned to France. And Wilson agreed to the French request for a security treaty guaranteeing Anglo-American assistance in the event of another war between France and Germany. To the dismay of the French the security treaty was buried in the Senate as a result of the defeat of the Versailles Treaty.

In order to complete the treaty, Wilson was forced into making a number of distasteful concessions. Hoping to mollify his Senate critics, Wilson—painful as it must have been for him—reassembled the League of Nations Commission and by force of personality succeeded in revamping the League Covenant. The amended Covenant exempted the Monroe Doctrine and questions of domestic jurisdiction from League interference, recognized the right of members to quit the League, and guaranteed that no member state could be required to accept a mandate. One of the most objectionable concessions, agreed to with great reluctance by Wilson, was the transfer to Japan of Germany's economic concessions in the Chinese province of Shantung. At the outbreak of the conflict Japan had ousted the Germans, claiming its ultimate intention was to return Shantung to China. Wilson got no support from Lloyd George or Clemenceau who had agreed in secret treaties to Japan's annexation of Shantung. At least Japan vaguely agreed to return Shantung to China at an unspecified date in the future. But Wilson's defense of self-determination was selective as he agreed that Italy might annex the Austrian Tyrol.

In its final form the Versailles Treaty, completed May 29, 1919, stripped Germany of its colonies without compensation, assigned Germany the sole guilt for the war (article 231), and assessed Germany an undetermined reparations bill, which ballooned to $33 billion when finally presented in 1921. As a product of coalition diplomacy, the final product was necessarily imperfect, representing as it did the competing material and moral interest of the diverse signatories. Did Wilson's investment of six months abroad improve the treaty? The fairest answer is an emphatic yes, notwithstanding the president's concessions on self-determination and his acquiescence in the document's hard and shortsighted treatment of Germany. But in the process Wilson repeatedly demonstrated questionable judgment by stubbornly refusing to enlist the opposition in the Paris peace process or to consult the Senate either before or after the conference. Wilson's belief that public opinion would rescue the treaty proved one of the worst political blunders in all of American history. And his self-righteous demeanor thoroughly provoked his opponents.

When the defiant Wilson returned to America on July 8, 1919, prospects still looked superficially rosy for Senate ratification. The public opinion poll was yet to be devised. However, the *Literary Digest* noted that only 181 of the nation's 1,380 newspapers opposed the treaty, whereas 481 conditionally approved, and 718 approved without reservation. Moreover, with the exception of two Democratic irreconcilables—James A. Reed of Missouri and Charles Thomas of Colorado—Wilson could count on the support of forty-five Democratic senators. To secure ratification he needed the support of eighteen Republicans. When he personally presented the Versailles Treaty to the Senate on July 10 Wilson struck a defiant note. Self-righteously he challenged his opponents with the rhetorical statement, "Shall we or any other free people hesitate to accept this great duty? Dare we reject it and break the heart of the world?" In a tone of moral superiority, Wilson asserted that America's role of world leadership was determined by "the hand of God who led us into this way." Under his leadership, said Wilson, the nation was embarking "with uplifted eyes and freshened spirit" upon a brightly lit path toward a destiny foreseen by America's founders. Predictably Wilson's critics were offended, probably as much by his tone as by his substance, and they characterized the speech as "utterly lacking in true Americanism" (Senator Warren G. Harding of Ohio); "soothing, mellifluous, and uninformative" (Senator Joseph Medill McCormick of Illinois); "mere soap bubbles of oratory and soufflé of phrases" (Senator Frank Brandegee of Connecticut); and "a fine lot of glittering generalities"

(Senator George W. Norris of Nebraska).[22] Wilson's best hope for ratification was to secure a quick Senate vote while public opinion was in his favor. Here the loss of the 1918 election proved costly because now the Republicans controlled the Senate machinery and were able to set the agenda. Wilson's strategy was to structure the treaty so as to include the League of Nations, making it necessary to reject the entire package to defeat the League. Senate majority leader Henry Cabot Lodge of Massachusetts, a twenty-five-year veteran of legislative battles, hit on a cynical but effective counterstrategy. He would delay action while building opposition. To avoid a direct yes or no vote on Wilson's treaty, Lodge planned to attach reservations unacceptable to Wilson. Often hailed as a masterful psychologist and tactician, Lodge would not have seemed so brilliant had Wilson accepted his reservations. Lodge gambled correctly that Wilson would remain stubborn to the end.

Wilson was infuriated (which was the intention) when Lodge deliberately wasted two months in reading the treaty aloud and then holding a hostile hearing before his Senate Foreign Relations Committee. Although the members of the Committee possessed basic literacy as well as copies of the Versailles Treaty, Lodge had the audacity to read the document word for word. In the six weeks of hearings Lodge made no pretense of fairness and turned the proceedings into a travesty at Wilson's expense. Indirectly Wilson testified by inviting Lodge and his committee to lunch at the White House. For the most part Wilson effectively parried the questions directed at him. Yet he was less than convincing in explaining America's commitment to preserve the territorial integrity and political independence of states belonging to the League of Nations. Wilson's contention that the United States had only a moral—not a legal—obligation left the senators wondering what was the distinction between the two? But Wilson's worse faux pas was his denial that he was aware of the secret treaties prior to attending the Peace Conference. Most likely Wilson made a snap decision to graze the truth on this point and felt compelled to stick to his answer even though it was demonstrably untrue.

Rejecting the advice of his physician, Wilson unwisely determined to rally public opinion through a nationwide speaking tour. The route of the president's "swing around the circle" was cleverly planned to start at Columbus, Ohio, and then proceed through the northern states of the Midwest to the Pacific with the return scheduled through the nation's midsection. But it was a physically and mentally exhausting undertaking inasmuch as Wilson had to write and deliver more than forty speeches without the assistance of microphones or loudspeakers (which were not yet in general use). Had the president's health withstood the ordeal, he would presumably have been able to generate a wave of support for the treaty. Even that is uncertain, as Wilson's irreconcilable opponents formed "truth squads" that shadowed his movements and at least partially neutralized Wilson's oratorical efforts. All the time during Wilson's tour, the Senate Foreign Relations Committee continued to hold critical hearings, which culminated in the adoption of forty-five amendments. Unlike reservations, amendments required the renegotiation of the treaty, which was for all practical purposes impossible. Their purpose, therefore, was to enrage Wilson, and they fully achieved their intent.

Modern neurologists have available to them diagnostic tools—such as the cerebral angiogram, the CT scan, and the MRI—which were not yet invented when Wilson, after speaking at Pueblo, Colorado, on September 25, suffered excruciating headaches. At the insistence of his doctor Wilson was forced to cancel the remainder of his trip. The lack of definitive tests and the disappearance of Wilson's medical records make it impossible to determine whether he had suffered a stroke or possibly a transient ischemic incident. No ambiguity surrounded the stroke that felled Wilson on October 2 after his return to the White House. By any definition Wilson experienced a major medical emergency that left him in critical condition for two weeks and paralyzed his left side. The president suffered as well from distorted vision and speech, and his power of concentration and his emotional equilibrium were affected. Wilson's ability to lead through graceful and idealistic phrases was lost forever. No longer was he a man who whistled when happy or who cultivated a store of jokes and limericks for amusing friends and cabinet officers. The stroke transformed Wilson from a leader of stature and great intellect to a caricature of his former self. In his own interest and that of the nation he should have resigned his office, but he was apparently not well enough to appreciate his diminished abilities.

As devastating as the stroke was for Wilson personally, it was even more tragic for the overall direction of American foreign policy. The death of Theodore Roosevelt in January 1919 had left Wilson as the country's leading advocate of an internationalist foreign policy (although the Rough Rider in his last years, perhaps for partisan reasons, seemed to be moving away from internationalism). Wilson's illness produced a vacuum of enlightened presidential leadership at the very moment the Senate was about to take up the Versailles Treaty. For Wilson the stroke could not have come at a worse time; for his opponents the illness could not have been better timed. Two months later (December 5, 1919) the bedridden Wilson received a vivid reminder of the real feelings of his opponents toward him when he received a senatorial "smelling" committee sent to ascertain his mental condition. To the hypocritical remark of the irreconcilable Senator Albert Fall of New Mexico, "Well, Mr. President, we have all been praying for you." Wilson rejoined, "Which way, Senator?"[23]

Although Wilson didn't realize it at the time his cause was already a lost one. A month after the president's stroke, Senator Lodge produced his malevolently designed reservations to the Versailles Treaty. Reflecting

Lodge's shrewd psychological strategy, it was no coincidence that he managed to produce exactly fourteen reservations—to go with Wilson's Fourteen Points. In their phraseology the Lodge reservations were legalistic, malicious, and insulting. Many of the reservations were unnecessary because they duplicated provisions already contained in the treaty. Article X was Lodge's main target: he provided that the United States could withdraw from the League by concurrent resolution of Congress, which did not require the signature of the president and was not subject to veto; that the United States assumed no obligation to defend foreign territory or accept League mandates; that the United States reserved from League interference questions of "domestic jurisdiction," including the Monroe Doctrine; and that the United States refused to accept the transfer of Shantung to Japan, or be bound by any League decision in which any member cast more than one vote (a slap at the British Empire).

To bring the number of reservations to the desired fourteen, Lodge added several extraneous reservations: asserting the power of Congress to name representatives to League commissions; requiring congressional approval of America's share of League expenses; permitting the United States to disregard any League disarmament agreement if the nation faced the threat of invasion; allowing Americans to trade with citizens of a state censured by the League, if those citizens lived outside the territory of the Covenant-breaking state; and reserving the right of American citizens to sue in American courts for any property seized under the provisions of the peace treaty. Whether Wilson was well enough to read or comprehend the maddening technicalities of Lodge's work is doubtful. Twice Senate Minority Leader Gilbert Hitchcock of Nebraska was permitted brief interviews with the ailing Wilson and found the president as uncompromising as before. On November 18, Wilson instructed "all true friends" of the treaty to vote against the Lodge reservations because they provided for the "nullification" of the treaty.[24]

Given Wilson's determination not to accept Lodge's reservations to his treaty, it was not a great surprise that the treaty failed when it came to a vote on November 19. What was unexpected was Lodge's margin of victory; the treaty with the fourteen Lodge reservations was defeated by a vote of 55 to 39 (with the Democrats and the irreconcilables voting in the negative); without reservations the treaty failed by almost the same vote, 53 to 38 (with the Republicans and the irreconcilables voting no). Even the irreconcilables, celebrating at the Washington home of Alice Roosevelt Longworth, expressed amazement that Wilson had played into their hands. The president's fierce opposition to the Lodge reservations remained unshaken over the winter even as he slowly regained physical strength. Before the final vote on March 19, 1920, he again urged Democratic senators to reject Lodge's "nullifying" reservations. Lodge was so confident of victory that he accepted numerous modifications and clarifications of his work, while adding a fifteenth reservation calling for Irish freedom from England. Even though twenty-one Democrats deserted Wilson and supported the treaty with Lodge reservations attached, the final tally read 49 yes, 35 no, or seven votes short of the two-thirds majority required by the Constitution. In his naivete, President Wilson hoped the election of 1920 would serve as a "solemn referendum" on the question of American membership in the League. But at their San Francisco nominating convention, the Democrats and their nominee, Governor James M. Cox of Ohio, showed only perfunctory enthusiasm for the League. At Chicago the Republicans also selected an Ohio candidate, Senator Warren G. Harding, who artfully confused the issue by endorsing a modified league while simultaneously calling for a return to "normalcy." Not surprisingly the "solemn referendum" got lost in the shuffle as Harding won a decisive victory.

Explaining the defeat of the Versailles Treaty does not require complicated analysis. Pride, prejudice, and partisanship on the part of both parties and both Wilson and Lodge produced a disgraceful debacle. Lodge, often cast in the role of a villain, thoroughly deserved his unsavory reputation. Had Lodge ended his career prior to 1919, he might have been remembered as a patrician scholar who advanced progressivism and a conception of "national interest." Instead, as Sir Arthur Willert of the *Times of London* wryly observed, Lodge revealed himself to be "as unscrupulous as any low-born boss." By purporting to favor "Americanizing" the treaty with reservations, he barely concealed his destructive opportunism. "He masks under the appearance of an elderly country peer a complete lack of broad convictions," noted Willert. "He is in fact deceptively parochial and slippery." At the same time Wilson, who sought to impose a revolutionary shift upon traditional American foreign policy and who inexplicably rejected innocuous if insulting reservations, hardly deserved his reputation as a starry-eyed martyr. In Willert's coldly realistic judgment, "The President negotiated single-handed, and then sneeringly told the Senate to ratify or be damned to eternity as traitors to humanity. His clumsy pride had really as much to do with the defeat of the treaty as the desire of the country to be faithful to George Washington's dicta and remain aloof from European entanglements."[25]

Finally, it is tempting to surmise that the history of the interwar era would have been dramatically different had the United States taken an active role in the League of Nations. Given the opaque nature of history and the hypothetical nature of the query, the question—like all "what if" questions—remains ultimately unanswerable. What is certain is that the League, without American participation, proved weak-kneed, especially after 1931, in maintaining international peace and stability. In response a national consensus emerged during World War II that held that the United States' refusal to join the League had been an error. Few believed American participation would have guaranteed a different result. But, with the destruction of World War II fresh in their minds, they felt that the effort ought to have been made. Ironically, the national determination not to repeat the errors of the interwar era helped to convince American leaders of the 1960s to embark on a bloody error of their own in Vietnam.

A common criticism of American foreign policy between the world wars has been that it seemed to drift from day to day without clear direction. Such a generalization would be an apt description of the six-month interregnum following Wilson's stroke. Routine government business was transacted by inertia, but basic policy decisions languished—including policy toward revolutionary Mexico and Bolshevik Russia, to say nothing of mounting a coordinated administrative strategy for the Senate fight over the Versailles Treaty. Diplomatic vacancies were left unfilled, and foreign diplomats could not present their credentials. Wilson remained secluded from his cabinet, sheltered by his wife and press secretary. Secretary of State Robert Lansing found that he could communicate with Wilson only by writing his press secretary who would then request permission from Mrs. Wilson to speak to her husband. Lansing, who never saw Wilson after his illness, contemplated having Vice President Thomas R. Marshall named as acting president during the period of Wilson's disability. Presumably Marshall would have accepted the obnoxious Lodge reservations, ensuring the ratification of the Versailles Treaty and American membership in the League of Nations. But Wilson was shielded by his physicians, even though he was unable to prepare his State of the Union message or even sign his name legibly. From the perspective of the White House invalid, Lansing's greatest crime was his having presided over twenty-four cabinet meetings without presidential authorization. When Wilson accepted Lansing's resignation on February 13, 1920, the ostensible reason for his demise was the calling of cabinet meetings. Had Wilson been more candid he could have added as contributing factors that Lansing had often been disloyal in supporting the Versailles Treaty, that he had fallen out of favor with Mrs. Wilson, and that the secretary of state, a foreign policy realist, was fundamentally out of sympathy with Wilson's idealistic internationalism.

Wilson surprised his party and the country by selecting as Lansing's replacement the New York attorney, progressive politician, and former member of the Shipping Board Bainbridge Colby. In contrast to Lansing, Wilson regarded Colby as a loyalist who could be trusted; equally important was Colby's literary ability, since Wilson needed assistance in drafting diplomatic notes and state papers. Calling Colby "a great man," Wilson (indirectly reflecting unfavorably on his two previous secretaries of state) remarked: "I can tell you that for the first time, I have a man who can write a note for me. You know, heretofore, I have always had to write them myself."[26] In his brief one-year term as secretary of state, Colby established a close working relationship with Wilson, although the friendship was never as intimate as that once enjoyed by Colonel House. In office Colby quietly sought to moderate harsh French demands upon Germany, to restrain Japanese economic expansion into Manchuria, and to improve relations with Latin America by liquidating interventionism. His least successful endeavor was to restate Wilson's policy of nonrecognition toward Soviet Russia. In the process Colby managed to please Wilson, and he foreshadowed the general direction followed by secretaries of state under presidents Harding, Coolidge, Hoover, and Franklin D. Roosevelt. On the whole, Colby's tenure demonstrated that there was more continuity between Wilsonian diplomacy and Republican diplomacy in the 1920s than is usually assumed.

Toward Europe Colby became increasingly skeptical. However, as a caretaker secretary of state for an ill president, Colby had little opportunity to initiate bold new policies. France, regarded by Washington as Europe's chief troublemaker, accounted for Colby's displeasure. Therefore, Colby deplored French militarism in the Rhineland, and he recommended that the United States participate in setting the German indemnity to restrain French rapacity. Wilson, embittered by the Senate's rejection of the Versailles Treaty, overruled Colby and declined an invitation to participate in the process. Possibly Wilson was concerned that the Allies would try to link Germany's payment of reparations to their payment of war debts to the United States.

In the Far East Colby continued the anti-Japanese role begun by Wilson after Japan seized Shantung from China in 1914. The State Department took the lead in organizing (in May 1920) a new, but ineffective, international bankers' consortium for the purpose of making loans to the Chinese Republic and lessening Japanese influence. In a related effort, Colby protested Japan's occupation of the northern half of Sakhalin Island (the southern half of the island had been annexed by Japan in the Russo-Japanese War of 1904–1905). Colby flatly refused to believe Japan's defense that the occupation of northern Sakhalin was justified to prevent atrocities by bloodthirsty Bolsheviks against innocent Japanese civilians. The alleged crimes described by Japan, Colby believed, were merely "fake massacres."[27] (Eleven years later the Hoover administration was to have a similar experience when the Japanese Army staged a fake atrocity near Mukden, Manchuria, which became the pretext for the occupation of Manchuria.) To restrain Japanese economic domination of Manchuria, Colby tried to block Japan from acquiring the Chinese Eastern Railroad—a shortcut from the Trans-Siberian Railroad across Manchuria via Harbin to Vladivostok. Outwardly London cooperated with Colby's efforts to prevent Japan from acquiring the railroad, while privately expressing sympathy with Japan's desire for a special interest in Manchuria. Such duplicity led President Wilson to complain in a cabinet meeting that Britain's two-faced diplomacy was based upon its past record of "grab everything it can."[28] Cooperation with Britain was also limited by the existence of the Anglo-Japanese Alliance of 1902 which was due to expire in 1921. As long as it remained in existence the United States and Britain were potential adversaries in the Pacific. In reality, Britain hoped to scrap the alliance, but the method for modifying the antiquated pact was not discovered until Wilson and Colby were out of office.

A hard-line policy toward Bolshevik Russia was already in place when Colby became secretary of state. But under Colby, whose views about Russia were influenced by a confidential adviser, American anti-communism became more virulent than ever. Hostility toward the Bolsheviks dated from the moment Lenin easily overthrew the pro-Western Provisional Government on November 7, 1917. The unwelcome news came as a complete surprise to Washington. Other surprises followed: the publication of the secret treaties and Lenin's peace offensive, both of which greatly embarrassed the Allies, who were counting on Russia's continued participation in the war. Just as distasteful was propaganda urging the masses to overthrow capitalism. Then, in the Treaty of Brest-Litovsk, on March 3, 1918, the Bolsheviks withdrew from the war by accepting the loss of 1.3 million square miles of territory and 62 million in population. By making peace with Germany, Lenin enabled the Germans to transfer their army on the eastern front to France.

From the Allies, the State Department, the Foreign Service, and such advisers as House and Lansing, Wilson came under heavy pressure to intervene. After "sweating blood" over what to do, Wilson finally capitulated on July 17, 1918, citing the need to keep military supplies sent to Russia out of German hands and expressing sympathy for the plight of the Czechoslovak Legion—two divisions of former prisoners of war who were fighting their way across Siberia to Vladivostok. In part, Wilson's decision to intervene was motivated by a desire to cooperate with America's coalition partners. Naively Wilson felt he could restrict the role of the 5,800 American troops sent to North Russia to the role of noncombatants. When the 339th Infantry left Archangel in July, 1919, 222 members had succumbed to disease and hostile action. Just as Colby was taking office, the Siberian phase of the Russian intervention came to an end with the withdrawal of the 9,000 American troops stationed as guards along the Trans-Siberian Railroad.

Until Wilson's presidency, diplomatic recognition of a government had not implied moral approval of that government. Following traditional practice, the United States had routinely recognized governments that held power and were capable of maintaining law and order. Wilson first broke with tradition when he refused on moral grounds to recognize the military government of Mexico, which seized power in a bloody coup just before Wilson took office. In the case of Russia, Wilson's policy was to withdraw the American ambassador (David R. Francis of Missouri) and to await further developments in the hope that the Bolshevik problem would just go away. It fell to Colby to formulate a more definitive policy.

Colby's crusading anti-communism was formulated during the great "red scare" that swept the nation in 1919 and 1920. Communist conspirators were claimed to have initiated every strike of the period, including the Seattle general strike, the Boston police strike, and strikes in coal and steel. Communists were also blamed for bombs addressed to prominent Americans. The scare culminated in a series of raids initiated by Attorney General A. Mitchell Palmer against suspected radicals, and Palmer warned of a Communist *coup d'état* against the United States government planned for May 1, 1920. Even though no uprising occurred, the idea was widely accepted in the United States that the machinations of Lenin were responsible for unrest throughout the globe.

At the height of the red scare, Lenin's regime was actually severely weakened by the effects of civil war and foreign intervention. This time the invader was not one of the "imperialist" powers of the west, but a historically familiar aggressor—Poland, a nation which had been partitioned by Prussia and Russia at the end of the eighteenth century and reestablished as an independent nation at the Paris Peace Conference. In the Russo-Polish War (April-October 1920), Polish forces advanced as far as Kiev before retreating. The prospect that a Russian counteroffensive might disrupt the territorial integrity of Poland prompted Colby's August 10, 1920, pronouncement regarding American policy toward Russia. The vehicle he chose was an unusual one: a diplomatic note addressed to the Italian ambassador in reply to his request for an expression of America's views about the Polish situation. Colby was credited with authorship of the note, and it is true that he wrote the introduction and conclusion. But the main section was contributed by the intensely anti-communist journalist John Spargo, who was Colby's private adviser on Russian matters. In his previous writings Spargo had characterized Bolshevism as "militarism gone mad," and he deeply felt that America's honor would be "sullied" by the establishment of relations with Lenin. Spargo urged Colby to make public a nonrecognition statement, which would presumably lead other nations to isolate Lenin's "outlaw nation."[29]

Colby's tone of moral indignation was similar to Wilson's own moralistic style. He contended forcefully that the regime of Lenin was undeserving of recognition because it was "based upon the negation of every principle of honor and good faith, and every usage and convention underlying the whole structure of international law; the negation, in short, of every principle upon which it is possible to base harmonious and trustful relations, whether of nations or individuals." And, as specific examples of Bolshevik negation Colby cited the intent of the Russian government to use its diplomats as revolutionary agitators and to sign agreements with no intention of keeping them. Essentially, Colby concluded, the Bolsheviks were a diabolical menace to western civilization. Wilson approved Colby's work as "excellent and sufficient," and subsequently cited the note on Russia to a reporter as an example of Colby's excellence as a wordsmith.[30]

A basic assumption of Colby, Spargo, and Wilson was that the Bolsheviks would soon collapse. It became practically an article of faith that was unhesitatingly embraced by American presidents from Wilson through Hoover. Nonrecognition of Russia on moral grounds became a basic American foreign policy bequeathed by the Wilson administration to the incoming Republicans. Whether consciously or not, they also emulated Colby's inclination to lecture the world on the wages of sin, without having any intention of assuming responsibility for remedial measures.

The most farsighted foreign policy contributed by Colby to his successors was a modest start at terminating the American military presence in the Caribbean. Under Wilson there had often been a conspicuous gap between Wilson's Pan-American ideals and his military interventions during chaotic revolutions in Mexico (1914 and 1916), Haiti (1915), and the Dominican Republic (1916). By the time Colby took office, the final phase of the Mexican intervention—which sought the capture of the bandit and patriot Francisco Pancho Villa—had ended, and both Haiti and the Dominican Republic were under American military occupation. Presidential politics may have influenced the decision of the State Department to act. A series of muckraking articles in *The Nation* criticized the military occupation as autocratic and cruel. The Republican candidate, Ohio Senator Warren G. Harding, then criticized Wilson's Caribbean interventions and promised that if he were elected he would not tolerate misconduct on the part of occupation personnel. The Democratic vice presidential candidate, Franklin D. Roosevelt, inadvertently added to the controversy by flippantly claiming to have drafted the Haitian constitution while serving as assistant secretary of the navy. In response Colby announced (September 20, 1920) that the United States was nearing the completion of its "benevolent purpose" in Haiti and "hopes to withdraw and leave the administration of this island to the unaided efforts of the Haitian people."[31] In the case of the Dominican Republic, Colby and Wilson approved a proclamation prepared by the chief of the State Department's Latin American Division, Sumner Welles, announcing the United States' intention to return control of the government to the Dominican people. No schedule for the withdrawal was outlined. However, in 1924 the Republicans terminated the Dominican occupation, although United States troops remained in Haiti until 1934.

Colby's one-year tenure as secretary of state concluded with a two-month tour aboard the battleship USS *Florida* to Brazil, Uruguay, and Argentina. The trip was designed as a goodwill tour to allay Latin American suspicions and reaffirm America's commitment to hemispheric solidarity. Colby would not have been human had he failed to perceive the personal advantages of spending the months of December and January at government expense visiting a warmer climate. By all accounts the trip went extremely well; Colby and his flowery oratory were universally well received. The secretary's graciousness, as well as his knowledge of and interest in Latin American affairs, impressed his audiences. At least symbolically the final months of the Wilson administration saw modest efforts to liquidate past interventionism and to establish the spirit of the good neighbor.

With one major exception, the Senate's rejection of the Versailles Treaty, the last year of Wilson's presidency was a lucky one. No major crisis or exterior threat materialized to expose the power vacuum at the top of the United States government. In the absence of leadership from the White House, Lansing and his successor, Colby, avoided major mistakes and dealt with problems as they arose. Colby did take the initiative in condemning Lenin's Russia as a blot on the history of civilization, a policy based upon the unquestioned assumption that Lenin's regime was not long for this world. The most positive legacy of Wilson's final year in office was the effort of his administration to initiate a modest good neighbor policy toward Latin America. At the same time the Wilsonians became increasingly disenchanted with America's wartime partners due to their perceived ingratitude, greed, and militarism. Disillusionment with Europe combined with a tendency to deliver self-righteous moral lectures to the world were two of the more prominent features of Democratic foreign policy passed on to the Harding administration.

NOTES

1. William Gibbs McAdoo, *Crowded Years: The Reminiscences of William G. McAdoo* (Boston, 1931), 376.

2. Oscar T. Crosby, "The American War-Loans and Justice," *Atlantic Monthly* 130 (December 1922), 825.

3. *Congressional Record*, 65 Cong., 1 Sess., 119 (April 2, 1917).

4. Thomas A. Bailey, *Woodrow Wilson and the Lost Peace* (New York, 1944), 333–34.

5. Eugene Trani, "Woodrow Wilson and the Decision to Intervene in Russia: A Reconsideration," *Journal of Modern History* 48 (September 1976), 458.

6. Thomas A. Bailey, *Woodrow Wilson and the Great Betrayal* (New York, 1945), 385.

7. Daniel M. Smith, *The Great Departure: The United States and World War I, 1914–1920* (New York, 1965), 121.

8. Smith, *Great Departure*, 128.

9. Bailey, *Woodrow Wilson and the Lost Peace*, 193.

10. Ralph Stone, *The Irreconcilables: The Fight Against the League of Nations* (Lexington, 1970), 159, 163.

11. Bailey, *Woodrow Wilson and the Great Betrayal*, 11.

12. Stone, *Irreconcilables*, 75.

13. John Maynard Keynes, *The Economic Consequences of the Peace* (New York, 1920), 41.

14. Bailey, *Woodrow Wilson and the Lost Peace*, 158–59.

15. Herbert Hoover, *The Memoirs of Herbert Hoover* (New York, 1951), Vol. 1, 449–50.

16. In a Senate speech on April 1, 1926, Senator Kenneth McKellar of Tennessee charged that the king of Italy had been bribed by Mussolini during the fascist march on Rome in 1922. The Italian ambassador responded by lodging a formal protest. Consequently, the State Department prepared a summary of insulting remarks made by Italians at the time of the Adriatic crisis in the spring of 1919, including the offensive remark attributed to the poet D'Annunzio. Memorandum by H. Carter, April 2, 1926, General Records of the Department of State, File No. 800.51W89 Italy/144, RG 59, National Archives.

17. Diary of Edward M. House, January 4, 1919, Papers of Edward M. House (Yale University).

18. Thomas W. Lamont, "Reparations," in Edward M. House and Charles Seymour, editors, *What Really Happened at Paris: The Story of the Peace Conference, 1918–1919* (New York, 1921), 289.

19. Glass to Wilson, December 19, 1918, United States Senate, Hearings Before the Special Committee Investigating the Munitions Industry, 74 Cong., 2 Sess. (Washington, 1936), 10448–49.

20. Rixey Smith and Norman Beasley, *Carter Glass: A Biography* (New York, 1939), 158.

21. Woodrow Wilson to Norman H. Davis, January 4, 1919, Carter Glass Papers (University of Virginia).

22. Bailey, *Woodrow Wilson and the Great Betrayal*, 5–6.

23. Stone, *Irreconcilables*, 150–51.

24. Bailey, *Woodrow Wilson and the Great Betrayal*, 185.

25. Sir Arthur Willert, "An Appreciation of the Republican and Democratic National Conventions held at Chicago and San Francisco in June and July, 1920," undated, FO414/246/6815, Public Record Office.

26. Daniel M. Smith, *Aftermath of War: Bainbridge Colby and Wilsonian Diplomacy, 1920–1921* (Philadelphia, 1970), 20.

27. Smith, *Aftermath*, 86.

28. Smith, *Aftermath*, 88.

29. Smith, *Aftermath*, 62–64.

30. Smith, *Aftermath*, 65–68.

31. Smith, *Aftermath*, 126–27.

CHAPTER 3

Harding, Hughes, and Republican Moral Diplomacy

Historians of American foreign policy during the interwar period all have available to them the same basic facts. Yet, in their writings, they give the impression of being on completely different pages. Traditionalists, who view world events as determined by such factors as balance of power, physical force, public opinion, and/or domestic political considerations, see the interwar era as one of shortsighted American diplomacy characterized by self-deluded efforts to ignore legitimate world responsibilities. In short, the period was a tragic retreat to isolation. The opposing viewpoint emphasizes economics as the decisive factor in shaping foreign policy and concludes that the period was actually one of vigorous expansion. Led by Secretary of State Charles Evans Hughes and Secretary of Commerce Herbert Hoover, the Republicans sought through the use of American bankers and trade expansion to establish a new international structure for world order. Anything but passive, Republican policy aggressively sought foreign markets and repayment of war debts, and financed European recovery through two bailouts of German reparations. Traditionalists would say that the United States' refusal to play an active role in the balance of power—especially in Europe—amounted, for all practical purposes, to a near isolationist policy. They would contend that shortsighted American foreign policies had, by the mid-1930s, under Democrats and Republicans, left the nation without a single close friend in the world, with the possible exception of Finland. It is not the facts used by the two historical schools that are in dispute. The issue is how to interpret those facts.

"Republican" foreign policy began with the inauguration of Warren G. Harding on March 4, 1921. Except for the partisan disagreement about the League of Nations, there were many points of similarity between the foreign policies of the two parties. From the Democrats the Republicans inherited and continued to possess an attitude of skepticism toward Britain,

France, and Japan. The new administration continued Wilson's policies on war debts and reparations, refused to recognize Russia, and sought, without spending any money, to improve relations with Latin America. Even on the topic of the League of Nations, the Republicans demonstrated some flexibility, establishing a policy of informal cooperation, but refraining from active membership. And, to the dismay of the irreconcilables, the new administration advocated joining the World Court, an institution established under the auspices of the League of Nations.

Warren G. Harding is usually relegated to the bottom ranks of United States presidents because of his unsavory Ohio cronies, his White House drinking and poker parties, his extramarital affairs, and above all, his administration's scandals involving the naval oil reserves and the Veterans Bureau. Harding was lucky in the sense that he won the Republican nomination because he was handsome and because his rivals canceled each other out. He was unlucky in that, once elected, he was over his head and knew it. Like his predecessor, Harding was not deeply interested in foreign policy, despite having been a member of the Senate Foreign Relations Committee. But Harding was not a provincial simpleton. Prior to his election, for example, he had traveled fairly widely: three times to Europe and once to Hawaii. His bombastic, convoluted speaking style and his background as editor of the *Marion Star* made him appear hopelessly unsophisticated. Wilson's new world order based on universal justice and world government was too radical a concept for Harding and his supporters. But Harding's vision of a return to normalcy, in which the nation sought to advance its national interest through traditional balance-of-power tactics, was a more pragmatic foreign policy concept than Wilson's.

Harding did not intend to be his own secretary of state. He made that clear when he named the fastidiously bearded New York lawyer Charles Evans Hughes to the post. "From the beginning," announced Harding, "the Secretary of State will speak for the State Department."[1] Hughes was the son of a strict Baptist minister who immigrated from Wales in 1855. He was educated at Baptist colleges; he first attended Madison University (the name was later changed to Colgate University) and graduated from Brown University. His legal training was completed at Columbia University at the precocious age of twenty-two. In his practice of law, as a mountain climber in the Swiss Alps, as governor of New York (1906–1910), and as an associate justice of the Supreme Court, Hughes demonstrated self-control and efficiency combined with emotional detachment. In 1916 Hughes almost defeated Wilson for the presidency; his narrow loss was attributable to continued divisions within Republican ranks between conservatives and progressives and the interventionist antics of Theodore Roosevelt. In selecting Hughes, Harding followed Wilson's example of 1913 when Bryan was chosen as secretary of state. Both Hughes and Bryan were former presidential candidates who were named secretary of state to unify their respective parties. For all his expertise as a technical lawyer, Hughes was almost as naive and moralistic in his approach to foreign policy as had been Bryan. A practitioner of the legal-moralistic approach, Hughes hoped to establish international rules and agreements promoting such worthy goals as conciliation, arbitration, and disarmament. The good faith of the signatories would ensure the sanctity of the resulting agreements.

Hughes's reputation as a great secretary of state is largely based on a dramatic speech he delivered at the opening of the Washington Conference of 1921. That Hughes, through oratory and force of personality, took the conference by storm is indisputable. Less certain is whether the naval limitations Hughes negotiated were in the long-term national interest of the United States. Actually it was neither Harding nor Hughes, but the unpredictable Senator William E. Borah of Idaho who took the first steps to head off a world naval race. Even before Harding's inauguration Borah introduced a Senate resolution (December 14, 1920) proposing a naval limitation conference. The United States, Great Britain, and Japan would be invited, with the goal being a fifty percent reduction in naval construction over a five-year period. In a second resolution (January 25, 1921) Borah proposed a six-month moratorium on American naval construction while the nation pondered whether to concentrate on reducing battleships, submarines, or aircraft carriers. When Hughes (on July 11) invited four major powers (Great Britain, Japan, France, and Italy) and four lesser powers (China, Portugal, Holland, and Belgium), he included not just disarmament as a topic for discussion, but the stability of the Chinese mainland and the Pacific as well. Ten days later, as Hughes was immersed in preparations for the conference, General William Mitchell of the Army Air Service performed the spectacular feat of sinking the German battleship *Ostfriesland* off the Virginia coast with 2,000-pound bombs dropped from the air. Because the vessel was anchored as a sitting duck, the demonstration—said defenders of the battleship—failed to prove the vulnerability of battleships to air power. The bitter truth did not sink in until December 1941 when Japanese aircraft caught and sank off the Malay coast the British cruiser *Repulse* and the battleship *Prince of Wales* just three days after the Pacific fleet of the United States had been decimated at Pearl Harbor.

Hughes's preparations for the conference were exceptionally thorough and imaginative. Shrewdly he outflanked the irreconcilables by appointing as delegates Senator Henry Cabot Lodge and Elihu Root, a former senator and secretary of state. Senator Oscar W. Underwood represented the minority Democrats. Then on November 11, the third anniversary of the Armistice, the delegates to the conference, together with 100,000 onlookers, witnessed an impressive state ceremony: the burial of the Unknown Soldier at Arlington Cemetery. The next day the conference opened at Constitution Hall with welcoming speeches by Harding and Hughes. The only hitch in the proceeding occurred when Aristide Briand, the chief French delegate, was assigned a seat at the corner rather than at the head of the table. Sir Auckland Geddes, the British ambassador to the United States and the second-ranking British delegate next to Arthur Balfour, diplomatically relinquished his seat in favor of Briand.

In his opening address to the conference Hughes rose magnificently to the occasion by dramatically spelling out the sacrifices he expected from each participant. Hughes took the delegates by surprise; they were expecting a typically harmless welcome to the national capital. And to be sure, Hughes's opening was mundane enough, but before he was through he had proposed the abandonment of 1.8 million tons of existing and planned capital ships; the American contribution was to be 845,740 tons. A common cliché held that Hughes in thirty minutes had destroyed more ships than had gone down in all the naval battles in world history. Fearing a possible leak, Hughes boldly decided to announce his proposals at the very beginning of the conference. The ratio he proposed for limiting battleships (5:5:3:1.75:1.75 for the United States, Great Britain, Japan, France, and Italy respectively) roughly maintained the status quo. Hughes's idea was to extend the battleship ratio to other classes of ships, combined with a ten-year moratorium on further construction.

Three months of bargaining elapsed before Hughes's efforts met success. Three principal treaties were signed by the time the conference adjourned in February 1922. First of all, the Five Power Treaty limited battleships according to the "Rolls Royce: Rolls Royce: Ford" ratio proposed by Hughes. In the process Hughes made several compromises, such as permitting Great Britain to construct two new battleships and agreeing that Japan might retain the battleship *Mutsu*, the sister ship of the infamous *Nagato*, which served as Admiral Isoroku Yamamoto's flagship during the Pearl Harbor attack and which was sunk by an underwater atomic blast at Bikini Atoll in 1946. The agreement provided for a ten-year "holiday" on the new construction of capital ships. Furthermore, aircraft carriers were limited to 135,000 tons for the United States and Great Britain, 81,000 tons for Japan, and 60,000 tons for France and Italy. An effort to limit submarines failed, due to the opposition of France.

The key to the success of the conference was the willingness of the western powers to accept the Four Power Treaty, which replaced the Anglo-Japanese Alliance by, in effect, expanding it into a four-power arrangement between the United States, Great Britain, Japan, and France. Specifically the treaty guaranteed the status quo in the Pacific "with regard to fortifications and naval bases." In practical terms this meant that the United States and Great Britain were forbidden from fortifying such bases as Hong Kong, the Philippines, or Guam. The final major treaty, the Nine Power Treaty, was signed by all the Washington participants. Principally drafted by Elihu Root, the document guaranteed the independence and territorial integrity of China and proclaimed the principle of equal commercial opportunity for all in China. And, in separate agreements negotiated outside the conference, Japan agreed to return Shantung to China and to withdraw all its remaining soldiers from Siberia.

At the time, Hughes was hailed as the greatest secretary of state in the history of the United States. Hughes was praised for his open diplomacy and credited with singlehandedly ending the naval race. Through a combination of charisma and morality he was credited with an accomplishment that, in the words of Arthur Balfour, was "unique in history."[2] Actually the secretary hid behind his beard the fact that he had not hesitated during the conference to read the mail of others. In a New York brownstone, nicknamed the "Black Chamber," American cryptographers deciphered Japanese code messages provided courtesy of American cable companies. A cable decoded in late November revealed that Japan would not insist on battleship parity with the United States and Great Britain if the western powers would accept the status quo in the Pacific. Subsequently Hughes commended the cryptographers for facilitating the success of the conference. Yet, when tension with Japan intensified after 1931, the quest for naval disarmament seemed less and less farsighted because the United States found itself lacking in adequate bases, ships, carrier planes, and workable torpedoes to back up an increasingly tough policy toward Japan. Belatedly it dawned on Americans that a high price had been paid for the Washington treaties. Japan had acquired de facto naval superiority in the Pacific and had prevented the United States and Great Britain from fortifying their bases in the region. In view of the enormous human and financial expenditures of World War II, Hughes did not seem so clever after all. However, in defense of Hughes it can be argued that depression economy measures also explained American naval weakness, leaving the United States Navy more than 100 ships short of treaty strength by 1934. Hughes, in defending himself from criticism after Pearl Harbor, contended that his diplomacy had averted a naval race between the United States and Great Britain. He further held that the United States had ample time under the New Deal to modernize the fleet and to fortify Guam, but that Washington complacently failed to take action.[3] Human reputations are fragile, and by the end of the interwar era Hughes's reputation as a miracle worker had faded badly, even though it was hardly fair to have blamed America's glaring military weakness solely on one man.

Less dramatic and less productive of publicity than the Washington Conference, but ultimately more farsighted, was the Harding administration's effort to follow in Colby's footsteps and improve relations with Latin America. In just his second month as president Harding was able to convince the Senate to approve a $25 million indemnity to Colombia for Theodore Roosevelt's 1903 "Rape of Panama." Roosevelt had enraged

Latin Americans by quickly recognizing the Republic of Panama when the former province of Colombia declared its independence in November 1903. Latin Americans were further infuriated when Roosevelt transformed Panama into an American protectorate by acquiring a ten-mile-wide canal zone in perpetuity. Under Wilson a treaty had been drafted with Colombia expressing America's regret and providing a $25 million payment. During Roosevelt's lifetime his friends kept the treaty bottled up. But Roosevelt's premature death of a stroke in 1919 combined with the desire of American oil companies to develop Colombian oil fields improved the treaty's prospects. Thus, minus the apology, the treaty, which provided an opening for American oil interests and demonstrated new American good-neighborliness, received Senate approval. Likewise the American evacuation of the Dominican Republic, but not Haiti, made a minor contribution to lessening Latin American resentment. The withdrawal was arranged by Hughes and Sumner Welles and completed in September 1924. Another tangled Latin American policy inherited from Wilson was nonrecognition of Mexico on moral grounds. For two and a half years a deadlock ensued, which was largely attributable to Hughes's insistence that Mexico must guarantee American property rights prior to recognition. Several decisions by the Supreme Court of Mexico favorable to foreign investors paved the way for American recognition of the government of General Alvaro Obregon in August 1923. On a modest scale Harding and Hughes had made the good-neighbor policy bipartisan.

The new administration could also take credit for a badly needed overhaul of the State Department. Originally drafted by Wilbur Carr, the director of the Consular Service, the reorganization bill was introduced in 1919 by Massachusetts Representative John J. Rogers. Sensibly the Rogers Act proposed the elimination of an illogical feature of American diplomacy, namely the existence of two branches: the Diplomatic Service and the Consular Service. The former was designed as a visible, socially prestigious service for negotiating with foreign governments. On the other hand, the Consular Service, founded in 1792, was designated to perform the routine, unglamorous work of facilitating commercial relations and issuing passports and visas. Hughes strongly supported combining the two services and raising salaries so as to open diplomatic careers to a broad range of candidates and not restrict the field to the affluent. The measure, which also provided for pensions, merit appointments, and promotions, finally cleared the Senate in May 1924, more than a year after its passage by the House of Representatives. In theory the consuls now enjoyed equal opportunity with the diplomats in all respects, but in practice men of means and social status continued to dominate the State Department bureaucracy. (According to the journalist Drew Pearson, their motto was borrowed from the placards displayed in the vestibules of Pullman cars: "Quiet is requested for the benefit of those who have retired.") Notwithstanding the bill's administrative improvements, the Foreign Service remained predominantly white, male, eastern educated, and socially arrogant—the very embodiment of "a pretty good club."[4]

Harding and Hughes were not isolationists in the sense that they wanted to bury their heads in the sand and abolish the Department of State. Unlike the irreconcilables, Harding and Hughes were not sullen and selfish in purpose. They were representatives of a party that had rejected Wilson's internationalism at great political profit. Considering the entrenched isolationism within their own party, the new leaders showed imaginative practicality in promoting peace through disarmament as an alternative to Wilson's program of peace through world government. They looked upon themselves as inheritors of traditional American concepts of non-entanglement in European politics, not as isolationists. Culturally and intellectually the vast majority of Americans and their leaders during the 1920s were anything but isolationist as they vigorously exported American films, music, and art, as well as concepts of business efficiency and peace through international cooperation. Economically, Americans were extroverted; they invested over $80 billion in Europe, Latin America, and Asia. When Germany experienced difficulty in making reparations payments, it was American, not European, bankers who arranged the Dawes Plan in 1924 and the Young Plan in 1928. Prodded by the Department of Commerce, American exporters made American goods ubiquitous abroad: American foreign trade doubled between 1913 and 1929 despite the maintenance of an illogically high tariff policy. To the extent that there was an American plan to establish world order, it was understated and unstructured. Politically Americans still took as little responsibility as possible for international stability. The country was essentially hoping for the best by neglecting to maintain close ties with the League of Nations and the British Empire, by taking a hard line against its World War I debtors, and by seeking to isolate Soviet Russia while waiting for communism to collapse. If America was internationally engaged culturally and economically during the interwar period, the nation was politically disengaged.

America's platonic political relationship with Europe during the interwar period can be illustrated by the hesitant connection established by the Harding administration with the League of Nations. Harding's overwhelming election victory in 1920 had decisively settled in the negative the question of American membership in the League of Nations. Although thirty-one prominent Republicans, including Hughes and Hoover, had signed a manifesto advocating membership in a revised league, Harding had no intention of wrecking his administration at the beginning by starting a bitter fight with the irreconcilables. The new president, therefore, ignored "The Thirty-One" and told Congress the League "can have no sanction by us."[5] Hughes likewise had no stomach for a fight that he believed was unwinnable. Nevertheless, without American participation, the League of Nations was organized at the neutral site of Geneva, Switzerland. By the spring of 1921 forty-three nations had already joined. At first, as revealed by a series of embarrassing articles in the *New York Times*, the State Department refused even to acknowledge communications from the League; a minor State Department official had relegated all League mail to the dead-letter file. Even though the error was rectified, Hughes's correspondence with the League was as technical, legalistic, and impersonal as possible. By the second year of the Harding administration, Hughes permitted Joseph Grew, the American minister to Switzerland, to establish direct contacts with League officials and to convey informally the American point of view without committing the United States in any way. Under Harding the United States began to participate in League humanitarian activities such as the control of anthrax in cattle and suppression of traffic in opium, prostitutes, and obscene publications. The United States quietly participated in League activities that were in America's interest while holding the League at arm's length. The idea of membership or the assumption of financial responsibility for League activities was anathema.

Less stealthy was the new administration's attitude toward the World Court, which was established in 1922 under the auspices of the League of Nations. Both Harding and Hughes, and later Coolidge, were unambiguously in favor of American participation. Hughes had long supported the principle of international adjudication of disputes. As the leading advocate of American membership in the World Court, Hughes showed flashes of the brilliance he had displayed at Washington. But this time there was to be no miracle at Washington. The irreconcilables were waiting in ambush to employ the same tactics against the World Court that had previously defeated Wilson's League of Nations. Led by Borah and Hiram Johnson, the opponents of the World Court saw American membership as a traitorous first step toward joining the League itself. The struggle began in February 1923, when Hughes recommended to Harding that the United States join the World Court and proposed four reservations designed to disarm the irreconcilables. Hughes's reservations were: first, that membership in the World Court carried with it no legal obligation to the League; second, that America could participate equally with the members of the League in the selection of judges; third, that Congress would determine America's fair share of World Court expenses; and fourth, that the regulations establishing the World Court could not be altered without American approval. Harding risked much of his political capital in challenging his former Senate colleagues and forwarding Hughes's proposal to the Senate. Henry Cabot Lodge, still chairman of the Senate Foreign Relations Committee, responded with determined tactics of delay. Taking his cue from Borah, Lodge tried to trap Hughes by demanding that he explain whether the United States would be required to submit to the judgment of the court all disputes that could not be settled through diplomacy. Lodge added that, as Congress was about to complete its session, a reply was not expected prior to adjournment. Hughes then scored heavily by immediately responding. First, he rejected Lodge's thesis that it was necessary for the United States to submit every dispute to the World Court; that would be futile and a waste of time, he contended. Hughes then pointedly denied that international arbitration of disputes would constitute an entanglement in European politics. Instead, he argued, membership in the World Court was in the national interest of the United States and was consistent with America's past support of arbitration (a point that Hughes exaggerated, since the United States had usually arbitrated only if dealing with minor matters or with stronger powers). Despite Hughes's heroics, the irreconcilables held together and were able to delay a vote during the tenure of Harding and Hughes. The opponents of the World Court retained a potent weapon of their own which they were prepared to unleash in due course—namely, crippling irreconcilable reservations after the model of those employed by Lodge in 1919–1920.

With the benefit of hindsight, one of the more shortsighted aspects of American interwar foreign policy was the failure to maintain amicable relations with the two powers that served as America's allies in World War II: Great Britain and Soviet Russia. Regarding Britain, relations were never outwardly hostile, but they were consistently testy. A case in point was the Anglo-American quarrel over overcrowding and unsanitary conditions at Ellis Island, the dilapidated immigrant reception station maintained by the United States in New York Harbor. The trouble coincided with the passage of the 1921 Immigration Act, which established a quota system based upon national origin. Only twenty percent of a country's quota could be admitted each month. Thus, it was not uncommon for immigrants to arrive at Ellis Island only to discover that their national quota had been exhausted for the month in which they arrived; to be admitted they would have to remain in confinement until the next month's quota began. Immigrants from the British Empire were frequently caught in an administrative limbo and forced to stay in close proximity with Eastern European immigrants who had crossed the ocean in steerage.

Sir Auckland Geddes, the forty-one-year-old British ambassador, was first instructed to protest Ellis Island congestion and confusion in the fall of 1921. Lord Curzon of Kedleston, the Foreign Secretary, formally objected to the lack of governmental machinery warning travelers that they might be denied admission if the quota for their country was exhausted. Furthermore, complained Curzon, travelers to the United States were not warned in advance that they might "be subjected to detention in conditions unworthy of a civilized country."[6] Hughes, playing the role of defense attorney, vigorously denied each and every British allegation. The congestion at Ellis

Island, he implausibly maintained, was the fault of British steamship companies, especially the Cunard Line, which deliberately transported inadmissable persons to the United States. Hughes's sole concession was to admit that the physical conditions at Ellis Island were "not satisfactory," but he maintained that the British had greatly exaggerated the shortcomings of the facility.[7]

Hoping to quiet the controversy, Labor Secretary James J. Davis invited Geddes, who had been trained as a medical doctor at the University of Edinburgh, to tour Ellis Island on December 28, 1922. From the perspective of the former anatomy professor, the facility at Ellis Island failed to pass muster. First of all, Geddes was struck by the inefficient arrangement of the buildings and their shocking lack of maintenance, as evidenced by peeling paint and a leaking roof. One of the most unpleasant features was the location of the toilets directly adjacent to the sleeping and living rooms. Everywhere he observed "impacted greasy dirt," combined with a "flat stale smell" and "the pungent odour of unwashed humanity." If given the choice, Geddes said, he would prefer incarceration at Sing Sing Prison to Ellis Island. For the next day and a half Geddes found he was accompanied by a distasteful souvenir of the experience. As he explained to Curzon: "After leaving the island, it took me thirty-six hours to get rid of the aroma which flavoured everything I ate or drank."[8]

For more than half a year the existence of Geddes's thoughtful report remained unknown to the general public. However, in the latter part of June 1923, in answer to a parliamentary question, the undersecretary for foreign affairs alluded to Geddes's visit and report. Responding to questions about Englishmen "incarcerated in cages" at Ellis Island, the official disclosed that Geddes had made an inspection and communicated his findings to the Foreign Office and the State Department. Following press reports that fifty British citizens had been hostilely questioned and then deported for being in excess of the British quota, it was decided to make the report public as a Parliamentary White Paper. A brief newspaper controversy ensued in which Geddes was attacked for having unjustly depicted Ellis Island as a "modern Black Hole of Calcutta." But by luck the furor was pushed to the back pages of the press because it coincided with the unexpected elevation to the presidency of Vice President Calvin Coolidge. Moreover, Ambassador Geddes, already blind in his left eye, was in London undergoing unsuccessful surgery to repair a detached retina in his right eye. Unable to read or see facial expression, he was forced into a premature retirement at age forty-four. Ultimately the United States did accept Geddes's suggestion that immigrants to the United States be examined at American consular offices in Europe rather than at Ellis Island. But instead of modernizing Ellis Island, Congress in 1924 imposed more restrictive quotas that slowed immigration from a flood to a trickle. The dispute illustrated the contentious state of Anglo-American relations as well as the cavalier attitude of Congress and the executive branch toward maintaining America's image as the world's asylum.[9]

One American foreign policy of the interwar era attracted the attention of the common man to a far greater degree than any other. It was not the League of Nations, the World Court, or disarmament, but the payment of war debts by Europe to the United States Treasury. Europe's notable lack of enthusiasm for repaying the $10.3 billion loaned by the United States during World War I occasioned great finger-pointing and head-shaking from American irreconcilable politicians. Spokesmen such as Senator Kenneth McKellar of Tennessee and Senator Henry W. Ashhurst of Arizona characterized the American loans as valid commercial obligations. Europe should promptly honor its obligations, they sermonized, instead of spending on armaments. If Europe failed to pay with interest, the American taxpayer would be saddled with the bill. On the other side, a phalanx of international bankers warned that debt repayment would depress Europe's ability to purchase American goods. The war debts were political, not commercial, said the bankers, and therefore they were subject to cancellation or substantial reduction. When Harding took office, Americans were divided into two distinct camps: those (the majority) who favored the payment of every dollar of principal and interest owed by Europe, and those who believed that collection would inevitably ruin the economies of Europe and America.

Soon after taking office, Andrew W. Mellon, Harding's Secretary of the Treasury, ordered a review of the foreign loans made under Wilson. A Pittsburgh banker and collector of art, Mellon was one of the world's richest men. But as secretary of the treasury he rejected the cancellationist views of his fellow bankers. Mellon concluded that the most efficient solution would be for Congress to confer upon him discretionary power to negotiate terms of settlement with each debtor including maturity dates and the interest rate. In Congress, which was seeking to regain power lost during the war to the executive branch, questions were raised as to whether it was wise to delegate so much authority to Mellon. The final version, delayed in passage until February 1922 by efforts to attach a veterans' bonus, sharply altered Mellon's proposal. Instead of granting sole negotiating authority to the secretary of the treasury, Congress created a five-man collection agency known as the World War Foreign Debt Commission. According to the strict terminology of the bill, the Debt Commission was instructed to collect the loans at an interest rate of 4.25 percent. To close any possible loophole, the commissioners were forbidden to agree to "cancellation of any part of such indebtedness except through payment thereof."[10]

In practice the members of the Debt Commission appointed by Harding were practical moderates. Mellon was designated by statute as the chairman. The other appointees were Hughes and Hoover, both cabinet officers, and two members of Congress, Senator Reed Smoot of Utah and Representative Theodore Burton of Ohio. Repeatedly the Debt Commission, ignoring the stringent terms laid down by Congress, negotiated the best terms it could get and then submitted each settlement to Congress for separate approval. The Debt Commission hoped that Great Britain, America's largest debtor to the tune of $4.6 billion, would be the first to negotiate. Until 1922 Great Britain's policy on debts had been to stall for time, hoping for a general cancellation of debts. In 1920, for example, Prime Minister David Lloyd George had broken off debt discussions between the United States and British treasuries and appealed unsuccessfully to President Wilson to accept an "all-round arrangement of inter-allied debts."[11] A final cancellationist ploy on the part of the British, which badly backfired, was the so-called Balfour Note of August 1, 1922.

The Balfour Note, signed by Arthur J. Balfour, the British Acting Secretary of State for Foreign Affairs, was sent to each of Britain's debtors—France, Italy, Yugoslavia, Rumania, Portugal, and Greece. The purpose of the communication was to inform the debtor countries that the British government had decided "with the greatest reluctance" to require them "to make arrangements for dealing to the best of their ability" with the loans advanced by the British Treasury. The note portrayed Great Britain as a magnanimous, generous creditor which had always favored a policy of "writing off, through one great transaction, the whole body of inter-allied indebtedness." The United States was depicted as a hard-hearted Shylock. Particularly distasteful to American officialdom was the statement: "In no circumstances do we propose to ask more from our debtors than is necessary to pay our creditors. And while we do not ask for more, all will admit that we can hardly be content with less. For it should not be forgotten, though it sometimes is, that our liabilities were incurred for others, not for ourselves."[12]

Contrary to the intentions of Balfour, his note was universally condemned in the United States. The Treasury Department was especially irritated. According to his nephew, Andrew Mellon was "really mad" and described the Balfour Note as "a lie."[13] According to Undersecretary of the Treasury S. Parker Gilbert, the Balfour Note was "dangerously near to an attempt at repudiation." Furthermore, added Gilbert: "The insistence of the British on the theory that our loans to them were made in order to help their allies is about as irritating a piece of nonsense as has been pulled in the whole discussion about inter-governmental debts." The statement that Britain's debt was incurred for others, Gilbert told Mellon, "is absolutely untrue and the British Government knows it, though for some years past it has lost no opportunity to spread this theory as to the advances made to the British Government by this Government."[14] The American press also criticized the Balfour Note, stressing that cancellation would be a gift to Britain while the American taxpayer remained saddled with a crushing burden.

Gradually the furor subsided. First, the Treasury was greatly pleased when the British made a goodwill payment of $100 million to cover interest due on the debt. Then, in January 1923, a seasick British delegation headed by Chancellor of the Exchequer Stanley Baldwin arrived in Washington for two weeks of talks before returning to London. The stumbling block was the rate of interest. On the basis of capacity to pay, Mellon offered to fund the $4.6 billion debt over sixty-two years at 3.3 percent interest. Prime Minister Andrew Bonar Law had been erroneously led by George Harvey, the indiscreet American ambassador to Britain, to expect an interest rate of only 1.5 to 2 percent. Baldwin and Geddes urged Law to accept the American terms so as to avoid "serious damage to our prestige," and Geddes argued it was "beyond doubt" that any better terms could be negotiated.[15] For the time being the prime minister resisted and called Baldwin home for consultations.

A revealing insight into the real state of Anglo-American relations came in the form of an exceptionally candid dockside interview given by Baldwin on his return. He spoke of being "bound in regard to that debt in the most stringent hands you can possibly imagine." He criticized American provincialism ("The people in the West merely sell wheat and hogs and other products and take no further interest in connection with the international debt. . . . A great many people in America think all we have to do is send the money over"). To Baldwin's shock his interview was widely publicized and criticized in America. A typical response came from Senator Kenneth McKellar of Tennessee who characterized Baldwin's statements as "coarse and uncouth." In Britain's hour of need Americans greeted the Balfour Mission (of 1917) with respect and esteem, said McKellar, but "when pay day comes around they send another commission over here that deals in the dark."[16] The controversy over the Baldwin interview subsided when Geddes announced on February 1, 1923, that the cabinet had accepted the American terms. A few irreconcilables, such as Senator James Reed of Missouri and Senator McKellar, contended that no concessions should have been made on interest, and the *Chicago Tribune* expressed disappointment that Britain had not ceded the British West Indies to the United States.[17] In Congress the settlement easily passed both houses and was signed into law by Harding on February 28, 1923.

The official signing ceremony for the British settlement was finally held on June 18, 1923, a scant week before the first payment was due. Actually Finland, a month and a half earlier, had become the first debtor to sign and seal a war debt settlement with the United States. Shrewdly, Finland agreed to pay its tiny debt of $9 million (which included $1 million in back interest) at the British terms over a sixty-two-year period at 3.3 percent interest. From the perspective of the Harding administration the British and Finnish agreements were ideal models for future settlements because they were reasonable, businesslike, and based on the principle of capacity to pay.

Harding called the British agreement "the first clearing of the war-clouded skies in a debt-burdened world, and the sincere commitment of one great nation to validate its financial pledges and discharge its obligations in the highest sense of financial honor."[18] Temporarily and superficially the British agreement improved Anglo-American relations until the British began to have second thoughts about the wisdom of the terms they had accepted. Lacking a crystal ball, the statesmen of 1923 can be excused for failing to foresee that their work would soon end in instability, illwill, and default. But the fault lay not exclusively with "Republican" foreign policy, since Harding was carrying out a policy that originated with Wilson.

A final Harding policy inherited from Wilson and adhered to with great rigidity was nonrecognition of Soviet Russia. In this case the state department of Charles Evans Hughes and the intensely anti-Bolshevik Assistant Secretary of State Robert Kelley took the anti-communist lead so vociferously that the few advocates of normal relations with Russia were overwhelmed. Justified on the basis of the highest moral principle, the nation's anti-communist paranoia led to another lost opportunity for American interwar diplomacy. In practice, Charles Evans Hughes proved even more rabid an anti-communist than his predecessor. In the first month of the Harding administration the Soviets approached Hughes requesting the opening of trade and diplomatic ties. Using the same arguments advanced by Colby, Hughes told the cabinet that the Soviets would use recognition to distribute revolutionary propaganda; besides, they would not pay legitimate debts, nor would they protect life and property in Russia. With the approval of the cabinet, Hughes announced that the United States saw "no proper basis" for trade relations. Diplomatic ties could only be established when the United States was satisfied that the Soviets would guarantee sanctity of life, contract, property, and the freedom of labor.[19] Despite this unpromising start, a strange two-year interlude of Soviet-American friendship and cooperation began quite unexpectedly a few months later. The cause of the unusual rapprochement was the work of neither statesmen nor conspirators, but a product of drought and civil war: a devastating famine that was most acute in the lower Volga region, the Crimea, the Urals, and even in Ukraine.

The catastrophe produced a human wave of refugees fleeing the devastated countryside to cities where they had heard there was food. For those with money, ample supplies of food, with the exception of bread and flour, were available even in the famine region. But for the penniless, exhausted, and vermin-infested refugees, the results were often tragic, as children were lost or abandoned and hospitals and children's homes overwhelmed. Epidemics of typhus and cholera added to the desolation. To subsist the destitute consumed seed grain, draft animals, cats, dogs, and nearly indigestible, greasy bread made from such substitutes as grasses, roots, bones, bark, acorns, straw, sawdust, clay, weeds, and manure. Numerous cases of cannibalism, corpse eating, insanity, and suicide were reported. A famous appeal for aid by the writer Maxim Gorky made the world aware of the calamity. "I ask all honest European and American people for prompt aid to the Russian people," he wrote. "Give bread and medicine."[20] According to the estimate of the Norwegian humanitarian Fridtjof Nansen, two million people perished from hunger and disease in Russia during the famine years 1921–1922.

The residents of the famine region experienced one stroke of good fortune in that the United States happened in 1921 to have available the world's best prepared relief organization. Founded in 1919 as an official government agency by the mining engineer, financier, and humanitarian Herbert Hoover, the American Relief Administration (ARA) continued in existence after World War I as a private organization with close ties to the United States government. By the terms of an agreement reached at Riga with the Soviets, the ARA mounted a $60 million, two-year effort that required the efforts of more than 200 American supervisors, inspectors, and physicians, as well as numerous grain ships, port officers, and United States Navy destroyers. The ARA's first priority was to establish kitchens for feeding Russian children plain but nutritious meals of corn bread, corn grits, maize gruel, and maize pudding (a combination of number two grade mixed corn with canned milk, sugar, fats, and salt). Having complied with its rule of "Feed Them First," the ARA then turned its attention to providing dry rations to hungry adults and to the distribution of food remittance packages, seed grain, clothing, shoes, socks, and medical supplies. The work of unloading, shipping, preparing, and serving ARA food required the services of almost 80,000 Russian employees and the setting up of 15,700 kitchens. At its high point in August 1922, the ARA was feeding more than ten million people every day. The exact number of lives saved can only be guessed but certainly numbered in the millions. Herbert Hoover's estimate was somewhere between ten and twenty million lives, although the Moscow office of the ARA leaned toward the more modest estimate of no fewer than five million.

Throughout the famine region the picture of Herbert Hoover became ubiquitous. Children playing in the streets would shout "Arah" when an ARA car or truck passed. American officials were inundated with emotional expressions of gratitude, often in verse and accompanied by illustrations showing intertwined Russian and American flags and the unloading of American food and medical supplies. According to the Riga agreement of 1921, which permitted the ARA to operate on Russian soil, the ARA was to confine itself solely to relief of the destitute. Political involvement was forbidden, at least in theory. But in practice many ARA workers and administrators, including economist Lincoln Hutchinson and former Indiana Governor James P. Goodrich, concluded that establishing trade and diplomatic relations with the Soviets was in America's best interest. Optimistically they believed the Soviets were moving inevitably toward capitalism and that recognition and trade would accelerate the abandonment of the foolish communist economic system. On June 19, 1922, Governor Goodrich and Stanford University historian Frank Golder met at the Kremlin with top Communist leaders including L.B. Kamenev, Maxim Litvinov, Aleksii Rykov, Leonid Krassin, and Grigori Sokolnikov. In a wide-ranging discussion, Goodrich found the Soviets had substantially met the conditions laid down by Hughes and that the two sides were not far apart on such issues as trade and debts. In combination with Senator Borah, Raymond Robins, and the Russian-American businessman Alexander Gumberg, Goodrich sought to interest the Harding administration in sending a commission to Russia to explore recognition. When that idea floundered, due to the opposition of Hughes, Goodrich received a promise from Harding to reassess his administration's Russian policy following his return in August 1923 from Alaska. Optimistically Goodrich wrote Alexander Gumberg, "I am really somewhat hopeful of getting results after the return of the President if nothing happens between now and then to complicate the situation. In the past something has always happened. I hope it won't this time."[21] Once again fate was against the advocates of normalizing Soviet-American relations as Harding became ill at San Francisco on his return from Alaska and died there on August 2, 1923. In the meantime the ARA operation in Russia was terminated and political contact between the two nations severed. Even the saving of millions of Russian lives failed to alter the political impasse. For all practical purposes the door to normal relations was closed for another decade.

NOTES

1. Betty Glad, *Charles Evans Hughes and the Illusions of Innocence: A Study in American Diplomacy* (Urbana, 1966), 132.

2. Mark Sullivan, *The Great Adventure at Washington: The Story of the Conference* (Garden City, 1922), 269.

3. Merlo J. Pusey, *Charles Evans Hughes* (New York, 1951), Vol. 2, 520–22.

4. Drew Pearson, *Washington Merry-Go-Round* (New York, 1931), 147. See also Martin Weil, *A Pretty Good Club: The Founding Fathers of the U.S. Foreign Service* (New York, 1978).

5. Robert K. Murray, *The Harding Era: Warren G. Harding and His Administration* (Minneapolis, 1969), 136.

6. Curzon to Geddes, September 16, 1921, FO414/248/A6238, Public Record Office.

7. Hughes to Curzon, October 3, 1921, General Records of the Department of State, File No. 150.08/92, RG 59, National Archives.

8. Geddes to Curzon, January 18, 1923, *Parliamentary Paper* (1923, XXV, Cmd. 1940), 4.

9. See Benjamin D. Rhodes, "A Modern 'Black Hole of Calcutta'? The Anglo-American Controversy Over Ellis Island, 1921–1924," *New York History* (July 1985), 229–48.

10. World War Foreign Debt Commission, *Combined Annual Reports of the World War Foreign Debt Commission with Additional Information Regarding Foreign Debts Due the United States* (Washington, D.C., 1927), 89.

11. Lloyd George to Wilson, August 5, 1920. *Combined Annual Reports*, 72–73.

12. Ambassador George Harvey to Hughes, August 4, 1922, Department of State, *Papers Relating to the Foreign Relations of the United States* [1922] (Washington, D.C., 1938), Vol. 1, 406–9 (hereafter cited as FRUS).

13. William Larimer Mellon, *Judge Mellon's Sons* (Pittsburgh, 1948), 447–48.

14. Gilbert to Eliot Wadsworth, August 17, 1922, and Gilbert to Mellon, August 17, 1922, "Fiscal Relationship of the United States and Foreign Countries, 1917–1941," Department of the Treasury, Records of the Bureau of Accounts, RG 39 (National Archives).

15. Law to Sir Robert Horne, January 22, 1923, FO371/8503/A440, Public Record Office (PRO); Geddes to Law, January 26, 1923, FO371/8504/A194, PRO.

16. *New York Times*, January 28, 1923; *Congressional Record*, 67 Cong., 4 Sess., 2669 (January 29, 1923).

17. *Literary Digest* 76 (March 3, 1923), 10–11; *Chicago Tribune*, February 2, 3, 1923.

18. World War Foreign Debt Commission, *Combined Annual Reports*, 98.

19. Murray, *The Harding Era*, 349.

20. Harold J. Goldberg, editor, *Intervention, Famine Relief, International Affairs, 1917–1933*, Vol. 1, *Documents of Soviet-American Relations* (Gulf Breeze, Florida, 1993), 198–99.

21. Quoted in Benjamin D. Rhodes, *James P. Goodrich: Indiana's "Governor Strangelove": A Republican's Infatuation with Soviet Russia* (Selinsgrove, Pennsylvania, 1996), 134.

CHAPTER 4

Foreign Policy Under Coolidge
and Kellogg: A Relative Bed of Roses

Calvin Coolidge was one of the unlikeliest American presidents and easily the most eccentric. The son of a Vermont politician, Coolidge was educated at Amherst College, then read law at Northampton, Massachusetts, and began a relentless climb up the Massachusetts political ladder. His election in November 1918 as governor of Massachusetts appeared to be a fitting pinnacle to a career founded exclusively on local and state issues. But a series of chance events brought Coolidge to national attention. First, he became a hero when he took a hard line during the Boston police strike of 1919. Styling the strikers "deserters," Coolidge supported the dismissal of those who had not reported for service. Then at the 1920 Republican convention at Chicago, to Coolidge's surprise, the delegates revolted against their party leaders and nominated him for vice president. When asked by his wife whether he would accept the post, the taciturn Coolidge replied, "I suppose I shall have to."[1]

Had it not been for the accident of Harding's death, Coolidge would likely have faded into the same political oblivion that had befallen such recent vice presidents as Charles Fairbanks, James S. Sherman, and Thomas R. Marshall. To the presidency he brought common sense, a conciliatory style of problem solving, and a reputation for remaining composed under fire. The latter quality he demonstrated in the early morning hours of August 3, 1923, when he learned of Harding's death while he and his wife were visiting the family farm at Plymouth Notch, Vermont. On the advice of Hughes, Coolidge secured a copy of the presidential oath, which his father administered by the light of an oil lamp amid a small audience of neighbors and reporters. Later when asked what had been his first thought on learning he had become president, Coolidge typically responded, "I thought I could swing it."[2]

In domestic affairs Coolidge was adequately equipped to "swing it," as evidenced by his efficient prosecution of the scandals he had inherited from Harding. Foreign policy, however, was an area where Coolidge found himself utterly inexperienced and uninformed and therefore dependent upon his secretaries of state, Charles Evans Hughes and Frank B. Kellogg. Coolidge's inclination was to solve problems as they came to him rather than to launch foreign policy initiatives. Basically he continued his predecessor's policies on war debts, disarmament, the League of Nations, the World Court, and nonrecognition of the Soviet Union. Toward Latin America his good-neighborliness was modified by fears of communist subversion. The boldest Coolidge foreign policy initiative, which in time made him look foolish, was the 1928 Pact of Paris for the renunciation of war.

For a position that required frequent public appearances and speech-making, Coolidge often appeared taciturn and introverted. Usually he went about the business of delivering a speech stoically, rarely acknowledging applause or the presence of friends through nods or smiles. And, although the silences of "Silent Cal" were very evident, he often combined awkward gaps in conversation with a dry Yankee sense of humor. Sir Esme Howard, who replaced Sir Auckland Geddes as British ambassador in 1924, observed during his first meeting with Coolidge that when the president chose to make a humorous remark his eye would suddenly show a sparkle "rather like that in the eye of a parrot that is about to give someone a tweak." When Howard presented Lord Robert Cecil to the president, he received his visitor with a painful silence. Then with a gleam in his eye Coolidge remarked, "When folks come to see me I expect them to do the talking." That broke the ice and permitted conversation to flow "as much as it ever did with Mr. Coolidge."[3]

Coolidge had never left the United States and often, in self-righteous platitudes, he conveyed the impression that he was a Vermont boy who had never left the farm. Once, probably with tongue in cheek, Coolidge shocked Lady Isabella Howard by stating that he would never visit Europe because America possessed everything he wished to learn. For all his apparent Yankee provincialism, Coolidge was not in sympathy with the irreconcilables, whom he regarded as obstructionists. Like Harding, Coolidge had no intention of being his own secretary of state and, as had been the case with Harding, Coolidge relied heavily on Hughes. One of Coolidge's first foreign affairs problems was finding a replacement for Ambassador to Great Britain George Harvey, who had long been in Hughes's bad graces due to his frequent indiscretions, including heavy drinking—prohibition notwithstanding. Coolidge first offered the post to Elihu Root and then to former Illinois Governor Frank Lowden, both of whom declined. Coolidge next interviewed former Minnesota Senator Frank B. Kellogg, who was in Washington arguing a case before the Supreme Court. By agreeing to go to

London, Kellogg won the confidence of the new president and became a likely candidate to head the State Department should a vacancy occur.

As long as Hughes headed the State Department, he dominated the formulation of foreign policy. That was made plain when, in his carefully prepared 1923 State of the Union message, Coolidge, at the urging of Raymond Robins, included a conciliatory overture to the Soviets. The United States, said the president, ought to be "the first to go to the economic and moral rescue" of Russia, provided the Soviets ended revolutionary propaganda, paid for confiscated property, and recognized repudiated debts. "We have every desire to help and no desire to injure," Coolidge concluded. Grigori Chicherin, the Soviet Commissar for Foreign Affairs, expressed a "complete willingness" to discuss outstanding problems.[4] However, instead of unconditionally accepting Coolidge's conditions, Chicherin called for basing discussions upon reciprocity and the principle of non-intervention in the internal affairs of others. The legalistic Hughes then decisively intervened and ruled out any thought of negotiation until Moscow first restored confiscated property, recognized its debt, and promised not to spread propaganda. Hughes's nonrecognition stance prevailed despite the decision of the British to recognize the Soviets in the spring of 1924. On July 1 Hughes reaffirmed his hard-line nonrecognition position, contending that the Soviets had refused to pay valid debts, engaged in subversive efforts to undermine the United States government, and had imposed the will of a small minority upon the Russian people. Strangely, Coolidge, preoccupied with the Harding scandals and his own election campaign, took no public notice of the contradiction between his State of the Union overture and the intense anti-communism of Hughes.

Much of Hughes's final year as secretary of state was devoted to seeking a solution to the German financial crisis, caused by runaway inflation and a default of German reparations payments to the Allies. Hughes had to move cautiously to avoid the scrutiny of the irreconcilables. Theoretically reparations were not a concern of the United States since, from the time of the Peace Conference, the official American position had been that the payment of German reparations to the Allies was unrelated to the Allies' payment of war debts to the United States. To everyone else the connection seemed clear enough. Hughes first suggested, in a speech to the American Historical Association on December 29, 1922, that the United States should assist in an adjustment of reparations. Specifically he suggested that "distinguished Americans" should prepare a payment plan. Behind the scenes Hughes engineered the appointment of Chicago banker Charles G. Dawes as chairman of a commission of experts to study currency stabilization. The plan proposed by Dawes provided for a sliding scale of German payments beginning with one million marks the first year, increasing to two and a half million marks annually after five years. An essential feature of the Dawes Plan was a $200 million loan to Germany to be extended by American and European bankers. Both Hughes and Kellogg played crucial roles in convincing the Allies and Germany to accept the arrangement. At London in mid-July, Kellogg used a Dawes Plan conference to pressure France and Germany to accept. Simultaneously Hughes made an unofficial European visit, masquerading in his role as president of the American Bar Association, to promote a reparations settlement. The American squeeze play paid off handsomely when French Premier Edouard Herriot capitulated and the Dawes Plan temporarily relieved the German financial crisis.[5] Typically the American role had been indirect, unofficial, and involved no governmental commitment.

Before leaving office, Hughes had to grapple with another minor Anglo-American dispute, but one that typified the less-than-cordial state of relations between Washington and London. This time the two nations clashed over national prohibition, which went into effect in the United States with the passage of the Volstead Act of 1920. The measure, which enforced the Eighteenth Amendment to the Constitution, banned the sale of any beverage containing more than one half of one percent alcohol. Immediately there appeared a lucrative liquor-smuggling industry, which was headquartered at Nassau in the Bahamas. To the highly taxed British liquor industry and the depressed Bahamas, prohibition proved a financial godsend. Seeking to avoid seizure by the United States Coast Guard, American rum runners rushed to secure the safety of British registry at Nassau. British liquor exports to the Bahamas, which were legal, soared from a mere 27,427 gallons in 1918 to 567,940 gallons in 1921, and the revenue of the Bahamian government increased correspondingly. Cooperative officials in the Bahamas encouraged smuggling by issuing bootleggers, for a fee, two sets of papers designed to outwit the Coast Guard. One set, to be produced if the vessel was halted, purported that the ship was legally transporting liquor from the Bahamas to Canada. The other, designed for use if the liquor was successfully unloaded into the boats of collaborators, stated that the ship was sailing empty from the Bahamas to the United States. By the summer of 1921 a "rum fleet" of as many as fifty-five British vessels began hovering off the coasts of New York and New Jersey (known as Rum Row), waiting for an opportunity to discharge Scotch whiskey into speedy rum runners.

Initially the liquor dispute fell into the category of a minor nuisance. However, on April 30, 1923, the Supreme Court in *Cunard v. Mellon* held that the attorney general had the power to seize foreign liquor within the territorial waters of the United States. In a test case, United States customs officials boarded the British liner *Berengaria* and removed its sealed store of liquor while leaving undisturbed liquor earmarked for medicinal purposes. Thereafter British liners were able to sell liquor only on voyages to the United States, with any excess thrown overboard upon reaching the three-mile limit. Hughes found an apparent solution to the imbroglio in the Anglo-American Liquor Treaty, which was ratified by the Senate on March 13, 1924. The British agreed to permit the visit and search of suspected smugglers and allowed the Coast Guard to apprehend fleeing bootleggers at a distance of up to one hour, depending upon the speed of the vessel concerned, from the coast of the United States. In practice the Liquor Treaty was hardly a landmark in Anglo-American friendship. One immediate benefit was that the size of the rum fleet was reduced to ten to twelve vessels hovering thirty to ninety miles off the coast. However, Britain had only signed the treaty to prevent further damage to its trans-Atlantic transit industry. And the one-hour limit contained in the treaty proved unworkable as a legal proposition. Moreover, the federal courts refused to permit Coast Guard entrapment techniques or the use of hypothetical measurements of the distance a smuggler could cover within an hour. The most serious disputes were the cases of the *W.H. Eastwood*, which in 1926 was struck by machine gun fire from a Coast Guard cutter engaged in "target practice," and the 1929 case of the *I'm Alone*, which was sunk by shell fire after a chase of 200 miles into the Gulf of Mexico. It was not the Liquor Treaty that ended the trans-Atlantic bickering over deliberate and flagrant British bootlegging, but the repeal of national prohibition in 1934.[6]

The Charles Evans Hughes era at the State Department ended in January 1925, when the sixty-three-year-old secretary of state announced his intention to return to the practice of law. After twenty years of public office, Hughes was said to be tired and in need of augmenting his income. At least that was the public explanation for his departure. In reality Hughes hoped and expected to remain in office following Coolidge's inauguration on March 4, 1925. As a formality he and other cabinet members submitted their resignations and to Hughes's shock his was accepted. The secretive Coolidge never offered an explanation, but his desire for a change was likely influenced by Hughes's distant, arrogant, and legalistic personality. "Silent Cal" apparently felt uncomfortable with the stiff, bearded, but not silent, Hughes.

Hughes was easily the most dominating secretary of state of the interwar era. He left office having won the respect of his associates for his hard work and keen legal mind. Theoretically he left a more professional foreign service, although in practice members of the diplomatic branch managed to control the promotion process to the detriment of the former Consular Service. Instead of creating a happy family of professionals, the Rogers Act left a legacy of bitter internal feuding. To contemporaries, Hughes seemed the greatest of American secretaries of state, with the possible exception of John Quincy Adams. But Hughes's reputation, like those of such other American interwar leaders as Harding, Coolidge, Mellon, and Hoover, faded badly with the collapse of prosperity and the perception that Hughes's legal and moralistic vision, as represented by the Washington Conference treaties, was irrelevant and impotent in meeting the fascist challenge of the 1930s. If Hughes was not quite the miracle worker described in legend, his was unquestionably a tough act to follow.

Former Minnesota Senator Frank B. Kellogg, sixty-eight years old, was Hughes's hand-picked successor. In terms of direct contact with foreign affairs, Kellogg was better prepared than his predecessor. A wealthy Minnesotan corporation lawyer, he was the successful Republican candidate for the Senate in 1916. He served on the Foreign Relations Committee, and during the debate over the Versailles Treaty he was a mild reservationist. Defeated for reelection in 1922, he was appointed ambassador to Great Britain in 1923. In that position he managed to keep his hot temper under control, but as secretary of state his temperamental outbursts became legendary. Behind his back he was often called "Nervous Nellie," a nickname which was malicious and mean spirited.[7] He was appointed secretary of state by a president who was anxious to maintain the status quo in foreign policy and to avoid fractious disputes within his own party. Coolidge later boasted he had been a president who minded his own business and he expected his secretary of state to do the same. Kellogg was appointed to keep the State Department on an even keel and to avoid rocking the boat, and within those parameters he succeeded.

From the beginning of his appointment (March 3, 1925), Kellogg followed paths previously charted by Hughes. On the topic of the Soviet Union, he disappointed the advocates of recognition by taking an even more dogmatic position than had Hughes. Senator Borah had now become the chairman of the Senate Foreign Relations Committee following the death of Henry Cabot Lodge in November 1924. But Borah found Kellogg's mind closed to any suggestion of recognition as he brandished "intercepted" documents supposedly proving a diabolical Kremlin plot to subvert American blacks. Former Indiana governor James P. Goodrich met a similar response. Following a Russian tour in the fall of 1925, Goodrich urged Coolidge to use his 1925 State of the Union address to endorse Russian recognition. The exchange of ambassadors, Goodrich advised Coolidge, would advance world stability, strengthen American business ties with Russia, and "accelerate rather than retard the march now going on from communism to capitalism." Coolidge dashed the hopes of the recognition advocates with a typically bland two-sentence reply thanking Goodrich for his "very interesting letter on the situation in Russia. I am always glad to have your views and am obliged to you for writing me so fully."[8]

Fear of possible Communist subversion in the vicinity of the Panama Canal lay behind the Latin American policy of the Coolidge administration, which represented a decided pause in the development of the Good

Neighbor Policy. Actually both Coolidge and Kellogg lacked basic information and interest in the region and heavily relied on those in the field for advice. Ambassador to Mexico James Rockwell Sheffield and Assistant Secretary of State Robert E. Olds, both wealthy and conservative attorneys, largely determined American policy toward Mexico. The immediate dispute between the two nations was an outgrowth of the great social revolution that had swept over Mexico during the presidencies of William Howard Taft and Woodrow Wilson. In 1917 Mexico adopted a new constitution designed to reverse the virtual giveaway of Mexican land and resources which had characterized the long dictatorship (1876–1911) of Porfirio Díaz. Article 27 of the 1917 Constitution vested ownership of subsoil mineral rights in the Mexican nation. If literally enforced, Article 27 would have expropriated the holdings of foreign oil companies. The threat of Plutarco Elías Calles, who was elected president of Mexico in 1924, to enforce the 1917 Constitution through legislation produced a new crisis in Mexican-American relations. Both Sheffield and Olds argued for a hard-line American response, and Olds made the sensational, but unsubstantiated, charge that Bolshevik influence was spreading southward from Mexico toward the Panama Canal.

In 1927 the crisis subsided almost as quickly as it had appeared largely due to a rare example of successful personal diplomacy. To replace the unpopular Sheffield, Coolidge named the New York financier Dwight Morrow, who had just ended his ties with J.P. Morgan and Company. The new ambassador employed unconventional methods, including traveling to Mexico City in his private railroad car and hiring a competent personal staff out of his own pocket. Morrow also displayed old fashioned charm and succeeded in establishing a flexible and conciliatory relationship with Calles. The controversy was all but settled when the Supreme Court of Mexico, under pressure from Calles, handed down a favorable decision permitting American petroleum companies, which had begun development prior to the 1917 Constitution, to retain ownership.[9]

Nicaragua was the other major Latin American trouble spot during the Coolidge administration. As in the case of Mexico, relations with Nicaragua were complicated by repeated American interventions, the most recent of which had occurred in 1912 during Taft's "dollar diplomacy." A token legation guard of marines still was stationed at Managua until it was unwisely removed in August 1925. Former president Emiliano Chamorro, who had been fraudulently counted out in the 1924 election, maneuvered his way into power at the expense of President Carlos Solózano and Vice President Juan Sacasa. As revolution flared along Nicaragua's east coast in the spring of 1926, United States marines were landed with instructions to suppress the fighting. Nevertheless, the fighting spread by 1927 to the west coast. A few months previously, Chamorro had fallen from power and had been replaced by one of his confederates, Adolfo Díaz, whom Coolidge recognized. At the same time, Mexico recognized Juan Sacasa and encouraged his revolution against the Díaz government. The credibility of both Kellogg and Coolidge suffered when they attributed the instability of Nicaragua to Bolshevik plotting.

Coolidge managed to extricate himself from the dilemma by dispatching to Nicaragua, as he had to Mexico, a skilled troubleshooter in the person of Henry L. Stimson. Already Stimson had served Taft as secretary of war, a position to which he was again named in 1940. In between he served Hoover as secretary of state. Arriving at Managua in the spring of 1927, Stimson insisted that Díaz remain in power and that the United States supervise the 1928 election so as to guarantee fairness and stability and forestall the standard Latin American solution of a revolution. With the exception of the revolutionary Augusto C. Sandino, all parties agreed to the terms negotiated by Stimson. To the relief of Washington, the 1928 election, won by the liberal candidate José Moncada, was generally agreed to have been fair and peaceful.[10]

On the whole, the Latin American policy of the Coolidge administration had been improvised at the last minute and was based on the false assumption that Soviet agents were behind Latin American instability. Neither Coolidge nor Kellogg took much serious interest in the region and found it the path of least resistance to fall back on Theodore Roosevelt's policy of "big stick" intervention in the internal affairs of banana republics. Much more farsighted was the drafting in 1928, at Kellogg's request, of the J. Reuben Clark Memorandum rejecting any right for the United States to intervene in Latin America under the authority of the Monroe Doctrine. In 1905 Theodore Roosevelt had twisted the "hands off" theme of the Monroe Doctrine to justify American intervention in Latin America so as to avert chaos. However, the Clark Memorandum, named for Kellogg's undersecretary of state, was not published until 1930, and it did not categorically rule out intervention. As late as the 1928 Havana Pan American Conference, the American representative, Charles Evans Hughes, refused to endorse a statement denouncing the right of intervention under all conditions.[11] When Coolidge and Kellogg left office in 1929 American relations with Latin America were at their lowest level of the interwar era.

To contend that the Department of State was in mothballs during Kellogg's tenure would be going too far. But Kellogg had little direct influence on two major foreign policies of the period that made the United States appear narrow-minded as well as sullen and selfish in purpose. In fairness to Kellogg, both the question of joining the World Court and the conflict over repayment of European war debts were issues so enmeshed in partisan politics that probably no secretary of state could have made a difference. Both Coolidge and Kellogg advocated United States membership in the World Court. In his first State of the Union message, Coolidge urged the Senate to approve participation in the World Court with the four reservations suggested by Hughes. Likewise Kellogg, speaking to the American Society of International Law, endorsed American participation. All appearances were that the World Court proposal would pass, especially after the House of Representatives overwhelmingly approved membership by a vote of 302 to 28.

Senator Borah, taking his cue from the deceased Henry Cabot Lodge, denounced what he called the "League Court." He contended, rather transparently, that he favored the concept of a world court, but opposed one related to the League of Nations. Borah, and other World Court opponents, found a solution by adding a fifth reservation stating that the World Court could not, without American approval, hand down an advisory opinion on any matter involving the United States. (According to the League constitution, the League Council could request advice from the World Court on current matters that were before it.) In reality, rendering advisory opinions was a minor function of the World Court, but the strategy worked for the irreconcilables. With five reservations the proposal passed the Senate on January 27, 1926, by a vote of 76 to 17. But it proved impossible to secure acceptance of the reservations by all forty-seven World Court members.[12] With good reason, Coolidge abandoned hope, and the World Court issue faded into oblivion until debated for a final time in 1935. Given the determination and skill of the World Court opponents, it is hard to see what more Coolidge and Kellogg could have done to join the World Court; it is equally difficult to see whether American membership would have affected world events to any great extent.

It was during Coolidge's presidency that America's image abroad sank disastrously. The immediate cause was clear enough: European resentment against the United States' closing of the New York loan market and simultaneously imposing war debt settlements under duress. Instead of the wartime image of generous "Uncle Sam," the United States was widely stereotyped abroad as the sinister creditor "Uncle Shylock." The role played by the State Department in settling the war debts was only a peripheral one inasmuch as the basic collection policy had been established by Congress and was implemented through the World War Foreign Debt Commission headed by Treasury Secretary Mellon. Nevertheless, the unpopular debt settlements imposed by the Debt Commission complicated Kellogg's conduct of foreign policy and reinforced the American impression that Europeans were ungrateful.

When Coolidge took office, model debt settlements with Great Britain and Finland had already been completed. It was his intention to continue the process begun under Harding, and Coolidge supposedly summarized his views on the topic with the shallow remark, "They hired the money, didn't they?" To collect "the money" the Coolidge administration made use of a new method: closing the domestic loan market to countries with unfunded debts to the United States. In 1924 the Debt Commission used closure of the loan market to convince such minor debtors as Hungary, Lithuania, and Poland to accept the British terms; Czechoslovakia, Estonia, Latvia, and Rumania followed in 1925. At the same time Belgium, the United States' fourth largest debtor after Britain, France, and Italy, agreed to terms. Belgium's debt of $417,780,000 was unusually controversial because the Versailles Treaty had made Germany responsible for Belgium's pre-Armistice debt to the United States of about $172 million. Since the Senate rejected the Versailles Treaty, the Debt Commission included that amount in the total due. When Belgium sought a $50 million loan in May 1925 from J.P. Morgan and Company, Kellogg (who was now a member of the Debt Commission) told the bankers that the State Department would not look with favor upon the loan until Belgium funded its debt. To secure access to the credit market Belgium then came to terms; the Debt Commission agreed to charge no interest on Belgium's pre-Armistice debt, which was payable over the standard sixty-two-year period. The British terms (3.3 percent interest over sixty-two years) were required on the remainder of $246 million. Although the Belgian settlement was the most liberal made by the Debt Commission up to that time, it was highly unpopular in Belgium. The Belgian press printed news of the settlement under the headline "THE AMERICAN SHYLOCK WANTS TO BE PAID AT ONCE," and charged that the signature of President Wilson had become a mere scrap of paper.[13]

Even more generous terms were extended to Italy, which, including back interest, owed just over $2 billion. The Italian government of Benito Mussolini pleaded poverty and suggested that the debt be retired over a century without interest; if Germany failed to pay reparations, Italy asked for the right to suspend payments. Both Mellon and Kellogg adopted a hard line. The Italian proposal did not constitute a valid offer, they said. Mellon bluntly told the Italians that he would insist on payment of the principal at once plus five percent interest if Italy did not modify its terms. So almost immediately the Italians capitulated and for the usual reason: they needed access to the New York loan market. In November 1925 an Italian debt commission arrived in Washington and, accompanied by economists with skillfully prepared pamphlets and statistics, presented a convincing description of Italy's dubious capacity to pay. After two weeks of negotiations the Debt Commission extended Italy its most generous terms: the $2 billion debt was to be repaid over sixty-two years at just 0.4 percent interest. Despite the objections of congressional Democrats, who contended the low interest rate subsidized Italian militarism, Congress gave its approval.[14]

The most bitter recriminations of all emanated from the French who, including unpaid interest and the purchase of American surplus war stocks, owed the Treasury slightly more than $4 billion. In 1922 Premier Raymond Poincaré took the intransigent position that "France is not in a position to make any agreement concerning the payment of her political debts." The implication was that France's debt, incurred on behalf of a common cause, was subject to bargaining or cancellation. Two years later Myron T. Herrick, the American ambassador to France, was handed a typically unacceptable proposal by the French finance minister suggesting a settlement on the basis of a complete moratorium for ten years, no interest for the next ten years, and 0.5 percent interest for the following ninety years. French opinion passionately held that France had paid in blood at Verdun and the battles of the Marne. The French Chamber of Deputies gave Louis Marin, its former vice president, a demonstrative standing ovation when he proclaimed: "If in this world the power of gold has so much influence on the policy of nations, then farewell to justice and farewell to the power of conscience and the high influence of the great heart of humanity." When Senator Borah accused the French of "finessing for cancellation," Marin retorted that the United States had substituted a golden calf for the Statue of Liberty.[15]

Headed by Finance Minister Joseph Caillaux, a French debt commission arrived at Washington in an uncompromising frame of mind in September 1925. Prior to his departure, angry French war veterans presented to Herrick—for him to present to Senator Borah—a wooden leg, an American medal, khaki and blue helmets, and a history of the American Revolution. They stated to Herrick: "We attach a medal which one of our comrades received for saving the life of an American officer at the front. He does not want it any longer. He is returning it to Senator Borah: we owe him so much money. We also add a wooden leg such as those worn by thousands of French soldiers. All of it you have here in a blue helmet such as fought side by side with the American khaki helmet on the field of battle in 1918. Ask if Senator Borah would only understand that the day will come when the price in gold which he wishes to collect won't be worth the price in blood which we have shed."[16]

The primary stumbling block in the negotiations was Caillaux's insistence on a "safeguard clause," permitting France to suspend payments in the event Germany failed to pay reparations. Commerce Secretary Herbert Hoover, a member of the Debt Commission, rose to the occasion by devising a disarmingly simple statement: "This agreement is based upon the economic capacity of France to meet the annual payments set out. It is therefore agreed that if it shall be proved that these payments are beyond the capacity of France to pay the payments are to be jointly reviewed by the two governments." When the French rejected Hoover's statesmanlike proposal the talks collapsed and Caillaux returned home. Finally, in the spring of 1926, a new French ambassador, former Senator Henry Bérenger, reached a settlement with the Debt Commission. In return for relinquishing the concept of a safeguard clause, Bérenger secured significant concessions on the rate of interest. Over the sixty-two years of the agreement the average interest rate was just 1.6 percent. And under the Mellon-Bérenger Accord, France would pay only $160 million during the first five years as compared to $220 million agreed to by Caillaux.[17]

In theory the settlements negotiated by the Debt Commission provided that the United States, over the standard sixty-year payment period, would receive slightly more than $22 billion. Mellon maintained that the Debt Commission had achieved "a true balance . . . between the duty of the debt commission to the American taxpayer and fairness toward those nations to which was extended aid during and after the war."[18] American opinion accorded the issue more attention than it warranted from a purely economic viewpoint. The reality was that the debt payments were less important to the national finance of the United States than contemporaries believed because, with the exception of Great Britain, the payments were scaled down in the early years of the agreements. Italy and France received special treatment and France did not ratify the Mellon-Bérenger Accord until 1929. The significance of the war debts was political, not economic: they poisoned relations with the United States' former allies and intensified isolationism at home by convincing Americans that Europe was ungrateful, morally bankrupt, and unworthy of American attention. In France resentment against the "Shylock" American debt settlement took the form of a Paris demonstration (July 11, 1926) by 20,000 veterans, headed by the blind, the maimed, and the shell shocked parading in silent protest. Various other outrages and insults were directed at American tourists, and cynical editorials criticized America's love of money at the expense of ideals. Joining the criticism was Chancellor of the Exchequer Winston Churchill who, in the summer of 1926, attacked the "rigour" the United States had meted out to Britain in the 1923 debt settlement. Senator Borah accused Churchill of launching a "Gallipoli campaign," and Kellogg called in the British chargé to protest.[19]

The atmosphere of mutual recriminations did not help at all when the United States, Britain, and Japan met at Geneva, Switzerland, from June to August 1927 to consider further steps toward disarmament. The objective was simple enough: to extend the Washington Conference ratio to lesser ships, especially cruisers. Kellogg invited all the Washington Conference participants to attend, but France and Italy declined due to their growing naval rivalry in the Mediterranean. So, at Geneva only the three ranking naval powers were in attendance: the United States, Great Britain, and Japan. Three months of negotiation led precisely nowhere and the conference adjourned an obvious failure. Why did it fail? A standard answer was that a lack of preparation and prior agreement was the culprit; this was the view of Vice President Charles G. Dawes. A more convincing explanation is that the conference failed because of Anglo-American distrust and naval rivalry.

At the outset prospects seemed bright for success since both the United States and Britain paid lip service to applying to cruisers the 5:5:3 tonnage ratios agreed to at Washington for battleships. But the conference was dominated by the egos and professional aspirations of naval experts, such as Rear Admiral Hilary P. Jones of the United States and Sir William Bridgeman of Great Britain, rather than by the political leaders who had been in charge at Washington. Superficially the two positions were not far apart. The basic problem was how to apportion the tonnage quotas among heavy and light cruisers. United States naval policy emphasized the construction of heavy 10,000-ton cruisers with eight-inch guns and a long cruising range. The British stressed light cruisers of 6,000 tons and six-inch guns. Bridgeman insisted upon Britain's "absolute need" for seventy cruisers; fifty-five would be of the 6,000-ton class and only ten of the 10,000-ton category. Britain, said Bridgeman, must have a superiority in numbers of cruisers, although he would concede overall tonnage parity.

The conference was soon tangled in a semantic dispute. The American position was that the conference must first agree on maximum tonnage limits before considering a limit on numbers. On the other hand, the Admiralty insisted that the number of vessels should be agreed to before limiting tonnage. To the man on the street such a disagreement was unintelligible. In reality, the debate over technical matters disguised the fact that, in the event of another world conflict, the two nations were potential naval rivals. With the experience of World War I behind them, the British wanted a large fleet of light cruisers to protect commerce and their far-flung empire. Moreover, the light cruisers would be essential for enforcing maritime belligerent rights, including blockade. On the other hand, the United States Navy envisioned the heavy cruisers as useful commerce raiders and as essential weapons for breaking blockades. As aptly summarized by General Preston Brown in a conversation with the British military attaché in Washington, the British wanted more light cruisers so as to be able to establish a blockade; the United States Navy wanted the large cruisers so as to challenge potential British blockades. Kellogg and Coolidge regarded the British performance at Geneva as a stab in the back, and Coolidge recommended that the United States undertake a massive naval buildup, which was partially implemented in the Naval Construction Act of February 1929, which authorized the construction of fifteen cruisers. In fact the act proved to be a bluff, because it also provided for suspension by the president if a naval limitation agreement became reality. After the London Naval Conference of 1930 and the crisis in American finance produced by the Great Depression, the United States quietly capitulated, so that by 1932 the United States Navy had only nineteen cruisers to Britain's fifty-two.[20]

To later generations Kellogg's reputation as a muddleheaded statesman was established because he lent his name to what was one of the most

bizarre treaties ever conceived: the Kellogg-Briand Pact for the renunciation of war as an instrument of national policy. Originally conceived as a
Franco-American pact, it was endorsed by sixty-four nations when it went
into effect. Even Kellogg in his retirement became disillusioned and suspected that the treaty, for which he had received the 1930 Nobel Peace Prize,
had become (to use a phrase coined by Senator James A. Reed) an "international kiss."[21]

In retrospect it seems incredible that two such experienced statesmen as
French Foreign Minister Aristide Briand and Kellogg could have associated
themselves with such a strange document. In truth they brought much of
the problem upon themselves through opportunistic political maneuvering
on the part of Briand and misplaced idealism on the part of Kellogg. Skillful and energetic pressure generated by dedicated pacifists completed the
picture. Just who originated the concept of outlawing war is still a subject
of some dispute. Among American pacifists, Columbia University President
Nicholas Murray Butler, Columbia University historian James T. Shotwell,
and Chicago attorney Salmon O. Levinson played the major organizational
and public relations roles. Levinson and Raymond Robins combined to
enlist the critical support of Senator Borah behind the cause of renouncing
war. Briand, at the suggestion of Shotwell, took the first step by proposing
a Franco-American treaty outlawing war. His motive was primarily political:
to elevate French prestige and to send a message to Germany that the United
States' backing of France was unwavering. Briand followed up his proposal
by submitting a draft treaty.

Kellogg, who was at first skeptical of the outlawry concept, became by
1928 an enthusiastic convert. A barrage of pacifist pleading and the realization that a renunciatory pact could be his historical legacy as well as the
likely route to the Nobel Peace Prize accounted for his change of heart. The
fifteen signatories, "deeply sensible of their solemn duty to promote the
welfare of mankind," pledged "that they condemn recourse to war for the
solution of international controversies, and renounce it as an instrument
of national policy in their relations with one another." Only a few Latin
American nations failed to attach their approval when the document went
into effect in 1929; even today it remains harmlessly in force. Senators
James A. Reed of Missouri and George Moses of New Hampshire led a
movement to attach reservations so as to protect the Monroe Doctrine and
America's right of self-defense. Foreign Relations Committee Chairman
Borah, demonstrating his formidable ability as a debater and parliamentary tactician, outmaneuvered the opposition. In the closing weeks of the
Coolidge administration the opponents were routed as the Senate approved
the pact by a vote of 85 to 1. No American reservations were attached, although Borah read into the record a report of the Senate Foreign Relations
Committee explaining that the committee understood that the pact in no

way abridged the United States' right of self-defense. Kellogg treated the report as merely an expression of opinion that required no legal action or exchange of notes.[22]

The Coolidge administration departed office indulging in expressions of self-congratulation and praising itself for having brought peace and prosperity to mankind. Condescendingly Coolidge, in his final State of the Union message, announced: "We must extend to other countries the largest measure of generosity, moderation, and patience. In addition to dealing justly, we can well afford to walk humbly." A few skeptics such as Senator Carter Glass of Virginia regarded the Pact of Paris as a "worthless, but perfectly harmless peace treaty."[23] Privately many senators agreed with Glass but hesitated in a presidential election year to go on record against the sacred cause of peace. Hailed by pacifists as the triumph of conciliation, arbitration, and the rule of law, the outlawry movement expressed the near isolationist hope of the 1920s that war would just go away without the inconvenience and cost of binding obligations. The jubilation was short-lived once new conflicts broke out in the Far East—not only dooming the reputations of the authors, but making it clear that the world had bought not peace, but a mess of pottage.

NOTES

1. Claude M. Fuess, *Calvin Coolidge: The Man from Vermont* (Westport, 1976, reprint of 1939 edition), 265.

2. Fuess, *Coolidge*, 311.

3. Esme Howard, *Theatre of Life* (Boston, 1953–1955), Vol. 2, 491–92.

4. Coolidge, State of the Union Address, December 6, 1923, *Papers Relating to the Foreign Relations of the United States, 1923* (Washington, 1939), 1, 8–9 (hereafter cited as FRUS); Chicherin to Hughes, December 16, 1923, FRUS, 1923, 2, 787.

5. For the United States and reparations see Harold G. Moulton and Leo Pasvolsky, *War Debts and World Prosperity* (New York, 1932); Herbert Feis, *The Diplomacy of the Dollar, 1919–1932* (Baltimore, 1950); John D. Hicks, *Republican Ascendancy, 1921–1933* (New York, 1960); Bruce Kent, *The Spoils of War: The Politics, Economics, and Diplomacy of Reparations, 1918–1932* (Oxford, 1989); and Stephen A. Schuker, *The End of French Predominance in Europe: The Financial Crisis of 1924 and the Adoption of the Dawes Plan* (Chapel Hill, 1976).

6. For prohibition diplomacy see Lawrence Spinelli, *Dry Diplomacy: The United States, Great Britain, and Prohibition* (Wilmington, Delaware, 1988).

7. L. Ethan Ellis, *Frank B. Kellogg and American Foreign Relations, 1925–1929* (New Brunswick, 1961), 7–8; Robert H. Ferrell, *Frank B. Kellogg*, in Robert H. Ferrell and Samuel Flagg Bemis, editors, *The American Secretaries of State and Their Diplomacy* (New York, 1963), Vol. 11, 1–24.

8. Benjamin D. Rhodes, *James P. Goodrich: Indiana's "Governor Strangelove": A Republican's Infatuation with Soviet Russia* (Selinsgrove, Pennsylvania, 1996), 154.

9. Ellis, *Frank B. Kellogg and American Foreign Relations*, 23–57; Ferrell, *Frank B. Kellogg*, 28–44.

10. Ellis, *Frank B. Kellogg and American Foreign Relations*, 58–85; Ferrell, *Frank B. Kellogg*, 44–57.

11. Ferrell, *Frank B. Kellogg*, 58–61.

12. Robert J. Maddox, *William E. Borah and American Foreign Policy* (Baton Rouge, 1969), 168–70.

13. Kellogg to William Phillips, May 29, 1925, FRUS, 1925, 1, 114–15; World War Foreign Debt Commission, *Combined Annual Reports* (Washington, 1927), 171–77; Phillips to Kellogg, September 16, 1925, General Records of the Department of State, File No. 800.51 W89 Belgium/109, RG 59, National Archives.

14. Alexander DeConde, *Half Bitter, Half Sweet: An Excursion into Italian-American History* (New York, 1971), 192–200.

15. Benjamin D. Rhodes, "Reassessing 'Uncle Shylock': The United States and the French War Debt, 1917–1929," *Journal of American History* 55 (March 1969), 794.

16. *New York Times*, September 16, 1925.

17. Benjamin D. Rhodes, "Herbert Hoover and the War Debts, 1919–1933," *Prologue: The Journal of the National Archives* 6 (Summer 1974), 134–36.

18. World War Foreign Debt Commission, *Combined Annual Reports*, 59–60.

19. See Benjamin D. Rhodes, "The Image of Britain in the United States, 1919–1929: A Contentious Relative and Rival," in B.J.C. McKercher, editor, *Anglo-American Relations in the 1920s: The Struggle for Supremacy* (London, 1990), 202.

20. B.J.C. McKercher, *The Second Baldwin Government and the United States, 1924–1929: Attitudes and Diplomacy* (New York: 1984), 55–104; Brian McKercher, "Wealth, Power, and the New International Order: Britain and the American Challenge in the 1920s," *Diplomatic History* 12 (Fall 1988), 411–41.

21. Ferrell, *Frank B. Kellogg*, 115.

22. See Robert H. Ferrell, *Peace in Their Time: The Origins of the Kellogg-Briand Pact* (New Haven, 1952), esp. 266–69.

23. Ferrell, *Peace in Their Time*, 251.

CHAPTER 5

Foreign Policy Under Hoover and Stimson: A Bed of Pain

Prior to their inaugurations the three previous presidents of the interwar era (Wilson, Harding, and Coolidge) had been men without much, if any, exposure to foreign policy. Herbert Clark Hoover, Coolidge's successor, was a notable exception. Born at West Branch, Iowa, to Quaker parents in 1874, Hoover was not a provincial midwesterner. Both his parents died before he was ten, and he spent his formative years on the west coast, first in his uncle's home at Newberg, Oregon, and then as a college student of engineering and geology at the newly opened Stanford University. His reputation as the "great engineer" was a result of an international career in which the superefficient Hoover traveled the globe as a "doctor of sick mines." Simultaneously Hoover was highly proficient as a financier, an activity that he later preferred to minimize.

Hoover's fame as the "great humanitarian" was established by his hard driving organization in 1915 of the Commission for Relief in Belgium (CRB); all international relief to Belgium was funneled to that occupied nation through Hoover. During the Peace Conference many CRB men joined Hoover's American Relief Administration, which, on credit, fed the destitute of Europe. It was not Hoover's fault that Congress later ungraciously insisted on being repaid for American aid with interest. Continuing as chairman of the ARA in the 1920s, Hoover responded to Soviet pleas and supervised the distribution of bulk corn to the starving people of Ukraine and southern Russia. Between 1915 and 1923 Hoover had the distinction of having saved tens of millions of human beings from starvation. Serving as secretary of commerce under Harding and Coolidge, Hoover was easily the outstanding cabinet officer of the 1920s. He served on every important commission of the era, amazing his associates with his energy, even when his famous scowl and temper were evident. When Coolidge, in typically eccentric fashion, announced in August 1927, "I do not choose to run for president in 1928," Hoover staked out his claims. No strong candidate arose against him in the Republican Party, and in the November 1928 election he easily defeated the wet and Catholic Democratic candidate, New York Governor Alfred E. Smith.

Foreign policy was not a closed book to Hoover. At the Paris Peace Conference he had advised Wilson to take a hard line against establishing diplomatic relations with the Bolsheviks, a position that he consistently adhered to afterward. As secretary of commerce, Hoover aggressively promoted the growth of American exports, and he played a leading role in shaping United States war debt policy as a member of the World War Foreign Debt Commission. Raymond Moley, a member of Franklin D. Roosevelt's "brain trust," justifiably called Hoover "the best informed individual in the country on the question of the debts."[1] Sir Esme Howard, the departing British ambassador, shrewdly summarized Hoover as a man characterized by "complete self-reliance and belief in himself and his country, an immense power of work and talent for organization, a hatred of what he terms the 'European frozen strata of classes,' and of tyranny in any form which prevents completely free development of an individual who has merit above his fellows." In Howard's opinion, one of Hoover's few shortcomings was his dislike of criticism, "which is not likely to make the White House a bed of roses for him, nor perhaps his staff." Howard also detected a certain social awkwardness on Hoover's part, noting that he was "lacking entirely in those lesser graces of life which . . . help to make the wheels of the machine around him move smoothly." Unlike the passive Coolidge, Hoover appeared ready to solve problems in "a bold spirit of statesmanlike efficiency." The greatest problem confronting Hoover and the country, Howard prophetically observed, "was how to keep new wine in an old bottle without either damaging the taste of the old wine or bursting the bottle."[2]

For his first seven and a half months as president, Hoover experienced a relative bed of roses, at least in comparison with the bed of pain that materialized once the shattering of the economic bottle destroyed the bright promise of his presidency. Initially American business and political leaders underestimated the seriousness of the economic damage. Hoover's secretary of commerce assured the commercial attaché of the British Embassy that all was well: the period of recession would be confined to only three months, and the economy would then resume its upward momentum. Perhaps that rosy scenario would have played out had not a second and even more devastating financial crisis struck from Europe in 1931. Now American foreign lending practically ceased, giving some support to Hoover's often ridiculed argument that Europe, not the United States, was the source of the depression. The unwise Hawley-Smoot Tariff of 1930 was another contributing factor. Passed as the result of legislative log-rolling run amuck, Hawley-Smoot raised rates to a prohibitive fifty-nine percent level, producing a suicidal international trade war.

In the interim, before the economic storm clouds overshadowed everything else, Hoover managed several modest foreign policy achievements in Latin American policy and disarmament. In both cases Hoover built upon precedents set earlier in the interwar era. Moreover, unlike the two Republican presidents who had preceded him, Hoover took an active interest in foreign policy, even though he did not try to be his own secretary of state. Henry L. Stimson was not Hoover's first choice to head the Department of State. The job was first offered by Hoover to men he knew such as Kellogg, Hughes, and Borah, but they all rejected the offer. On the advice of Elihu Root, Hoover appointed Stimson, who was sixty-two years old and governor of the Philippines. In his forties Stimson had served Taft as secretary of war, a position to which he returned, somewhat traitorously, in 1940 under Franklin D. Roosevelt. Stimson belonged to the liberal, internationalist wing of the Republican Party, although (with the exception of his Nicaraguan troubleshooting mission of 1927) he had not been involved directly in shaping specific policies. The new secretary of state found Hoover a difficult taskmaster as the president thought nothing of starting the day with a vigorous game of medicine ball and then working long hours, even on weekends. As the depression deepened, the president became even more dour, humorless, and pessimistic than ever. Stimson, who purchased a sumptuous Washington estate called Woodley, preferred a more relaxed pace. Until the Manchurian crisis of 1931–1932 they managed to co-exist. As Hoover came to see Stimson as too assertive and too self-promoting, the influence of the secretary of state waned. Had Hoover been reelected in 1932, there is little doubt he would have looked for a different secretary of state, most likely Undersecretary William R. Castle, whom Hoover found more compatible in terms of policy and personality.

Improving relations with Latin America was one of Hoover's highest priorities. Even before his inauguration, Hoover (taking a cue from Bainbridge Colby) made an extensive ten-week tour of Latin America in which he dispensed goodwill and Wilsonian assurances that the United States wished to turn over a new leaf. Being human, Hoover wanted to visit one of the few regions of the earth that was foreign to him. Moreover, Hoover would not take office until March 4, 1929, and the trip gave him something constructive to do and kept him out of Washington while the outgoing president was in the process of leaving. Hoover's trip aboard the battleships *Maryland* and *Utah* was far more extensive than Colby's tour of 1920–1921. Starting at San Pedro, California, Hoover visited Honduras, El Salvador, Nicaragua, Costa Rica, Ecuador, Peru, Chile, Argentina, Uruguay, and Brazil. Hoover, in a day before presidents employed speech writers, composed all of the twenty-five addresses delivered on the tour. His only purpose, he told a Lima audience, was to seek pan-American unity and to increase his knowledge and understanding of the South American republics. The phrase "good neighbor" was repeatedly invoked by the president-elect. Furthermore, Hoover took pains to reject the paternalistic concept of the United States as a "big brother" to Latin America. At Santiago Hoover took leave of the *Maryland* and crossed the Andes by train to Buenos Aires. Montevideo and Rio de Janeiro were his final stops before returning to the United States aboard the *Utah*. Symbolically the tour demonstrated Hoover's commitment to the principles of the good neighbor. A few demonstrations and a bomb threat to Hoover's train suggested that not all were impressed by Hoover's pacific assurances, but Latin America could not help but feel flattered by the attention and interest demonstrated by the president-elect.

Once in office Hoover did not lose interest in the region. The most immediate result of the goodwill visit was Hoover's successful arbitration of the Tacna-Arica dispute among Chile, Peru, and Bolivia. At issue was a long-standing conflict left over from the War of the Pacific (1879–1883) in which Bolivia lost its outlet to the sea as Chile prevailed over Peru and Bolivia. Under Harding and Coolidge, repeated but unsuccessful efforts had been made to resolve the dispute through the scheduling of a plebiscite. Suddenly on Hoover's trip a solution appeared—one that appeased the national pride of Peru and Chile, but left Bolivia out in the cold. Acting as an arbitrator Hoover awarded Tacna to Peru and Arica to Chile. To make the settlement acceptable to Peru, Chile was required to extend commercial privileges to Peru in Arica and pay Peru $6 million in compensation. As Stimson noted in his autobiography, the Tacna-Arica arbitration was Hoover's "greatest personal triumph."[3]

With less success Hoover tried to arbitrate the Leticia controversy between Peru and Colombia over Peru's occupation of a remote jungle region in dispute between the two countries. Both sides were guilty of fanning the flames of nationalism, encouraging armed skirmishing, and rejecting Stimson's appeals to accept a peaceful solution. After Hoover was out of office, the dispute was submitted to a League of Nations commission, which found that Peru's claims to Leticia were invalid. The patience of Hoover and Stimson was also sorely tried when they sought to resolve the Chaco dispute between Bolivia and Paraguay over a remote and pristine region desired by Bolivia as a potential outlet to the Atlantic. Through a neutral commission, Stimson sought unsuccessfully to bring the adversaries to the peace table. Meanwhile small-scale fighting escalated into a formal war just after Hoover left office. As neither side was capable of conducting an extended conflict, the hostilities ended in a stalemate in 1935. The incidents demonstrated the difficulty, even in the western hemisphere, of securing the acceptance of such lofty principles as the renunciation of force and respect for established boundaries.

Hoover's intention to launch a new era in relations with Latin America was most emphatically illustrated by the publication in the summer of 1930 of the Clark Memorandum. Latin American press opinion approvingly greeted the repudiation of the Roosevelt Corollary, with the exception of a few dissenters who questioned Hoover's sincerity. Hoover followed up the publication of the Clark Memorandum by gradually withdrawing the marines from Nicaragua after the 1932 presidential election. And, in the case of Haiti, Hoover promised in a 1932 treaty to end the American occupation by December 31, 1934. Some of the goodwill was dissipated by the onset of the depression and the trade stagnation associated with the Hawley-Smoot Tariff signed by Hoover in 1930 under duress.[4] Hoover, nevertheless, can be credited with laying the groundwork for the expansion of the good neighbor policy by Franklin D. Roosevelt. Finally, Hoover's advocacy of better relations with Latin America was based on principle, not politics, as there was no major American voting bloc to reward Hoover for his idealistic vision. By sponsoring arbitration and liquidating imperialism, Hoover had taken a giant step toward making better relations with Latin America bipartisan.

All the frustrations and misconceptions of American interwar diplomacy were summed up in the deliberations of the London Naval Conference of 1930. It was called to resolve the cruiser issue that had stymied the Geneva Conference of 1927; it consumed, for the better part of a year, the energies of the highest American and British officials, and it produced a result that was ultimately futile. This time, profiting from the experience at Geneva, there was extensive high level advance preparation. First of all, the new American ambassador in London, former Vice President Charles G. Dawes, and disarmament expert Hugh Gibson discussed with the new British Prime Minister Ramsay MacDonald the American idea of a mechanical "naval yardstick" for gauging the strength of world navies. MacDonald, in principle, accepted the idea of parity between the American and British fleets. Hoover contributed the sensible suggestion that, to avoid another Geneva fiasco, the British and American naval officers should be locked in a room and only consulted on technicalities. Unlike the Washington Conference, there was to be no assistance from the "Black Chamber," as Stimson had disbanded the code-deciphering operation on the high moral ground that "gentlemen do not read each other's mail." Then in October, MacDonald, to the accompaniment of enormous publicity, sailed to New York for an eight-day American tour—the first time a sitting British Prime Minister had visited the United States. The highlight was MacDonald's visit to Hoover's "camp" in the Blue Ridge Mountains on the Rapidan River. Sitting on a log in their work clothes the two leaders "threshed out" (Hoover's phrase) the details of naval disarmament, namely that an agreement would be struck on the basis of giving the United States superiority in heavy cruisers, with Britain being compensated with a superiority in light cruisers.

The politicians, deftly outflanking the naval officers, had established the basis for the nominally successful London Naval Conference (January–April 1930) attended by the United States, Britain, and Japan. Hoover profited from Wilson's example by naming a bipartisan delegation including Senators Joseph Robinson of Arkansas, a Democrat, and David A. Reed of Pennsylvania, a Republican. Stimson, Dwight Morrow, Secretary of the Navy Charles Francis Adams, and Hugh Gibson, the disarmament specialist, completed the delegation. The end product, signed after four months of maddeningly technical and jargon-filled negotiation, was a complex treaty of twenty-six articles. The heart of the agreement (article 16) allotted the United States 180,000 tons of heavy cruisers to 146,800 tons for Britain and 108,400 for Japan. However, in the light cruiser category, Britain was assigned 192,200 tons, to 143,500 for the United States and 100,450 for Japan. A British effort to limit aircraft carriers was resisted by the United States, which under the Washington Conference treaties, had most of its 135,000-ton quota taken by the converted cruisers *Lexington* and *Saratoga*. In the destroyer category the London treaty assigned 150,000 tons each to the United States and Britain, while Japan accepted 105,000 tons (which worked out to a 10:10:7 ratio). In submarines Japan achieved parity with the other signatories, with each accepting a limit of 52,700 tons. The agreement was to last until 1936; it included a holiday on further battleship construction and an "escalator" clause (article 21) permitting the parties to disregard the agreement if they felt "materially affected" by naval construction by a power not a party to the treaty.[5]

Back in the United States the irreconcilables were unhappy. According to the Hearst press, Hoover had left the American merchant marine defenseless against British cruisers. Also critical was the *Chicago Tribune*, which argued that Hoover should have listened to the naval experts. In the Senate, Hiram Johnson attacked Hoover's "secret diplomacy." In support of Johnson, Tennessee Senator Kenneth McKellar introduced a resolution demanding that the White House turn over "all letters, cablegrams, minutes, memoranda, instructions and dispatches, and all records, files, and other information touching the negotiations of said London naval treaty." Senator Borah successfully urged the Senate to "rise in its majesty" and demand the documents. Although the resolution passed 53 to 4, Hoover asserted executive privilege on the ground the request "would be incompatible with the public interest." Hoover held the feet of the irreconcilables to the fire by calling a special session of the Senate, which ratified the treaty by a vote of 58 to 9 after adding an innocuous reservation repudiating any secret documents or understandings pertaining to the treaty.[6]

Whether the London Naval Treaty did any real good is questionable. In a sense the limitations were irrelevant since none of the participants, naval or civilian, had any appreciation of the role air power was to play in future conflicts. Furthermore, the London agreement, combined with the economic depression, led to the abandonment of the American cruiser program begun under Coolidge. So, numerically the United States Navy fell far behind its potential adversaries; by 1939 the United States had only thirty-two cruisers and nine under construction, compared to sixty-two cruisers built and seventeen under construction for Britain. Furthermore, Japan denounced the treaty in 1935 and launched a naval race that by 1941 gave its navy ten aircraft carriers to five for the United States. Whereas the participants hoped their efforts had set a precedent for future arms reduction conferences, the London Naval Conference used up bales of paper but failed to add to the reputations of the statesmen involved or to provide a lasting solution.

The year 1931 saw the domestic and foreign policy roof fall in for the Hoover administration. Domestically the economy failed to snap back despite government spending on public works projects and the purchase of farm surpluses. The dominant trends were growing unemployment, banking and farming bankruptcies, the omission of corporate dividends, a growing federal deficit, and a further decline in the stock market, all of which proved serious political liabilities for the unfortunate occupant of the White House. Already, according to his critics, Hoover's reelection slogan should have been, "Don't change toboggans in the middle of the slide." Hoover's bad luck continued in mid-1931 as the German economy collapsed and Japan launched a military venture in Manchuria.

The financial health of Germany was not just an academic question for the Hoover administration, since in 1924 the United States had taken a leading role in arranging the Dawes Plan, which temporarily restored Germany's reparation payments but set no final date for their completion. And in 1928, as Germany again experienced difficulty in meeting its obligations, the American financier Owen G. Young lent his name to the Young Plan, which reduced the reparations bill to about $8 billion. But in May 1931, the German and Austrian financial structure took a sudden turn for the worse. The largest bank in Austria, the Creditanstalt, teetered on the brink of insolvency, and the mood of panic began to engulf Germany, producing a flight from the mark. Hoover was concerned partly about the likely suspension of German reparations payments to the Allies. It is likely he had some awareness that a German default might have touched off a new financial crisis in the United States since New York bankers had an estimated $700 million in loans at stake. Hoover, who was anxious to avoid any implication that he had acted on behalf of bankers, gave the impression he had lacked full information about the risky exposure of American bankers until later.[7]

Hoover, in a conference on June 5, 1931, with Stimson, Treasury Secretary Mellon, and Undersecretary Ogden Mills, first suggested the idea of a one-year moratorium on intergovernmental payments. Stimson and Mills were enthusiastic, but Mellon, who was about to leave on a European vacation, questioned whether such drastic action was appropriate. Afterwards Hoover told Stimson that he "was leaving Mellon to find out for himself and he thought that it would be quite a shock to him."[8] For the next two weeks Hoover kept a close watch on the situation while trying to decide whether to act or not. While attending the dedication of the beautiful memorial to the discredited Harding at Marion, Ohio, Hoover learned that the Reichsbank had lost almost a third of its gold reserve in the previous two weeks. On his return to Washington, a fatigued Hoover (according to Stimson) seemed hesitant to act. As noted by Stimson after a discussion with Hoover on June 18: "The President was tired and as usual when particularly busy, he went through all the blackest surmises for it. It was like sitting in a bath of ink to sit in his room; and on top of the hard work that Mills and I had been doing, it pretty nearly took everything out of me. But I think he is moving at least."[9] Finally, following appeals for action from Mellon and J. Ramsay MacDonald, Hoover on June 20 released the text of his moratorium proposal. Boldly Hoover called for a postponement for one year of all intergovernmental obligation, meaning war debts and reparations, but excluding private debts. So far as the war debts were concerned, the moratorium would extend for a year and a half, since the June 15, 1931, payments had already been received. Assuming all parties accepted Hoover's proposal, the next payments would not be due until December 15, 1932—three weeks after the forthcoming presidential election.

Everywhere, except in France, the moratorium proposal was received with enthusiasm. Not only were the French offended by what Premier Pierre Laval called Hoover's "shock tactics," but they regarded the plan as the first step toward the permanent loss of reparations. Sixteen days of tortuous trans-Atlantic negotiation were required to induce the French to accept. Andrew Mellon, his vacation in shambles, and Ambassador to France Walter E. Edge presented the American case in Paris, with assistance from Hoover via the newly inaugurated trans-Atlantic telephone. Hoover also twisted congressional arms by securing an advance commitment from thirty-nine members of Congress that they would support the moratorium when Congress reconvened in December. Yet this tactic was not entirely successful, since many congressmen regarded Hoover's heavy handed methods as an infringement upon the powers of Congress. Congressional resentment over Hoover's moratorium resurfaced in December when Congress was asked to formally ratify the document. A final piece in Hoover's hastily improvised palliative was to stabilize short-term credits to Germany. In a short

London conference (July 20–23, 1931) the United States, Britain, France, Germany, Italy, Belgium, and Japan recommended a six-month "standstill" on short-term credits to Germany including the continuation of a $100 million credit advanced by the principal central banks on June 25.[10]

The breathing spell produced by Hoover's politically courageous moratorium and the "standstill" agreement proved of short duration. Pressure shifted from Germany to the London gold market, and on September 21 Britain was forced off the gold standard. The possibility that at the conclusion of the one-year moratorium the world could resume payments of debts and reparations was becoming more and more doubtful. The inevitability of revising the existing structure was squarely faced by Hoover on December 11, when he presented the moratorium to Congress for approval. Either courageously (the view of his defenders) or naively (the view of his critics), Hoover stated: "I recommend the re-creation of the World War Foreign Debt Commission, with authority to examine such problems as may arise in connection with these debts during the present economic emergency, and to report to the Congress its conclusions and recommendations."[11] Never has a president so misjudged the political climate of Washington as did Hoover in December 1931.

Determined resistance met Hoover's proposal. Borah stated, "I am not in favor of recreating the World War Foreign Debt Commission. There is no business for it to transact. I do not see any evidence that Europe proposes to reduce armaments or that she proposes to adjust reparations upon any proper basis." Mississippi Democrat John E. Rankin asked the House: "Why revive the debt Commission? There can be but one object and that is to further reduce or cancel these foreign debts to the United states. Postpone them? This postponement talk is mere camouflage."[12] The new British ambassador, Sir Ronald C. Lindsay, aptly described the congressional atmosphere as consisting of "fear, unreason and hostility." The congressional mood reminded Lindsay of the situation that confronted Wilson on his return from the Paris Peace Conference in 1919. "Throughout a week of unrelieved gloom and gaining alarm," reported Lindsay, "Congress has given an exhibition of irresponsibility, buffoonery and ineptitude that could hardly be paralleled in the Haitian legislature."[13]

When the House Ways and Means Committee approved a bill endorsing the Hoover Moratorium there was no mention of a new debt commission. By the terms of the bill, Hoover was authorized to sign agreements with each debtor whereby the deferred payments would be refunded in ten annual installments at four percent interest. Section five of the legislation contained a calculated rebuke to Hoover: "It is hereby expressly declared to be against the policy of Congress that any of the indebtedness of foreign countries to the United States should be in any manner cancelled or reduced; and nothing in this joint resolution shall be construed as indicating a contrary policy, or as implying that favorable consideration will be given at any time to a change in the policy hereby declared."[14] At first the Senate failed to take action because it was preoccupied with the selection of a president pro tempore, a position of only symbolic importance. A filibuster was directed against New Hampshire Senator George Moses because he had once referred to congressional progressives as "sons of the wild jackass." Hurriedly debating the moratorium one day prior to the Christmas recess, the Senators took a tough stand against debt concessions. According to Senator Hiram Johnson, "There is only one way in my opinion to deal with those debts, just one way. Stand our ground in reference to those debts! Let any nation default that desires to do so. Let any nation that wishes refuse to pay what we legitimately and rightfully ought to be paid."[15] Senator McKellar described the Hoover Moratorium as the "entering wedge for further cancellations."[16] And Senator Thomas Gore of Oklahoma facetiously suggested that the proviso "Provided, that this is no joke," be added to the statement that debt cancellation was contrary to the policy of Congress.[17] Hoover's hands were tied when the House denied Hoover's request for a new debt commission by a vote of 318 to 100; the Senate vote of 69 to 12 left Hoover with little maneuvering room. Sir Ronald Lindsay aptly described the congressional attitude of intransigence toward debt revision as "100 percent cowardice."[18]

Simultaneously the Hoover administration was forced to turn its attention to a Far Eastern dilemma that it had been doing its best to ignore in the vain hope that the League of Nations would take action. The problem had been festering since September 18, 1931, when the crack Kwantung Army of Japan staged the Mukden incident and commenced the conquest of Manchuria. From the notorious Twenty-one Demands of 1915, Japan had gained special privileges in Manchuria, including the right to guard Japanese-owned railroads with Japanese troops. Deliberate Chinese sabotage to the South Manchurian Railroad, it was claimed, compelled defensive countermeasures by the Kwantung Army. As testimony at the Tokyo war crimes trials later demonstrated, the Manchurian conquest was the daring brain child of officers of the Kwantung Army and had been carefully planned for months, including such details as quietly moving howitzers from Port Arthur to Mukden and arranging to shell the Mukden airfield to prevent the Chinese from using their French fighter planes. The young conspirators, led by Colonel Itagaki Seishiro, Lieutenant Colonel Ishiara Kanji, and Major Hanaya Tadashi, saw the seizure of Manchuria as vital to Japan's hopes for major power status and as essential for the spiritual regeneration of the Manchurian region and Japan itself under the principle of benevolent imperial rule.[19]

Watchful waiting was the initial response of the Hoover administration. In view of America's economic troubles at home and the British financial crisis, Washington hoped Manchuria would fade away and that the civilians in the Japanese government would gain control of the situation. Instead the Kwantung Army methodically and efficiently drove the Chinese "bandits" from Manchuria. As Hoover was absorbed with the domestic economic crisis, much of the Manchurian burden fell upon Stimson. At first he tried to work through the League of Nations, but found himself frustrated by its timorous response. Seeking to prod the League, Stimson authorized Prentiss Gilbert, the American Counsel at Geneva, to attend League Council sessions as an observer. He was only permitted to join the discussion if the possible invocation of the Kellogg-Briand Pact became a topic of debate. But since that subject never arose, Gilbert was compelled to sit in silence. On October 24 the League weakly pleaded with China and Japan to make peace and asked Japan to withdraw by November 16, 1931. When Japan paid no attention, the League appointed a commission to investigate, headed by the Earl of Lytton. Unimpressed, the Kwantung Army on January 2, 1932, occupied the port city of Chinchow in southern Manchuria.

Since Japan was flagrantly thumbing its nose at the peace structure assembled by previous Republican administrations, specifically the Nine-Power Treaty and the Kellogg-Briand Pact, Stimson decided to carry out an idea suggested by Hoover at a cabinet meeting on November 9. Hoover's thought was to refuse diplomatic recognition of military conquests that altered established national boundaries. It was not a new idea, but one borrowed from the Wilson administration (and an idea that had not worked all that well for Wilson). In 1915 Japan had presented China with the Twenty-one Demands, which aimed at turning China into a Japanese protectorate. As was the case in 1931, the Twenty-one Demands came at an awkward time, since it coincided with the *Lusitania* crisis—Germany's sinking of a famous British liner, drowning 1,198 persons. In the May Caveat (May 11, 1915), composed by Robert Lansing and sent to Japan under the signature of Secretary of State William Jennings Bryan, the policy was stated that the United States would not recognize any agreement impairing the territorial or administrative integrity of China. Although the May Caveat satisfied America's sense of moral outrage, it came too late to save China, since the Chinese had already capitulated to most of Japan's demands. In the case of Manchuria, history in a sense repeated itself, as the Hoover administration eventually followed Wilson's example of delivering an ineffective moral protest backed up by hollow threats.

With Hoover's approval, Stimson on January 7 sent Japan a famous note containing what is variously known as the Stimson Doctrine or the Hoover-Stimson Doctrine. In its wording Stimson's note was similar to Lansing's 1915 effort: he stated that the United States would not recognize any treaty, agreement, or de facto situation that impaired the rights of American citizens or the territorial and administrative integrity of China, or that violated the Kellogg-Briand Pact. As was the case with Wilson's May Caveat, the Stimson Doctrine satisfied the need to uphold the nation's moral purity. To have looked the other way would have constituted a moral defeat of the first order. However, Stimson's nonrecognition doctrine, which contained no threat of sanctions, did nothing practical to deter Japan, and received only lukewarm support from the League of Nations Council.

That Japan was not impressed was demonstrated by the punitive raid staged against Shanghai, which began on January 28, 1932. Launched by a glory-seeking admiral to punish the Chinese for anti-Japanese riots and boycotts, the invaders met determined Chinese resistance. In order to sack the city the Japanese landed 50,000 troops and bombed and strafed civilians. Assistant Secretary of State James Grafton Rogers suggested to Stimson, while they were horseback riding, that the secretary of state indirectly express his outrage by writing a letter to Senator Borah. Theoretically Stimson could have protested through diplomatic notes, but with good reason he feared he would receive "yellow-bellied" responses from the recipients. Hoover gave his approval, and Stimson's letter to Borah was delivered on February 24, 1932. After reiterating America's refusal to recognize territorial changes brought about by force, Stimson indirectly threatened Japan by referring to the Washington Conference treaties. As he put it: "The willingness of the American government to surrender its then commanding lead in battleship construction and to leave its positions at Guam and in the Philippines without further fortification, was predicated upon, among other things, the self-denying covenants contained in the Nine Power Treaty"[20] Although Stimson had used an imaginative device, the Borah letter proved no more effective than the Stimson Doctrine. Realizing that Stimson was bluffing, Japan was not deterred either by the Stimson Doctrine or the Borah letter. Instead, Japan organized and recognized the new state of Manchukuo. And Japan emphatically rejected the report of the Lytton Commission (October 3, 1932), which found that Japan had no legitimate reason for occupying Manchuria. When the League adopted the report, Japan withdrew from the League, retaining its Pacific mandates over the Mariana, Marshall, and Caroline Islands.

Considering the depression, the public mood of withdrawal, and America's lack of power in the region, the Manchurian incident placed the Hoover administration in a vise. To have ignored Japan's trampling of the Open Door Policy, the Nine Power Treaty, and the Kellogg-Briand Pact was morally out of the question for any American administration. Economic sanctions were ruled out by Hoover, who doubted—probably correctly— that they would do any good. An ineffective moral protest combined with an empty threat were the only avenues remaining open. Over the next four years the Manchurian situation calmed down temporarily as Japan consolidated its acquisition. Still only dimly perceived by public opinion was that the Manchurian controversy signaled that the peace structure erected by Hughes and Kellogg rested upon an increasingly unstable foundation.

The remainder of 1932 found the Hoover administration focusing less and less on foreign policy and more and more on the sinking economy and the forthcoming presidential campaign. The main exception was that the two parties competed over which would do more to collect the war debts when the moratorium expired in December 1932. In July, just as the campaign between Hoover and the Democratic nominee, Governor Franklin D. Roosevelt of New York, was heating up, the war debts reemerged as a political issue. Meeting at Lausanne, Switzerland, the Allies had just reduced Germany's obligation under the Young Plan to a nominal $715 million. And the payment of even that modest amount was to be made in nonnegotiable bonds deposited with the Bank for International Settlements. Theoretically the Lausanne reduction in German reparations was contingent upon a war debt reduction by the United States, but since no concessions were forthcoming from Washington the incomplete agreement went into effect anyway, ending the reparations dilemma.

American isolationists, as expressed by the *Chicago Tribune*, angrily described the Lausanne decision as a cynical European ploy to hand the American taxpayer the bill for World War I. William Randolph Hearst called the conference "a crooked conspiracy by European confidence men and their American confederates to rob the American people." Senator McKellar, without any proof, accused Hoover of giving Europe a secret assurance that the war debts would be cancelled. Senator James E. Watson of Indiana, the Senate majority leader, likewise castigated the Allies, stating "We are not going to revise or cancel the debts, no matter what agreement or promises were made at Lausanne. I do not believe any American Congress will ever revise or reduce those debts." The reaction of the unpredictable Senator Borah, however, was to propose that the adjustment of war debts and other economic questions should be referred to a world economic conference.[21] In reality such a conference was in the process of being arranged under the auspices of the League of Nations, although it was not held until Hoover was out of office and the subject of war debts was illogically excluded from the agenda.

Only the Democrats officially addressed the debts in their platform, promising to oppose "cancellation of the debts owing to the United States by foreign nations." Governor Franklin D. Roosevelt of New York, the Democratic candidate, criticized Hoover for lacking "the moral courage" to tell the debtors they must "acknowledge their debts." The Democrats also advanced the argument that it was an economic contradiction for the United States to demand payment and then impose a high tariff that made payment impossible. Recent scholarship suggests that, at least until the Hawley-Smoot Tariff, the nation's trade surplus was not an insuperable barrier to payment because debtor nations more than covered their trade deficit with such invisible payments as immigrant remittances and tourist expenditures. Hoover, in his acceptance speech, offered the debtors a vaguely defined reduction in payments if they would agree to increase their consumption of American products. Specifically Hoover was willing to offer America's debtors a payment reduction for every percentage point increase they accepted in American farm products above the 1932 level. In the case of Britain, Hoover's plan, according to Treasury Secretary Ogden Mills, would have reduced its payments by $30 million to $40 million a year. In a conversation with Andrew Mellon, now ambassador to Britain, Mills stressed that the credits would apply only to future payments and not to the payments due to resume on December 15, 1932. When Mellon noted that no one in Britain had yet raised a question about the December 15 payment, Mills correctly forecast, "I think they will raise it Mr. Mellon, a week from Wednesday morning, right after election."[22]

Mills's prediction proved almost accurate. Two days, not one, after the defeat of Hoover by Franklin D. Roosevelt, the British ambassador, in Stimson's words, "sprung a bombshell" about the debt payments. At the State Department's regular diplomatic hours on December 10, Sir Ronald Lindsay presented a formal note stating that "the regime of intergovernmental financial obligations as now existing must be reviewed." Since there was insufficient time to accomplish a revision prior to December 15, when the next payments were due, Britain asked for a postponement of that payment.[23] Within a few days similar requests arrived from France, Belgium, Czechoslovakia, Estonia, Latvia, Lithuania, and Poland. Mussolini shrewdly decided not to submit a request until it was seen how Washington responded.

Herbert Hoover was the last president required by the Constitution to serve as a lame duck for four entire months after being rejected by the voters. The Twentieth Amendment to the Constitution, ratified in 1933, mercifully provided for the presidential term to begin on January 20, instead of the traditional starting date of March 4, saving future presidents the "compound hell" endured by Hoover from November 3, 1932 to March 4, 1933. Painfully aware that his ability to function as president had been weakened by his election defeat, Hoover, on the advice of Stimson and Mills, decided to clear his course of action with the president-elect. Constitutionally, however, the president-elect was not obligated to consult with the president or to assume responsibility for policy. The first Hoover-Roosevelt meeting at the White House (November 22, 1932) was polite but strained. Despite pitchers of orangeade and fine cigars, Hoover and Roosevelt found it difficult to put aside the partisanship of the campaign. Hoover brought Ogden Mills to the meeting as his witness, while Roosevelt was accompanied by Columbia University Professor Raymond Moley. Falling back on his earlier plan, Hoover suggested recreating the debt commission and inviting Roosevelt to participate in the selection of its members. Hoover came away with the impression that Roosevelt had agreed to cooperate, probably because Roosevelt had an affable habit of saying "yes" when he really meant "I see what you are saying." In a statement, Roosevelt refused to endorse the creation of a new debt commission on the ground that regular diplomatic channels presented the best method for dealing with debtor nations. Afterward Hoover told Stimson he had spent much of the meeting educating "a very ignorant [but] well meaning young man," a remark that may have been meant to apply to Moley rather than Roosevelt.[24]

On December 15, the day of reckoning, Britain, to the great relief of the weakened Hoover administration, paid its full installment, making it clear that Britain expected a revision of the 1923 settlement prior to the next payment due June 15, 1933. In France Premier Edouard Herriot, who made the December 15 payment a vote of confidence, was voted out of office. The Chamber of Deputies by a vote of 380 to 57 justified France's default on the ground that the cessation of German reparations had rendered the Mellon-Bérenger Accord "no longer executory." Joining France in defaulting were Austria, Estonia, Greece, Hungary, and Poland. Mussolini, veiling his intentions until the last minute, paid in full.

In the eyes of isolationist spokesmen and newspapers, Hoover was the hero of the hour for refusing to recommend a suspension of the December 15 payments. In a self-styled campaign of "sound Americanism," Hearst argued that Europe had sufficient money for everything except a debt of honor. "Mr. Hearst and his papers," stated Senator McKellar, "have performed a wonderful service to the American people in fighting efforts to unload these foreign debts onto the backs of the American taxpayer." The *Chicago Tribune* contended that the United States, in the original debt settlements, should never have forgiven a penny of principal or interest. If the debtors could not pay in cash, the United States should accept French territories in the Pacific, or British colonies such as Bermuda or the Bahamas, or battleships, cruisers, submarines, and works of art. The *Washington Post* agreed on the ground that accepting capital ships from the debtors would relieve them of the burden of making cash payments as well as the expense of maintaining excessive armaments. Both the *Denver Post* and the Columbus *Ohio State Journal* advised insisting on payment without change even if such a policy led to repudiation. A few dissenting voices (the *Baltimore Sun* and the *San Francisco Chronical*) suggested that the United States should revise the debts downward to stimulate world trade, but they were drowned out by a chorus of isolationism and xenophobia.[25]

When Hoover left office very little progress had been made in resolving the dispute. A second Hoover-Roosevelt meeting on January 20, 1933, ended in a procedural stalemate. About the only hopeful development was Roosevelt's announcement that he would receive British representatives early in March to discuss debts and other world economic problems. What possible solution did Roosevelt have in mind? On January 29 the president-elect disarmingly told Sir Ronald Lindsay he was only interested in the moral side of the debt question and was prepared to justify to Congress a settlement based on forgiving interest. When Lindsay objected that payments under Roosevelt's plan would far exceed what was due to Britain under Lausanne, Roosevelt responded in the manner of a practical politician. As reported by Lindsay, Roosevelt said "it would be quite impossible to get Congress to agree to more than remission of interest and that if he and Hoover and an archangel from Heaven were all to be united in asking for more it would not avail."[26] In a second meeting with Lindsay (February 20), Roosevelt backed away from cancelling Britain's interest payments, admitting to Lindsay he had no specific plan in mind, but would look for something that might "gild the pill for Congress."[27] Thus the four months of the Hoover interregnum produced little forward movement. The bitter recriminations over the December 15 payments merely stimulated renewed isolationist bashing of Europe as ungrateful and unworthy of American association. Finding a solution had defied the best efforts of Hoover and Roosevelt, and had even baffled Roosevelt's figurative archangel from heaven.

NOTES

1. Raymond Moley, *After Seven Years* (New York, 1939), 72.

2. Howard to Lord Cushendun, November 16, 1928, FO414/262/A8126, Public Record Office (PRO); Howard to Chamberlain, March 8, 1929, FO414/263/A1973, PRO.

3. Henry L. Stimson and McGeorge Bundy, *On Active Service in Peace and War* (New York, 1948), 185.

4. For United States policy toward Latin America, see Alexander DeConde, *Herbert Hoover's Latin American Policy* (Stanford, 1951). See also Robert H. Ferrell, *American Diplomacy in the Great Depression: Hoover-Stimson Foreign Policy, 1929–1933* (New Haven, 1957), 215–30.

5. B.J.C. McKercher, *The Second Baldwin Government and the United States, 1924–1929: Attitudes and Diplomacy* (New York, 1984), 193–99; Ferrell, *American Diplomacy in the Great Depression*, 87–105.

6. Raymond G. O'Connor, *Perilous Equilibrium: The United States and the London Naval Conference of 1930* (Lawrence, 1962), 114–18.

7. Edward W. Bennett, *Germany and the Diplomacy of the Financial Crisis, 1931* (Cambridge, 1962), 136–38.

8. Diary of Henry L. Stimson, June 5, 1931, Yale University.

9. Stimson Diary, June 18, 1931.

10. Harold G. Moulton and Leo Pasvolsky, *War Debts and World Prosperity* (Washington, D.C., 1932), 333–37; Bennett, *Germany and the Financial Crisis*, 274–77; and Elting Morison, *Turmoil and Tradition: A Study of the Life and Times of Henry L. Stimson* (Boston, 1960), 297–302. See also Louis P. Lochner, *Herbert Hoover and Germany* (New York, 1960), chapter 7.

11. Special message to Congress from President Hoover, December 11, 1931, *Papers Relating to the Foreign Relations of the United States*, 1931 (Washington, 1946), Vol. 1, xxiii–xxv.

12. Benjamin D. Rhodes, "Herbert Hoover and the War Debts, 1919–1933" *Prologue: The Journal of the National Archives* 6 (Summer 1974), 138–39.

13. Lindsay to Sir John Simon, December 17, 1931, FO414/268/A7539, PRO.

14. *Congressional Record*, 72 Cong., 1 Sess., 996 (December 22, 1931).

15. *Congressional Record*, 72 Cong., 1 Sess., 1081 (December 22, 1931).

16. *Congressional Record*, 72 Cong., 1 Sess., 1097 (December 22, 1931).

17. *Congressional Record*, 72 Cong., 1 Sess., 1090 (December 22, 1931).

18. Rhodes, "Herbert Hoover and the War Debts," 139; Lindsay to Simon, December 31, 1931, FO371/15905/C394, PRO.

19. Takehiko Yoshihashi, *Conspiracy at Mukden: The Rise of the Japanese Military* (New Haven, 1963), 132–43.

20. Robert H. Ferrell, *Henry L. Stimson* (New York, 1963), 219–260; Ferrell, *American Diplomacy in the Great Depression*, 120–93; Morison, *Turmoil and Tradition*, 303–33.

21. *Literary Digest* 114 (July 23, 1932), 3–5; *New York Times*, July 17, 1932.

22. *New York Times*, June 21 and 30, 1932; memorandum of a trans-Atlantic telephone conversation between Stimson, Mills, and Mellon, October 31, 1932, General Records of the Department of State, File No. 800.51 W89 Great Britain/ 336 1/2, RG 59; Stephen A. Schuker, *American "Reparations" to Germany, 1919–1933: Implications for the Third-World Debt Crisis* (Princeton, 1988), 97–101.

23. Stimson Diary, November 10, 1932; Lindsay to Stimson, November 10, 1932, FRUS, 1932, I, 754–56.

24. Moley, *After Seven Years*, 73; Arthur M. Schlesinger, Jr., *The Crisis of the Old Order* (Boston, 1957), 441–45; Herbert Hoover, *The Memoirs of Herbert Hoover* (New York, 1951–1952), Vol. 3, 179–84.

25. *New York American*, December 1, 1932; *Chicago Tribune*, November 24, 1932; *Washington Post*, December 3, 1932; *Literary Digest*, 114 (November 26, 1932), 1–2.

26. Lindsay to Simon, January 30, 1933; E.L. Woodward and Rohan Butler, editors, *Documents on British Foreign Policy, 1919–1939* Second Series (London, 1956), Vol. 5, 748–49.

27. Lindsay to Simon, February 21, 1933; Woodward and Butler, *Documents*, Vol. 5, 769–71.

CHAPTER 6

Early New Deal Foreign Policy: The Limits of Improvisation

Three of the five presidents of the interwar era have left behind voluminous records that serve as a vital resource to historians seeking to judge their characters and reconstruct the human drama of their administrations. The exceptions are Harding, some of whose papers were burned by his wife, and Coolidge, who left very little in his own hand. Franklin D. Roosevelt, the first chief executive to have established a presidential library, left an unusually rich legacy of personal correspondence, public papers, press conferences, speeches, recordings, and photographs. But in Roosevelt's case, the quantity of documentation notwithstanding, his basic character has remained as elusive as ever.

The general outline of Roosevelt's career is familiar. Born on January 30, 1882, at Hyde Park, New York, he was the product of a marriage of two generations. An indifferent student, Roosevelt charmed his way through the exclusive Groton School and Harvard University. At the Columbia University Law School he learned enough law to pass the New York bar exam, although he never completed his degree requirements. His wife, Eleanor, was the niece of Theodore Roosevelt, yet Franklin Roosevelt entered politics as a Democrat, the party of his father. Not yet thirty, he was elected a New York state senator in 1910, then appointed by Wilson as assistant secretary of the navy, a post once held by Theodore Roosevelt. At age thirty-eight, mainly because of his famous name, he was nominated for vice president and together with Ohio Governor James Cox was decisively defeated by Harding and Coolidge. In the summer of 1921 Roosevelt contracted infantile paralysis, an illness which left him permanently paralyzed and which seemed to have ended his hopes for a public career. Roosevelt displayed qualities of fortitude and determination in facing his infirmity; instead of retiring as desired by his mother, Roosevelt remained an active and ambitious Democrat who kept an eye open for a return to politics.

During his recovery Roosevelt, who was philosophically a defender of Wilsonian internationalism, dabbled amiably in foreign policy. In 1923 he prepared, but did not submit, an entry for the Bok Peace Plan contest—a competition sponsored by a wealthy retired publisher. Roosevelt proposed American membership in a weak society of nations that would confine itself to affairs of the western hemisphere and would lack the territorial guarantee of the League of Nations. Senator Borah would have been pleased by Roosevelt's apparent retreat from Wilsonian internationalism. In his 1932 presidential campaign he called for collecting the war debts, and he specifically rejected membership in the League, contending (in a transparent effort to placate the publisher William Randolph Hearst) that it was no longer the league of Woodrow Wilson. As president-elect, Roosevelt combined a typically superficial command of foreign policy details with a brilliant ability to improvise. The war debts were not his baby, he quipped to reporters after his first White House meeting with Hoover. And he told Henry L. Stimson, during a six-hour conversation at his Hyde Park home, that he supported Stimson's Manchurian policy because of a family interest in the Far East. When he took office he continued to display his brilliance as an improviser, because he had developed few specific plans for either domestic or foreign policy. Using a sports metaphor, he told a press conference he regarded himself as a "quarterback," who would experiment or invent plays if the need arose.[1]

Was Roosevelt a Wilsonian internationalist in disguise during the early years of his presidency or a neo-isolationist? There are as many answers as there are historians since Roosevelt projected so many different personalities, moods, and roles. On the one hand he was charming, warm, gracious, photogenic, and capable of writing fighting speeches laden with memorable phrases delivered with a beautiful voice and an expert sense of timing and phrasing. Presumably it was these qualities that led the Reichsbank president Hjalmar Schacht to praise Roosevelt as reminding him "in every way of Hitler."[2] Roosevelt could also be hard-boiled, intimidating, manipulative, devious, self-centered, and ungrateful to those who had served him loyally. Most baffling of all was Roosevelt's serene and genial manner of seeming to agree with his visitors while actually keeping his own counsel. Revisionist authors (Charles A. Beard and Charles C. Tansill) criticized Roosevelt for abandoning internationalism and reverting to isolationism; his defenders portray the president as a Wilsonian internationalist who pragmatically decided to emphasize domestic recovery as his first priority.[3] Certainly there was a glaring gap between the New Deal's dynamic, clear direction in domestic policy and the corresponding inconsistency and drift in foreign policy. Much of the explanation for the futility of early New Deal foreign policy is found in the fact that Roosevelt hated to delegate authority and tried to do everything himself. Even a man of Roosevelt's energy, ambition, and ability as a diplomatic juggler found himself stretched thin.

Consistently during Roosevelt's first years in the White House, it was foreign policy that suffered from a lack of clear presidential attention and vision.

Taking office during a time of unprecedented economic crisis, Roosevelt displayed an infectious verve, self-confidence, and self-control. He was the first American president to master the art of speaking over the radio. Through his brilliant inaugural address and his equally brilliant fireside chats and press conferences, Roosevelt established his credentials as a leader and restored public confidence in the federal government. During the famous "one hundred days" session of Congress, Roosevelt launched an unprecedented program of "alphabet soup" agencies designed to restore and reform agriculture, banking, electric power, and public works, and to provide relief through jobs to the destitute. In the area of foreign policy the New Deal record, despite rhetorical flourishes to the contrary, continued many of the main themes of previous interwar presidents—in terms of the League of Nations, the World Court, disarmament, collection of war debts, and the good neighbor—usually with results that were less than impressive.

The indefatigable president immersed himself in every aspect of the foreign policy process. His appointment of Tennessee Senator Cordell Hull to the premier position in the cabinet left little doubt that Roosevelt intended to function as his own secretary of state. Hull was a veteran of Tennessee politics. He had served as a member of the Tennessee legislature and the House of Representatives, as chairman of the Democratic National Committee, and was elected in 1930 to the Senate. Hull had made his mark in Congress as the author of the first federal income tax law and as an opponent of the Republican war debt settlements, which he criticized as too generous. He was even better known as a crusader for reducing tariff barriers as a means for advancing world peace and improving the lives of people everywhere. Roosevelt viewed Hull as a link between northern and southern Democrats, and in 1928 he had favored Hull for vice president on the Democratic ticket. As had been true of Harding, Hull's appearance was one of his greatest assets: he was a dignified, soft spoken southern gentleman who carried himself like a state circuit judge—a position to which he had once been appointed. Behind his courtly image, Hull concealed the temper and profane vocabulary of a Tennessee frontiersman; in the 1930 Tennessee senatorial primary Hull denounced his opponent as the "damnest liar" in the state. Hull was self-righteous (in his entire two-volume autobiography he expressed no second thoughts about any of the policy issues that came before him), secretive (he carefully concealed his wife's Jewish ancestry), and unforgiving toward those, such as Raymond Moley and Sumner Welles, who disagreed with him. Roosevelt often treated Hull cavalierly by failing to furnish him with basic information concerning debts and the planned world economic conference. Sir Ronald Lindsay found his conferences with Hull inevitably pleasant but uninformative and a waste of time. Displaying what Lindsay described as "the utmost integrity, dignity and charm," Hull would patiently answer any question posed by visiting diplomats, "but when they return to their houses they usually have difficulty in remembering anything he has said that deserves to be reported."[4]

William Phillips, who had been assistant secretary of state under Wilson and undersecretary under Harding and Coolidge, was appointed by Roosevelt as undersecretary because of his experience, his social graces, and his personal friendship with the president—who had the effrontery to offer Phillips the position in a midnight telephone call. Roosevelt selected Columbia University professor Raymond Moley as assistant secretary of state, a member of the campaign "brain trust," who had accompanied Roosevelt during his meetings with Hoover about war debts. During the interregnum Moley served as Roosevelt's "man Friday," assisting the president-elect in selecting personnel for his administration. Moley's duties, as indicated by Roosevelt, included: "The foreign debts, the world economic conference, supervision of the economic advisor's office and such additional duties as the President may direct in the general field of foreign and domestic government."[5] The delegation of such sweeping responsibilities to an assistant secretary of state was personally galling to Hull, who admitted he "was not at all enthusiastic" about the appointment of Moley. The relations of the two men were less than cordial from the beginning, since Hull viewed Moley as a rival, not a colleague. For his part Moley managed to offend virtually every State Department employee due to the gruff, self-assured manner in which he threw his weight around. Behind his back Moley was known as "the General Patton" of the State Department. During the first weeks of the New Deal, Moley had an interview with Hull in which he stated that, rumors to the contrary, he had no ambitions for Hull's job. Hull's suspicions were not allayed, and his remark that "Moley at least has the subject on his mind" illustrated the internal strains within the new administration.[6]

The differences between Hull and Moley went much deeper than a mere personality conflict. Moley was a confirmed economic nationalist who was highly skeptical that international measures, such as tariff reductions or currency stabilization, would prove effective in fighting the depression. Instead, he stressed national recovery measures such as the New Deal's Agricultural Adjustment Administration and National Recovery Administration, as well as a devalued dollar to stimulate exports. On the other hand, Hull was committed to an international tariff reduction of ten percent, and an international tariff truce, to be followed by further tariff reductions through reciprocal agreements. As for Roosevelt, he displayed a blithe willingness to tolerate widely differing policy approaches. Personally he was convinced that economic questions were not as complicated as professional economists would have him believe. Thus as Roosevelt launched the New Deal, his administration had embarked with bickering personnel upon a contradictory foreign economic policy of simultaneously pursuing internationalist and nationalist agendas.

The immediate foreign policy problems for Roosevelt were interrelated: preparing for the London Economic Conference and resolving Britain's request for a revision of war debts. Somehow Roosevelt found the energy to guide his domestic program through Congress and to receive a parade of foreign dignitaries, the most prominent of whom were British Prime Minister J. Ramsay MacDonald and former French Prime Minister Edouard Herriot. The economic conference was inherited by Roosevelt from the Hoover administration. The idea for a world economic conference originated in a British proposal at the conclusion of the Lausanne Conference in the summer of 1932. A preparatory committee of experts met at Geneva in October and, had Hoover been reelected, the conference would probably have met early in 1933. With the understanding that he was not going to the United States to reach a debt settlement, MacDonald accepted Roosevelt's invitation to visit Washington to survey the economic landscape. While in mid-ocean MacDonald received the shocking news that Roosevelt had abandoned the gold standard in an effort to stimulate the domestic economy and American exports. MacDonald could hardly protest publicly since Britain had done the same thing in 1931, but he was irritated by Roosevelt's timing, which smacked of diplomatic blackmail.

The talks themselves were productive of few concrete results. For five days (April 22–26, 1933) Roosevelt and MacDonald ranged over the field of world politics. Much of their time was spent in what Moley called "we must work shoulder to shoulder to save the world talk."[7] A case in point was Roosevelt's enthusiastic endorsement of MacDonald's arms reduction proposals to be presented to the Geneva Disarmament Conference. In reality the Geneva Conference proved an exercise in futility due to the determination of Nazi Germany to rearm. Against his better judgment, MacDonald agreed to Roosevelt's proposal for a tariff truce to last the duration of the conference. Privately MacDonald compared Roosevelt's truce plan with a man who, having finished his breakfast, says to his friend, "Let's have a truce on breakfasts."[8] On the fourth day the debt question was discussed without much success, as MacDonald ineptly confused millions and billions of pounds and dollars. Their joint statement, which emphasized that they had achieved "a clearer understanding of the situation" and had commenced "preliminary explorations of many different routes" toward a solution, was a masterpiece of ambiguity. (Without Hull's knowledge Sir Frederick Leith-Ross, the Chief Economic Advisor of His Majesty's Government, remained in Washington to discuss debts with Moley. When Hull inadvertently learned from Sir Ronald Lindsay of the talks, he was understandably infuriated.) Finally, in their last session, the leaders agreed that the Economic Conference should open at London on June 12. That date was chosen because the special session of Congress would then be over, and besides, MacDonald facetiously noted, a later date would interfere with the grouse hunting season and "all the British statesmen would walk out" of the conference.[9]

Next Roosevelt received Edouard Herriot, Italian Finance Minister Guido Jung, Hjalmar Schacht of Germany, and representatives of China, Chile, Mexico, Brazil, and Japan. The public statements following these meetings were replete with the usual mutual protestations of friendship and recognition of the urgency of international economic cooperation, but other than endorsing Roosevelt's tariff truce, no definitive agreements were concluded. The need for international action to combat the depression was also a theme sounded by Roosevelt in his second fireside chat on May 7. The Economic Conference, he said, "must succeed. The future of the world demands it and we have pledged ourselves to the best joint efforts to this end."[10] The urging of international action was again stressed on May 16 when Roosevelt appealed to fifty-three governments to "end economic chaos." That worthy goal would be achieved at London, said the statement, "by a stabilization of currencies, by freeing the flow of world trade, and by international action to raise price levels."[11] By endorsing currency stabilization, Roosevelt carelessly placed himself in the embarrassing position of advocating a program he soon decided to repudiate.

Also careless was Roosevelt's last-minute selection of the delegation and the drafting of its instructions. The chairman was Secretary of State Cordell Hull, who undertook the mission with the understanding that Roosevelt would submit to Congress a reciprocal agreements bill demonstrating America's desire to reduce tariff barriers. Former Ohio Governor James M. Cox of Ohio, Roosevelt's running mate in 1920 and a low-tariff advocate, was selected as vice chairman. Senator Key Pittman of Nevada, the chairman of the Foreign Relations Committee, went to look after the interests of western silver producers. The chairman of the House Foreign Affairs Committee, Representative Samuel McReynolds of Tennessee, who shared the tariff views of the secretary of state, was talked into making the trip. The last two delegates were not chosen until virtually the last minute. They were Senator James Couzens of Michigan—reputedly the only Republican senator willing to attend, after Hiram Johnson had declined—and a retired San Antonio banker and cotton dealer, Ralph W. Morrison, who was chosen on the recommendation of Vice President John Nance Garner.

The instructions for the delegates were also a last-minute production. The delegates were permitted to discuss a tariff truce, the coordination of monetary and fiscal policy, the removal of exchange restrictions, the "laying of the groundwork" for an international monetary standard, the gradual abolition of trade barriers, and the "control of production and distribution of certain basic commodities." As for currency stabilization, that topic was purposely removed from the jurisdiction of the delegation. Now that the dollar had fallen against the pound, and the stock market and domestic prices had risen, Roosevelt was becoming hesitant to stabilize until it was known how far the dollar might fall. A further consideration was that stabilizing currency too early might reverse the rise in American domestic prices. Two separate delegates were named by Roosevelt to discuss stabilization: Oliver Sprague of Harvard University and George Harrison, governor of the Federal Reserve Bank of New York. Their discussions in regard to stabilization, according to Roosevelt's instructions, were to be carried on "wholly independently of the Economic Conference."[12] The delegation that sailed for London was unclear about what they were expected to accomplish as well as divided among themselves.

In the meantime British and American representatives in Washington were making little progress in resolving the impending crisis over the British war debt, the next installment of which was due on June 15, 1933. For several weeks Sir Ronald Lindsay and Sir Frederick Leith-Ross studied an imaginative plan, known as the "Bunny," which was dreamed up by the financier James P. Warburg, whereby Britain's payments would be reduced to about $2.5 billion, twenty-five percent of which would be in gold. On the basis of the British gold payments the Treasury would issue new treasury bills to be used for financing American public works. However, as was so often the case during the interwar era, the participants decided not to take action. In this case the British cabinet was lukewarm to the idea, unless Britain's debt was cut to $1 billion and the requirement for gold payments eliminated.

As a revised debt agreement was out of reach, MacDonald turned to the June 15 payment. In a personal letter to Roosevelt, the prime minister urged Roosevelt to suspend the June installment on the ground it would imperil the economic conference and interfere with the negotiations for a final settlement. Roosevelt's response was to suggest a partial payment, noting that such a procedure "would make it clear in both countries that there had not been a default. It avoids a debate on terminology."[13]

As the deadline approached, Lindsay vigorously pleaded Britain's inability to pay its installment of $75,950,000, even alluding to the "we forgive our debtors" phrase of the Lord's Prayer. Twice Lindsay met with Roosevelt to explore possible solutions. His impression was that Roosevelt was "extraordinarily fresh and vigorous," although there were "plenty of contradictions" in his understanding of international finance. On behalf of the cabinet, Lindsay offered a token payment of $5 million, but when Roosevelt objected that in the United States a "token" was considered a small worthless coin, London raised the offer to $10 million. A formal note explained that the June payment could not be made "without gravely imperiling the success of the [London Economic] Conference and involving widespread political consequences of a most serious character." The $10 million payment was made "as an acknowledgment of the debt pending a final settlement." Lindsay confessed to Sir John Simon, "I don't know how my nerves can stand a third such crisis."[14]

Britain's example of a token payment was followed at the last minute by several other debtor governments. Italy paid only $1 million on a total due of more than $13.5 million, despite Roosevelt's suggestion that the amount was similar to the "kind of tip which one gave in a very unfashionable restaurant."[15] Czechoslovakia made a token payment of $180,000 and Latvia paid $6,000. Hungary ostensibly met its obligation, but deposited its payment in a blocked account. Rumania and Lithuania notified the State Department of their inability to pay, but recanted when other debtors made partial payment. Rumania then paid slightly more than $29,000, and Lithuania belatedly remitted $10,000. With the exception of Finland, which paid in full, all the remaining debtors, including France and Belgium, defaulted.

At London nothing seemed to go well for Chairman Cordell Hull and his diverse collection of delegates. On his arrival, Hull learned that Roosevelt, believing he had pressured Congress as far as was possible, had decided not to submit a reciprocal trade agreements bill until 1934. The news came as a "terrific blow" to Hull because he had hoped to be able to display the bill as evidence of America's willingness to reduce trade barriers. Hull, in his *Memoirs*, bitterly recalled that he had "left for London with the highest of hopes, but arrived with empty hands."[16] Hull was also upset when Prime Minister MacDonald, in his opening address to the conference, boldly brought up a subject that, even he freely admitted, was officially excluded from the conference agenda. "I refer," he stated, "to the question of the war debts, which must be dealt with before every obstacle to general recovery has been removed, and it must be taken up without delay by the nations concerned. Lausanne has to be completed and this vexed question settled once for all in the light of present world conditions."[17] Ambassador Robert W. Bingham, expressed the mood of the Americans in London, when he wrote Roosevelt that he was "simply aghast" at MacDonald's "breach of faith."[18]

As the conference organized during its first week, Sprague and Harrison negotiated a stabilization agreement with the British and French. The agreement would have maintained existing exchange rates of the dollar, pound, and franc for the duration of the conference, and it obligated the Treasury to expend up to $60 million in defense of the dollar and to compensate the Federal Reserve Bank of New York for any losses incurred. Earlier Roosevelt had endorsed currency stabilization, but once the conference began he reconsidered his position, fearing that stabilization at too low a level would be premature. General Hugh Johnson, the outspoken director of the National Recovery Administration, put the position of the more nationalistic New Dealers bluntly when he told Moley, "an agreement to stabilize now on the lines your boy friends in London are suggesting would bust to hell and gone the prices we're sweating to raise." Roosevelt sided with the nationalists in his administration when he quickly rejected the Sprague-Harrison plan as too vague. "As a general principle," wrote Roosevelt, "I am at present opposed to any agreements aimed at close stabilization of pound and dollar with small leeway either way, especially at present approximate levels."[19]

Roosevelt's reversal of his position on stabilization threw the American delegation and the conference into a state of confusion. Even Hull, still demoralized by the rejection of his tariff reduction hopes, felt "the conference was showing unmistakable signs of bogging down."[20] Moreover, the behavior of several members of the delegation, with the conspicuous exception of Cox, was bizarre: attendance at meetings was sporadic, especially on the part of McReynolds and Morrison. Couzens repeatedly criticized Hull's policies in press interviews. Hull appeared despondent and later complained to Moley that the delegation had been "disobedient and recalcitrant."[21] And Pittman disgraced himself by lapsing into a state of chronic intoxication, by picking quarrels, and physically assaulting staff members of the delegation. In a conversation with Henry L. Stimson a few weeks later, MacDonald burst out: "How on earth did Roosevelt ever send such a delegation to the conference? It had no cohesion or initiative. It could act only on daily reports and instructions from Washington."[22]

An equally bizarre performance was Raymond Moley's voyage to London. It was preceded by Moley's descent, by seaplane and destroyer, upon Roosevelt's vacation schooner *Amberjack*. Roosevelt, cordial as ever, wrote out in his illegible handwriting a memorandum stating that Moley was being sent at the president's request to act as a "messenger or liaison officer," that he would bring the delegation firsthand information, and that after about a week he would return to brief the president. Hazily the president indicated to Moley that he could accept a limited stabilization agreement to keep the conference from failing, or at least that was Moley's impression. For the reputations of both Moley and Roosevelt, the mission to London proved singularly ill-advised.

During the six days it took for Moley to reach London, the conference came to a virtual standstill. Hull was deeply mortified as the Moley mission gave at least the tacit impression that Hull had proved incapable of adequately representing American interests. Therefore, it was rumored, Roosevelt was sending his "man Friday" to replace Hull as secretary of state. On his arrival, to Hull's acute embarrassment, Moley was lionized by the press, while Hull was ignored. At one point MacDonald asked Hull if he would "send Moley over to me? I'd like to talk to him," adding as an afterthought, "and you can come too if you like." Hull's impression, contained in his *Memoirs*, was that Moley "appeared to act as if he were in entire charge for the United States Government, notwithstanding his transparent protests and denials as to occupying such a status."[23]

Subsequently Moley, at the urging of MacDonald and with the approval of Sprague, Harrison, Bernard Baruch, Secretary of the Treasury Will Woodin, and his Undersecretary Dean Acheson, endorsed an exceptionally ambiguous stabilization proposal designed to keep the conference from collapsing. In vague generalities the agreement spoke of restoring international monetary stability "as quickly as possible" and endorsed the abstract desirability of ultimately restoring the gold standard "when the time comes." To control currency speculation, central banks were requested to coordinate their operations. In trans-Atlantic telephone conversations, which were then a novelty, Roosevelt's economic advisers endorsed the plan (in one telephone conference an inadvertent $400 charge was incurred when Woodin, who was suffering from cancer, suddenly fainted and the phone was left off the hook). Moley magnanimously arranged for Hull to announce the president's acquiescence when the expected favorable reply was received from the USS *Indianapolis*, where Roosevelt was headquartered.[24]

Instead Roosevelt surprised everyone, especially Moley, by dispatching his "bombshell" message of July 3, 1933, in which he emphatically rejected stabilization, saying it would be a world tragedy if the conference were to be "diverted by the proposal of a purely artificial and temporary experiment affecting the monetary exchange of a few nations only." Realizing that Moley "had reached the end of his rope," Hull rebuked him with the advice, "You had better get back home. You had no business over here in the first place," and Hull continued "to elaborate along those lines." In discussing Moley with Stimson, Hull remarked, "You can properly call him a son of anything you please," and in a conversation with James P. Warburg, Hull referred to Moley as an untrustworthy "piss-ant." As for MacDonald, he was devastated by Roosevelt's "bombshell." In frustration MacDonald burst out, "This doesn't sound like the man I spent so many hours with in Washington. This sounds like a different man. I don't understand."[25]

To save face the conference remained in session until July 27 when it "recessed," never to reconvene. But the remaining three weeks were largely wasted in what Hull called "a kind of paper chase during which we sought to find odds and ends of topics that could be discussed."[26] First, an effort to agree on a new agenda ended in a stalemate between the gold and nongold nations. The efforts of the Monetary and Economic Commission, headed by Cox, produced almost nothing of substance: a harmless resolution calling on debtors to make every effort to pay their debts, as well as resolutions that urged central banks to cooperate in making agricultural loans available, to discourage the circulation of gold coins, and to establish central banks in countries where they did not already exist. The effect of these resolutions was aptly summarized for Roosevelt by Pittman, who reported "all these resolutions were innocuous, gave opportunity for unobjectionable speeches and seemed to satisfy Near East groups."[27] The other major branch of the conference, the Economic Commission, was just as unsuccessful, adopting a report stating that the lowering of tariffs was "indispensable," but agreement could not be reached even on a generalized resolution. Equally futile were the results achieved by the division's subcommissions on the coordination of production and marketing, on timber, on governmental subsidies to shippers, and indirect protective measures (meaning customs regulations, quarantines, and administrative red tape). The subcommission reports merely called for further study or admitted that the deliberations had revealed conflicting positions. Somewhat ironically the chief accomplishment at London, achieved outside the framework of the conference, was the handiwork of Senator Pittman. The so-called London Silver Agreement established quotas for sales to the international silver market for the major silver producers, and committed the United States to purchase the current production of the American silver industry.

For all parties concerned the London Economic Conference had been an exercise in futility. Ramsay MacDonald was humiliated by the waste of time. But if Roosevelt felt any embarrassment for "torpedoing" the conference, he hid it behind bravado and contended he had preserved the nation's integrity against the greedy designs of European central bankers. In 1937, in discussing the "bombshell" message with the journalist Arthur Krock, Roosevelt made the ridiculous statement: "I'm prouder of that than anything else I ever did." The reality was that there was much in Roosevelt's diplomacy of which he should have been embarrassed: his selection of a weak, poorly instructed delegation; his adoption of a contradictory policy of simultaneously pursuing a nationalist policy at home while calling for international action at London; his apparent failure to even read Moley's stabilization proposal; and his casual humiliation of a loyal, if abrasive, assistant. One of the more unflattering explanations for Roosevelt's angry "bombshell" is that he wrote it at a time when he was upset as a result of the inevitable frictions that occur in even the best of marriages, namely that his wife had spoken sharply to him about what she regarded as Moley's excessive influence and had raised objections when Roosevelt served a cocktail to his teenage son, and then criticized her husband for being thirty minutes late to dinner; his excuse was that he didn't know what time dinner was being served.[28] In defense of Roosevelt's unsteady economic diplomacy, it has been argued that the gold standard nations should share the blame for the failure at London by insisting on stabilization as a precondition for accomplishing anything else. Moreover, even if Roosevelt had accepted Moley's stabilization agreement, it is unlikely much would have been accomplished. But Roosevelt and the United States would have escaped the blame for torpedoing the conference and retreating to isolationism.

The adjournment of the London Economic Conference by no means ended the New Deal's foreign economic troubles. By the fall of 1933 the White House, the State Department, and the Treasury Department were forced once again to turn their attention to the unpleasant topic of war debts, this because the six debtors who had made token payments in June had requested further negotiations. According to Moley, Roosevelt conceived the idea toward the end of the London Economic Conference of offering Finland, the only debtor paying in full, a substantial reduction of its debt, which would presumably serve as a model for general debt revision. To the surprise of the State Department the Finns, whose payments were insignificant and who enjoyed a favorable balance of trade with the United States, showed no interest. Likewise Czechoslovakia declined to be the first to negotiate, noting that they would be criticized by other debtors if they broke ranks. By default, therefore, the British, who sent Sir Frederick Leith-Ross to Washington in October, became the sole debtor to negotiate, while the remaining token payment debtors watched and waited.

Typically, few preparations were made on the American side until virtually the last minute. Undersecretary of State William Phillips plaintively wrote Hull, "Someone has got to talk to Leith-Ross, who will arrive in Washington in a few days. Someone ought to be studying the voluminous information which our Embassy in London has sent us, under the Department's instructions with respect to Great Britain's financial situation."[29] Belatedly it was decided to divide the negotiations between the treasury and state departments. Undersecretary of the Treasury Dean Acheson was placed in charge, and Assistant Economic Adviser Frederick Livesey was named as his assistant. The selection of the urbane Acheson was not entirely fortunate because Acheson was rapidly falling out of favor with Roosevelt due to his opposition to the bizarre theory of Professor George Warren that buying of gold by the Treasury would increase agricultural prices; a few weeks later the dispute led to Acheson's forced resignation. No doubt it would have been more sensible to have named a negotiator with the full confidence of the president. In practice it soon became evident that the two sides were so far apart that the lack of rapport between Roosevelt and Acheson was irrelevant.

It did not take Acheson long to discover that he had been "garlanded for sacrifice" and dispatched on a "kamikaze mission." The futility of the negotiation was immediately apparent as neither side was prepared to alter the positions taken the previous spring. Roosevelt told Acheson to hear Leith-Ross sympathetically, but to accept no settlement involving a drastic sacrifice. Fundamentally, British strategy also remained unchanged. Chancellor of the Exchequer Neville Chamberlain, showing no hint of being a weak appeaser, insisted on a settlement that would pass on to the United States the remnants Britain had received at the Lausanne Conference. Roosevelt, thinking of the congressional reaction to any drastic reduction, was adamant. The most he could offer, Roosevelt told Acheson, was to reduce Britain's debt to $2.26 billion and spread the payments over fifty years without interest. If Britain accepted, its annual payments would be reduced to about $40 million and in Roosevelt's opinion, conveyed to Leith-Ross through Acheson, "it was nonsense to say [the] British Government could not pay this."[30]

At the cabinet meeting of October 13, Acheson embarked upon an ill-starred effort to modify Roosevelt's views. Believing the situation presented a unique opportunity to direct public opinion away from the mentality of Calvin Coolidge, Acheson enlisted the support of Hull and Secretary of Labor Francis Perkins. But the president brusquely indicated he was holding out for more favorable terms. When Acheson stated that it was time to face the facts, Roosevelt decisively interrupted him with the comment: "Nothing new. I was afraid so. I must go into it with you later. It's not a matter of general interest here." Hull cleared his throat, but perhaps intimidated by Roosevelt's demeanor, declined to enter the fray. Afterward Hull, who pronounced his Rs as Ws, explained that the President "didn't give me a chance to begin maneuvewing."[31]

Two weeks of further negotiation failed to discover a middle ground. Tentatively the British suggested a temporary settlement involving a lump sum payment of perhaps $50 million to cover three or four years. Again Roosevelt was critical, and by October 27 Leith-Ross confided to Stimson that he was "not getting anywhere, but simply batting the air." Nor was the impasse broken by a White House conference between Lindsay, Leith-Ross, and the president on November 1. "His mind seemed to be quite decided," reported Leith-Ross, "and he brushed aside all the arguments which we put forward in favour of a longer period of agreement. There seemed no chance therefore of getting anything except another temporary arrangement covering the December 15 payment."[32] Roosevelt freely conceded that the 1923 debt settlement had been too severe, but in his political judgment neither the American public nor Congress was ready for a settlement that would reduce Britain's payments to only $10 or $15 million a year. The same objection applied to a temporary settlement of three or four years. Congressional authorization would be required for such an expedient, explained the president, and he argued it would be futile to approach Congress until a permanent settlement could be achieved. There was common agreement that the only course of action was to repeat the token payment procedure, and Roosevelt said he was willing to state again that he did not consider the British to be defaulters.

But Roosevelt, who liked to pride himself on his ability as a horse trader, was outsmarted on the amount of the token payment. Originally Chancellor of the Exchequer Neville Chamberlain had authorized a $10 million payment. Leith-Ross and Lindsay, neglecting to mention that they were able to pay the same amount as on June 15, shrewdly offered $7.5 million and Roosevelt readily accepted. A carefully worded statement drafted by Roosevelt artfully announced that the two governments had decided "to adjourn the discussions until certain factors in the world situation—

commercial and monetary—become more clarified." In view of the token payment Roosevelt added, "I have no personal hesitation in saying that I shall not regard the British Government as in default."[33]

The British debt issue was not the only relic of World War I to intrude upon Roosevelt's thoughts. For months the president had been exploring the possibility of ending the United States' sixteen-year diplomatic blackout of the Soviet Union. Like his predecessors Roosevelt found that a major obstacle to recognition was the Soviet government's repudiation of loans made by the Wilson administration to the Provisional Government totaling nearly $193 million. By 1933 the logic behind nonrecognition was no longer persuasive. Its permanency established, the Soviet Union appeared less and less as a diabolical menace, and its purchases under the first Five Year Plan seemed to offer hope for the United States' sagging export trade. Moreover, Roosevelt and Hull believed it unnatural for two such pivotal nations not to maintain diplomatic relations.

Roosevelt took the initiative by writing directly to the president of the Soviet Union inviting the Russians to send a representative "to explore with me personally the questions outstanding between our countries." No advance conditions were mentioned either by Roosevelt or in the Soviet reply accepting the invitation. On the sixteenth anniversary of the Bolshevik Revolution, Soviet Commissar for Foreign Affairs Maxim Litvinov arrived in Washington to conduct the negotiations. At the outset Roosevelt found that Litvinov was as intractable on the question of debts as were the United States' capitalist debtors. In the Roosevelt-Litvinov Agreement, announced on November 16, 1933, it was Roosevelt who made most of the concessions. In return for diplomatic recognition, Litvinov made paper promises to refrain from propaganda and to guarantee freedom of worship to Americans living in Russia. On the question of the Soviet debt the two leaders initialed an exceptionally imprecise "gentleman's agreement." In this remarkable document, seemingly dictated by Roosevelt, the president agreed to accept a minimum settlement of $150 million and expressed his opinion that Congress probably would reject a smaller sum. Litvinov, describing Roosevelt's figure as excessive, stated that he would, "without making any commitment," advise his government to accept $100 million as a fair compromise. But in the same breath Litvinov expressed confidence that "when the President had looked into the facts he would not feel that a sum greater than $75 million was justified."[34] Immediately the agreement was subject to conflicting interpretations, and by 1935 the negotiations reached an impasse over Soviet insistence that an American loan must precede a settlement. Years later Roosevelt was derided by critics for what they described as his hopelessly naive "Be Good to Russia" policy of wartime collaboration with Stalin. But in this case it is highly unlikely Roosevelt entered into an understanding with the Soviets in a spirit of childlike naivete. More likely Roosevelt accepted the agreement with Litvinov as an expedient, believing that the potential benefits of recognition outweighed whatever might be received on the comparatively small debt inherited by the Soviets. Not surprisingly the Treasury is still waiting for the first debt installment.

Simultaneously with the opening of diplomatic ties with Moscow, Roosevelt, playing the role of foreign policy quarterback, took the initiative in improvising a promising and imaginative debt revision agreement with Finland, which could have served as a prelude to a general debt revision and at least a nominal improvement in relations with the European debtors generally. At the same time Roosevelt kept a keen eye on how any reduction in payments, even in the case of the faithful Finns, would be received by Congress. A few months previously Finland had shown no interest when the subject of modifying its 1923 agreement was first floated. But by November 1933, the Finnish government changed its mind as opposition politicians were asking why only Finland should pay in full when America's other debtors were defaulting or making token payments. At Roosevelt's invitation a White House conference was convened on November 13. In attendance were Dean Acheson, William Phillips, the president, and the Finnish minister, Axel Leonard Aström. Roosevelt opened the discussion by expressing his gratitude to Finland for scrupulously observing its signed obligations. He added that to express his full appreciation to Finland, he wished to propose a debt revision that would reduce Finland's interest rate from three and a half percent to a "purely nominal" rate. The president's words were conveyed in so cordial a spirit that the minister wept. Phillips and Acheson were instructed to work out the details.[35]

The new agreement was not ready by the December 15 deadline, so Finland paid its installment ($229,623) according to the existing schedule. Again Finland was the only debtor to pay in full, although five debtors made token payments: Britain ($7.5 million), Italy ($1 million), Czechoslovakia ($150,000), Lithuania ($7,000), and Latvia ($8,500). Based upon a penciled memorandum by Roosevelt, the Treasury prepared alternatives for revising Finland's 1923 agreement. By recalculating Finland's debt on the basis of the Italian settlement of 1925, the Treasury concluded that the remaining principal due totaled $5,854,903.25. Roosevelt enthusiastically recommended that Finland be offered a revision that would retire the principal over thirty years without interest. "If you think this will attract them and that they will go through with it," Roosevelt wrote Phillips, "I take it the next step will be a tentative agreement, and you can tell them that I would submit such an agreement to the Congress for approval."[36] By mid-January 1934, the agreement was ready for signing. However, due to his contracting a case of political cold feet, Roosevelt never carried through his promise to send the agreement to Congress.

From Capitol Hill came strong indications that Congress, even under Democratic control, was as violently opposed as ever to even the slightest debt concession. What caught Roosevelt's attention was a bill introduced in March 1933, by Senator Hiram Johnson of California that proposed to ban the further purchase or sale in the United States of the bonds or securities of countries that were in default of their war debts. The exact definition of the term "default," however, was not spelled out in the legislation. The purposes of the measure, according to the favorable report of the Senate Judiciary Committee, were "to curb the capacity of those engaged in the sale of foreign obligations, [and to serve] as an admonition to governments well able to pay but which nevertheless repudiate their written engagements."[37]

In a little more than three months the Johnson Act made its way through Congress. On January 11, 1934, the bill passed the Senate without opposition, but it was reconsidered when Hull sought to modify its more extreme provisions. In its original form the bill would have banned further loans to individuals, as well as governments, of countries in default. At Hull's direction, Assistant Secretary of State R. Walton Moore urged that Latin America be excluded from the loan ban since defaults in that area had been attributable largely to financial chaos. However, no exemption was requested for the five debtors making token payments. Senator Johnson promptly agreed to accept the changes suggested by the State Department, thereby ensuring passage. To the shock of the British Embassy, the Johnson Act passed the Senate without opposition on February 6.

With Roosevelt and Hull standing aside, the Johnson Act sailed through the House. A theme frequently sounded during the House debate was that a ban on loans to defaulting governments would compel America's wayward debtors to pay. "This bill now before us," stated Democratic Representative Frank L. Kloeb of Ohio, "may bring them [defaulting debtors] to a sudden recognition of the fact that the backs of the taxpayers can no longer be lashed by debt defaulters who breach their solemn obligations." Representative Samuel McReynolds of Tennessee, the chairman of the House Foreign Affairs Committee, agreed stating, "By voting favorably on this bill we can say that we do not propose to have this Government or the citizens of the Government lend money until the defaulting governments have settled what they owe us. In other words we will protect the Government as well as the people of the United States."[38] By voice vote the measure passed the House on April 4 without dissent. In its final form the Johnson Act was cleverly constructed to eliminate any possible loophole. It banned not only loans to governments in default, but also the purchase or sale of the bonds, securities, or any other obligations of any foreign government "or political subdivision thereof or any organization or association acting for or on behalf of a foreign government or political subdivision thereof," while that government was in default of the payment of its debts "or any part thereof, to the Government of the United States."

Violators were subject to a fine of $10,000 or five years imprisonment or both.[39]

The passage of such a xenophobic law without a single dissenting vote must have demonstrated to Roosevelt the utter futility of further talk about reducing even the debt of Finland. Throughout, Roosevelt had approached the subject of revision with extreme caution, always bearing in mind the political implications of revision. Wary of committing his prestige on behalf of a losing cause, the president had not repeated in public his willingness to make concessions on the British and Finnish debts. That he had abandoned control of the debt issue to Congress was demonstrated by his signing of the Johnson Act on April 14.

The one remaining question raised by the Johnson Act was whether countries that had made token payments, such as Britain and Italy, were in default and subject to a loan ban. At the direction of the president, Attorney General Homer Cummings prepared an opinion to provide clarification. According to the ruling, handed down on May 5, Cummings took a flexible view of the term "default," holding that a government that had made only partial payment of its previous installments was not yet in default. Although he did not rule upon the question directly, the attorney general's opinion implied that full payment of the installments due on June 15 would be necessary to avoid the penalties of the Johnson Act.[40]

Without enthusiasm Chancellor of the Exchequer Neville Chamberlain agreed to make another $7.5 million token payment, provided Roosevelt would state again that he did not regard Britain as in a state of default. Lindsay, on instructions, met with the president to assess the possibilities. Displaying his "usual breezy optimism and amazing candour," Roosevelt made it plain that the mood of Congress ruled out further token payments. Throughout the conversation Roosevelt avoided appearing as a debt collector, and adopted the attitude of a friendly counselor whose only desire was to be helpful. When the ambassador asked for suggestions, the president recommended that the British divert attention from the distasteful word "default" by sending a prestigious mission to Washington for a new round of debt negotiations. Such a procedure, said Roosevelt, would "certainly improve" the situation regarding the June 15 payment and perhaps the next "pay-day" as well. Lindsay expressed his "absolute horror" at the idea, and according to William Phillips, the ambassador "did not seem to receive the President's suggestion in a very happy spirit." Repeatedly Roosevelt stressed the necessity of preserving Anglo-American friendship so that the two nations could respond jointly to any crisis that might arise in Europe or the Far East. "He actually said," reported an astonished Lindsay, " 'you have not yet completed Singapore and please let us know when you have.' " The president further startled Lindsay by audaciously saying he would like to draft the diplomatic note to be sent by Britain explaining its decision to default. His advice was to avoid formal language and to explain the current British budget surplus as the result of "unparalleled sacrifices." Clothed in his role as helpful adviser, Roosevelt "actually recommended" to the bemused ambassador that the British note stress the necessity of reducing the tax burden of the average British citizen so as to remove "social injustice."[41]

The passage of the Johnson Act ended any thought of debt revision on Roosevelt's part. Pragmatically he surrendered to the "Iron Cancellor," as Lindsay now called the irreconcilable senator from California. To the distress of the Finns, Roosevelt refused to carry out the revised debt settlement, noting that the political situation in Congress made its submission impossible. As William Phillips explained to the Finnish minister, a reduction in Finland's payments would raise embarrassing questions as to whether other debtors would receive the same treatment and would likely disrupt and prolong the congressional session. Roosevelt's capitulation on the issue was formalized by the publication on June 1 of the president's debt message to Congress. Drafted in the State Department by Assistant Economic Adviser Frederick Livesey and William Phillips, the statement displayed none of the stylistic flourishes characteristic of the president. Making no mention of the Warburg Plan, of his offer to cancel all interest on the British debt, or of the proposed Finnish settlement, the message emphasized the "sacredness" of the debtors' moral obligation to the American taxpayer, and noted that the American people would look critically upon foreign spending "for purposes of unproductive nationalistic expenditure or like purposes." His administration was open to holding further discussions relating "to means and method of payment," but Roosevelt frankly conceded that "the final power lies with the Congress."[42] In view of Roosevelt's unsympathetic tone, the five debtors that had remained in good standing by means of partial payment were confronted with a choice between full remittance of the June installments or default.

To no one's surprise the era of token payments now ended as a formal note announced the British decision to default. Ignoring Roosevelt's suggestion about "social injustice" and the heavy burden of taxation, the British employed more conventional justifications, citing the high American tariff, the "unreasonable" and "inequitable" debt settlement of 1923, and the incongruity of Britain's honoring its obligations to the United States while receiving nothing from its debtors. The actual term "default" was scrupulously avoided; technically Britain was only "suspending further payments until it becomes possible to discuss an ultimate settlement of intergovernmental war debts with a reasonable prospect of agreement."[43]

Italy, Czechoslovakia, Latvia, and Lithuania, having waited to see what Britain would do, followed the British lead and defaulted. Only Finland made full payment, a policy that continued during World War II (even after Finland joined Germany) because Finland had sufficient dollar reserves in American banks; in 1949 the remaining Finnish payments were diverted into a fund for educational exchanges. Semiannually after June 1934 the Treasury and State Departments went through a ritual of presenting each of the defaulting debtors a statement of the amounts due plus compound interest. In return the debtors politely expressed regret that the conditions that had compelled the suspension of payments had not changed. It was a practice that was not abandoned until after the outbreak of World War II. The entire war debt conundrum, which so fixated the American public and foreign policy makers, was in many ways typical of American interwar foreign policy. Legalistically both Democrats and Republicans insisted upon the United States' moral right of repayment, even if the financial returns were insignificant compared with the political costs of poisoning relations with potential allies. Every time a promising solution was suggested, the statesmen of the day, usually for fear of political retribution, decided not to act. From a purely material point of view the war debt policy of the interwar era proved shortsighted. Of the $10.3 billion funded by the World War Foreign Debt Commission, the United States collected only about $2.7 billion by 1934; and of this sum $2,024,000,000 was paid by Britain. Moreover, the punitive Johnson Act backfired in that, instead of forcing the debtors to pay, it made it easier for them to default. For their part the British, who were at first pleased to have escaped from the debt conundrum, did not look so clever when the Johnson Act blocked loans to Britain, which were badly needed for rearmament in the face of the Nazi threat. An incidental result of Britain's default was to further intensify the personal distrust between Neville Chamberlain and Franklin D. Roosevelt.

Historians often claim the "lessons" of history to which they are privy are ignored; but in this case learned historians were hardly required to instruct future generations about the folly of loaning huge sums and then expecting repayment over several generations. That the obvious implications of the defaults of 1932–1934 were not lost on President Roosevelt was soon demonstrated by his deft elimination of the dollar sign through his imaginative Lend-Lease program during World War II. The quiet repeal of the Johnson Act and a $2 billion loan to Britain followed in 1946.

NOTES

1. Arthur M. Schlesinger, Jr., *The Coming of the New Deal* (Boston, 1959), 193.

2. Stephen A. Schuker, *American "Reparations" to Germany, 1919–1933: Implications for the Third-World Debt Crisis* (Princeton, 1988), 73.

3. For a portrayal of Roosevelt as an isolationist see Charles C. Tansill, *Back Door to War: The Roosevelt Foreign Policy, 1933–1941* (Chicago, 1952), 43; and Charles A. Beard, *American Foreign Policy in the Making, 1932–1940* (New Haven, 1940), 132. For Roosevelt as an internationalist see William E. Leuchtenburg,

Franklin D. Roosevelt and the New Deal, 1932–1940 (New York, 1963), 197–230; and Robert Dallek, *Franklin D. Roosevelt and American Foreign Policy, 1932–1945* (New York, 1979), 20–97.

4. Lindsay to Anthony Eden, January 1, 1936, FO414/273/A308, Public Record Office (PRO).

5. Raymond Moley, *After Seven Years* (New York, 1939), 116.

6. Cordell Hull, *The Memoirs of Cordell Hull* (New York, 1948), Vol. 1, 247.

7. Moley, *After Seven Years*, 201.

8. Moley, *After Seven Years*, 204.

9. Moley, *After Seven Years*, 206.

10. *The Public Papers and Addresses of Franklin D. Roosevelt* (New York, 1938), Vol. 2, 167.

11. *The Public Papers and Addresses of Franklin D. Roosevelt*, Vol. 2, 185–91.

12. Hull to French Ambassador Andre Laboulaye, May 27, 1933, FRUS, 1933. I 619–20.

13. Roosevelt to MacDonald, May 22, 1933, Edgar B. Nixon, editor, *Franklin D. Roosevelt and Foreign Affairs* (Cambridge, 1969), Vol. 1, 153–54.

14. Lindsay to Hull, June 13, 1933, FRUS, 1933, I, 839–41; Lindsay to Sir John Simon, June 15, 1933, FO 794/17.

15. Moley, *After Seven Years*, 223.

16. Hull, *Memoirs*, Vol. 1, 255.

17. Walter Lippmann, editor, *The United States in World Affairs: An Account of American Foreign Relations, 1933* (New York, 1934), 103.

18. Schlesinger, *Coming of the New Deal*, 213.

19. Roosevelt to Hull, June 17, 1933, FRUS, 1933, I, 646.

20. Hull, *Memoirs*, Vol. 1, 259.

21. Moley, *After Seven Years*, 244.

22. Diary of Henry L. Stimson, July 15, 1933, Yale University.

23. Hull, *Memoirs*, Vol. 1, 260–61.

24. Moley, *After Seven Years*, 250–53.

25. Hull, *Memoirs*, Vol. 1, 261; Frank Freidel, *Franklin D. Roosevelt: Launching the New Deal* (Boston, 1973), 492; Moley, *After Seven Years*, 263.

26. Hull, *Memoirs*, Vol. 1, 129–30.

27. Pittman to Roosevelt, July 14, 1933, FRUS, I, 717–18.

28. Freidel, *Franklin D. Roosevelt: Launching the New Deal*, 478–89.

29. Phillips to Hull, September 25, 1933, Franklin D. Roosevelt Library, Official File 48.

30. Dean Acheson, *Morning and Noon* (Boston, 1965), 185–86; Lindsay to Simon, October 13, 1933, E.L. Woodward and Rohan Butler, eds., *Documents on British Foreign Policy, 1919–1939* (London, 1956), Second Series, Vol. 5, 845–48. See also Patricia Clavin, *The Failure of Economic Diplomacy: Britain, Germany, France and the United States, 1931–1936* (New York, 1996), 173–76.

31. Acheson, *Morning and Noon*, 185–87.

32. Lindsay to Simon, November 1, 1933, Woodward and Butler, *Documents on British Foreign Policy*, Second Series, Vol. 5, 852–53.

33. Press release issued by the White House, November 7, 1933, FRUS, 1933, I, 845–46.

34. Robert P. Browder, *The Origins of Soviet-American Diplomacy* (Princeton, 1953), 116–43; Donald G. Bishop, *The Roosevelt-Litvinov Agreements: The American View* (Syracuse, 1965), Chapter 5.

35. Memorandum by Phillips, November 13, 1933, FRUS, 1933, I, 864; William Phillips, *Ventures in Diplomacy* (North Beverly, Mass., 1952), 160.

36. Roosevelt to Phillips, December 22, 1933, Nixon, *Franklin D. Roosevelt and Foreign Affairs*, Vol. 1, 543–44.

37. Senate Reports, 73 Cong. 2 Sess., No. 20 (Serial 9769), 1–2.

38. *Congressional Record*, 73 Cong., 2 Sess., 6048, 6054 (April 4, 1934).

39. Department of the Treasury, *Annual Report of the Secretary of the Treasury*, 1934 (Washington, 1935), 238.

40. *Annual Report of the Secretary of the Treasury*, 1934, 238–42.

41. Lindsay to Simon, May 18, 1934, Woodward and Butler, *Documents on British Foreign Policy*, Second Series, Vol. 6, 926–28.

42. Roosevelt to the Congress, June 1, 1934, Nixon, *Franklin D. Roosevelt and Foreign Affairs*, Vol. 2, 126–34.

43. Lindsay to Hull, June 4, 1934, Department of the Treasury, *Annual Report of the Secretary of the Treasury*, 1934, 227–30.

CHAPTER 7

The Good Neighbor Policy:
A Bipartisan Accomplishment

Franklin D. Roosevelt possessed a wonderful ear for memorable phrases either of his own composition ("The only thing we have to fear is fear itself"), or those which he unabashedly borrowed from speech writers such as Raymond Moley ("I pledge you I pledge myself to a New Deal for the American people," or "In the field of foreign policy I would dedicate this nation to the policy of the Good Neighbor"). His predecessor had often urged the American people to cheer up and had taken substantial steps to improve relations with Latin America. Roosevelt, with his gift for language, got most of the political credit for a policy begun under Colby and expanded by his Republican successors. Unlike war debts, the economic conference, and recognition of the Soviet Union, Roosevelt's direct involvement in Latin American policy was sporadic as his domestic priorities took precedence. Illustrative of the unevenness of Roosevelt's attention to the region was a request received by the State Department on the afternoon of April 11, 1933, that a speech be prepared for the president to deliver the following morning at the Pan American Union.

Perhaps remembering Woodrow Wilson's Mobile, Alabama, address of 1913, Secretary of State Cordell Hull provided a suitable script pledging the United States' commitment to the ideals of mutual understanding, a sympathetic appreciation of others' views, and respect for territorial integrity.[1] But Hull made no pretense of being a Latin American expert. His direct contact with the region was limited to the five months he had spent in Cuba during the Spanish-American War. Simplistically he believed that expanding trade was the cure for the region's troubles. But Hull was well aware that he faced a formidable task in allaying Latin American suspicions of America's neighborly intentions because of past American interventions in Panama, Haiti, the Dominican Republic, Mexico, and Nicaragua. In particular, after his unhappy experience at the London Economic Conference,

Hull looked with foreboding to his enforced attendance at the Pan American Conference scheduled to meet at Montevideo, Uruguay, in December 1933.

Throughout his lengthy tenure as secretary of state, Hull frequently found that Roosevelt preferred to bypass him and work through intimates such as Raymond Moley or William C. Bullitt. In the case of Latin America, Hull often found himself playing second fiddle to another of Roosevelt's close friends, Sumner Welles. Socially and intellectually, Welles and Roosevelt were thoroughly compatible. Both had attended the same prep school (the Groton School), and both were Harvard graduates. A career foreign service officer, Welles had served in Argentina and, under Charles Evans Hughes, had headed the State Department's Latin American division at the tender age of twenty-eight. After temporarily leaving government service, Welles published a history of the Dominican Republic in which he praised Hughes's contribution to the Good Neighbor concept. In recognition of Welles's abilities and his financial and intellectual contributions to his presidential campaign, Roosevelt named him assistant secretary of state. Understandably, Hull was not enthusiastic about having ambitious assistants with easy access to the White House.[2]

Given the president's stirring inaugural commitment to the principle of the Good Neighbor and his appointment of Welles to the State Department, the path to improved relations with Latin America should have been a smooth one. In reality, Roosevelt's Good Neighbor Policy had a surprisingly shaky start. An implicit assumption is often made that the New Deal promptly liquidated the interventionism practiced by McKinley, Theodore Roosevelt, Taft, Wilson, and Coolidge. This was not true of Cuba, however. Since evacuating the island in 1901, the United States had possessed, in the form of the Platt Amendment, the right to intervene in Cuba as well as the right to occupy the Guantanamo Bay naval base. A Cuban-American treaty had formalized the concessions, making Cuba a de facto protectorate of the United States.

In the prosperous decade of the 1920s, Cuba, under President Gerardo Machado, set an example of welcome stability. As the price of sugar collapsed with the onset of the depression, so did the political stability of Machado's regime. When Roosevelt took office Machado was clinging to power with the support of the military. Welles was dispatched to Havana as ambassador and presidential troubleshooter. Instead of inaugurating a new era of good neighborliness, Welles's mission represented a throwback to interventionism. Three months after Welles' arrival, the military abandoned Machado, and he departed into exile in mid-August.

The hand of Welles was evident not only in the fall of Machado, but in the selection of his successor, Manuel Cespedes, the Cuban ambassador to the United States from 1914 to 1922. The new president proved a poor choice because he was beholden to Welles and seemingly bewildered by how to exercise his office. Three visits from Welles in one day were required to assist Cespedes in selecting a cabinet. Three weeks after taking office, Cespedes was sent into exile by a palace coup (September 5, 1933) masterminded by a junta of five enlisted men headed by Sergeant Fulgencio Batista. Welles's reaction was to request the landing of "a considerable force" of marines at Havana and other unspecified cities. But Hull convinced Roosevelt that armed intervention would produce a hostile reaction throughout the hemisphere and sabotage the forthcoming Pan American Conference. Vice President John Nance Garner also advised Roosevelt to refrain from an invasion. If the Cubans killed United States citizens, Garner counseled Roosevelt not to overreact, saying, in effect, that he should wait for those shot in the back to be rolled over and identified before taking drastic action. "Wait and see who the [dead] Americans are," was Garner's advice.[3]

Typically Roosevelt compromised between the views of his subordinates by sending twenty-four naval vessels as a bluff. Up to a point the threat worked as the junta resigned in favor of the nationalistic professor Ramon Grau San Martin. Recognition was delayed ostensibly to determine whether the new government was capable of maintaining law and order, but in reality because Welles regarded Grau San Martin as unacceptable both politically and personally. A break in the logjam did not come until Welles returned from Cuba to the State Department in mid-December 1933. His replacement as ambassador to Cuba, Jefferson Caffery, brought a fresh outlook and soon gained the cooperation of Batista to force Grau's resignation (January 20, 1934). With the selection of a new conservative president, Carlos Mendieta, Roosevelt ended nonrecognition and began negotiations to modify the 1901 Platt Amendment. In the final agreement, reached in June 1934, the United States kept the Guantanamo Bay Naval Base as a souvenir of the Platt Amendment, but relinquished the right to intervene in Cuban affairs. Hailed as a triumph for the New Deal's Good Neighbor Policy, the abrogation of the Platt Amendment had taken the better part of a year to accomplish and had required repeated threats of intervention as well as the nonrecognition of the Grau government. Moreover, Cuban stability came at the price of domestic repression by Fulgencio Batista, the de facto power behind the scenes from 1934 until his election as president in 1940. From the Cuban perspective, the Good Neighbor Policy had been as much illusion as reality.

In the meantime, Hull scored an unexpected and resounding personal triumph at the Montevideo Pan American Conference in December 1933. At first, prospects did not look very good for success due to the tensions associated with the economic depression and the adverse Latin American reaction to the United States' semi-intervention in Cuban affairs. Hull also had to contend with the well-known anti-Americanism of the Argentinean foreign minister, Saavedra Lamas, who, together with representatives from Brazil, Chile, and Colombia, urged a postponement of the gathering. A further obstacle was the indifferent attitude of the White House. Hull was told by Roosevelt's trusted assistant Louis Howe, "We don't think you need to undertake much down at Montevideo. Just talk to them about the Pan-American highway from the United States down through Central and South America."[4] As the first secretary of state to attend a Pan American Conference, Hull insisted on an ambitious program of stimulating hemispheric trade through reciprocal trade agreements and achieving peace through the mutual acceptance of the principle that war should be banned throughout the hemisphere.

Rebounding from his dismal experience at London, Hull extended himself and unleashed upon the delegates his ample reserves of southern hospitality and charm. On board his ship, the *American Legion*, Hull made a point of calling on all the Latin American delegates, especially those from Haiti, whom he was able to assure of America's intent soon to withdraw entirely from that island nation. Simultaneously Hull prepared resolutions for presentation to the conference urging the delegates to accept his program.

Upon reaching Montevideo, Hull effectively countered local manifestations of anti-Americanism ("Down with Hull" read one billboard) by making courtesy calls on the various delegations and giving the impression that he was a man of goodwill and earnest sincerity. He even had the effrontery to call on the skeptical Argentinean Foreign Minister Saavedra Lamas within an hour of his arrival at the conference in order to seek his cooperation. Surprisingly, the chain-smoking, volatile Argentinean and the courtly Tennesseean managed to find common ground. Within twenty-four hours Lamas agreed to support Hull's economic program as well as a resolution calling on the participants to ratify the Kellogg-Briand Pact. In return Hull agreed to support an anti-war pact drafted by Saavedra Lamas and signed by six Latin American nations two months before. The most serious crisis at Montevideo came when delegates from the Dominican Republic, Haiti, Nicaragua, El Salvador, and Cuba demanded that the United States endorse the principle that "No state has the right to intervene in the internal or external affairs of another." Hull wisely kept his poise and signed the nonintervention pledge, adding a reservation—which was widely overlooked—saying that the United States retained the right to intervene under existing treaty rights. When Hull returned to Washington via the west coast of Latin America and the Panama Canal, he had demonstrated that tactful personal diplomacy could, at least temporarily, transform the latent Latin American distrust of American motives. The unanswered question was whether he could convince President Roosevelt to rally behind his program. As before, the president had reservations about embracing Hull's idealistic foreign economic policies, fearing that trade concessions could derail his domestic policy of national recovery measures.

Having invested two and a half months of effort in preparing for and attending the Montevideo conference, Hull withdrew in favor of Welles from the active direction of Latin American policy. The courtly secretary of state found his time consumed by such issues as the unfortunate Johnson Act (which banned loans to defaulting debtor nations), the renewed movement to join the World Court, and especially his pet project: a reciprocal trade agreements act. Passing through the Panama Canal on his return from Montevideo, Hull had fulfilled a promise made by Roosevelt to Panamanian President Harmodio Arias that the United States would take steps to revise the 1903 Hay-Bunau-Varilla Treaty. Signed just two weeks after Panama had won its independence from Colombia, the controversial document had transformed Panama into an American protectorate. John Hay, Theodore Roosevelt's secretary of state, drove a hard bargain with Philippe Bunau-Varilla, the French engineer who was named as Panama's foreign minister. For a modest annuity of $250,000 plus a $10,000,000 down payment the United States received "in perpetuity" a ten-mile-wide canal zone and, in Article 7, the right "in perpetuity" to intervene in Panama City, Colon, and "the territories and harbors adjacent thereto" in order to enforce sanitary standards and maintain public order. At the time, Hay noted, "There are many things in this treaty to which a Panamanian patriot could object."

A further Panamanian grievance was the existence within the Canal Zone of a privileged American colonial enclave, which contrasted with the poverty and low pay of Panamanian employees. With the concurrence of Hull and the president, Welles was able to offer Panama an increase in the American payment to $436,000 as well as the abrogation of Article 7 of the 1903 treaty. In 1936, with Hull running interference among reluctant Democrats, the treaty passed the Senate.[5] Without altering the status of the critical canal, the New Deal refurbished the image of the United States as a good neighbor by relinquishing a treaty right that was hopelessly out of date.

Afterwards it was a frequent criticism of the Good Neighbor Policy that nonintervention had the unintended effect of entrenching repressive Caribbean dictatorships. Given the stark realities of Latin American governments combined with the United States' abandonment of military intervention, the only alternative to such relationships was continuous nonrecognition in the tradition of Woodrow Wilson—a policy which had failed spectacularly with Mexico and Soviet Russia. Unlike Wilson, Roosevelt pragmatically declined to teach the Latin Americans to elect good men. In practical terms, nonintervention required doing business with governments that were both corrupt and tyrannical.

Theoretically Haiti should have been a democratic model for the hemisphere. Since 1915 the island nation had been occupied by United States marines who supervised a plebiscite that approved a new constitution to which Franklin D. Roosevelt had contributed when he was assistant secretary of the navy under President Wilson. Under Hoover the United States had agreed to remove the marines on the condition that Haiti agree to pay its foreign debt, but the Haitian legislature balked and refused its approval. Roosevelt's minister to Haiti, Norman Armour, got around the obstinate legislative body by crafting the terms of the American evacuation of Haiti in the form of an executive agreement between Roosevelt and Stenio Vincent, the Haitian president. Vincent journeyed to Washington in April 1934 to complete the details of the withdrawal, which was carried out on August 15 after Roosevelt had visited Port-au-Prince during a tour of Colombia and the Caribbean. However, United States control of Haitian customs was not terminated until 1941. "We wish for the Government and people of Haiti stability, progress, and all success," Hull proclaimed.[6] Now that United States naval and marine forces had been removed, the fact was that Washington could only "wish" that the government of the repressive President Vincent respect the rights guaranteed by the American-sponsored constitution.

The Dominican Republic, the neighbor of Haiti, received special attention from Wells, who had a sentimental attachment to the island nation stemming from his diplomatic service there a decade before. As in the case of Haiti, the Dominican Republican presented the New Deal with another opportunity for liquidating longstanding American intervention. When the Dominican Republic defaulted on its foreign debt in 1905, Theodore Roosevelt proclaimed his Corollary to the Monroe Doctrine asserting the duty of the United States to avert chronic wrongdoing or disorder in the western hemisphere; as a result the Dominican Republic agreed by treaty to permit the United States to collect and manage its customs receipts. A full-scale intervention was authorized by Wilson in 1916 to restore order following a chaotic revolution; after eight years the marines were withdrawn in 1924, leaving the American-trained national guard in control. Raphael Trujillo, the personification of Latin American dictators, began his long career as president in 1930. In the fall of 1940, reflecting a desire to terminate a relic of the past, Welles rescinded the customs receivership. The fawning Dominican legislature than bestowed upon the nation's dictator the preposterous title "Restorer of the Financial Independence of the Republic." The unscrupulous Trujillo maintained himself in power by force, callously executing in 1937 thousands of Haitian laborers, whose only crime was trespassing on Dominican soil as they sought work in the sugar cane industry. The United States' association with the regime did not end until Trujillo's assassination by his own forces in May 1961.[7]

The price of stability in Haiti and the Dominican Republic was the acceptance of repressive regimes. A similar approach characterized the Good Neighbor Policy toward Nicaragua: recognizing a military tyrant was regarded as a realistic alternative to the old, failed policy of military and financial intervention. Since the Taft administration the presence of American troops had been a fact of life in Nicaragua. Under Coolidge the United States marines, who had been temporarily removed in 1925, returned in 1926 to suppress the Sandino rebels and to supervise the elections of 1928 and 1932. Ironically the 1932 election led to the selection as president of Juan Sacasa, who had once been castigated by Coolidge and Kellogg as a Bolshevik.

One of the first steps taken by the new president was the selection of General Anastasio Somoza as the commander of the Nicaraguan National Guard. Following Sacasa's inauguration, the marines, who had suffered 136 dead over six years but had failed to capture Sandino, departed to their base at Quantico, Virginia. As for Sandino, he was hailed as a national hero and unwisely agreed to a truce and the partial demobilization of his forces. Lured to a dinner (February 21, 1934) with the new president, Sandino, his brother, and two Sandino generals were executed by firing squad on the order of Somoza. Twenty years before, a similar incident in Mexico—the murder of President Francisco I. Madero—had resulted in American nonrecognition. In the case of Sandino, Arthur B. Lane, the American minister to Nicaragua, recommended the withdrawal of recognition to protest the assassination and the unfounded charge that it had been ordered by Washington. Welles, holding to nonintervention, denied the nonrecognition recommendation. And the State Department did not protest when Somoza deposed Sacasa in 1936. Roosevelt's attitude toward the Nicaraguan strongman, and by implication to other Latin American dictators, was summarized in the thoughtless (and probably apocryphal) remark, "He may be a son-of-a-bitch, but he's our son-of-a-bitch."[8] The acceptance of tyrants was essentially a cold-blooded alternative to Wilson's policy of moral nonrecognition and military intervention. Roosevelt, Hull, and Welles came to the frank recognition that Washington could not (as Wilson had hoped) teach Latin Americans to elect good men because in many cases the alternative to the existing tyrant was another tyrant.

To the average citizen of the hemisphere the most visible feature of the Good Neighbor Policy was the liquidation of intervention. Less obvious to the naked eye, but no less important to the success of the Good Neighbor, was the gradual improvement of hemispheric trade. For Cordell Hull the dream of a lifetime came true on June 12, 1934, when Roosevelt signed Hull's cherished Reciprocal Trade Agreements bill. Convinced that Congress could never be induced to repeal the Hawley-Smoot Tariff of 1930, Hull designed an end-run strategy. His bill authorized the president to increase or decrease existing rates by up to fifty percent in return for trade concessions. Once negotiated by the executive, the bilateral trade agreements required no further congressional approval. Latin America, which in 1932 had seen its imports from the United States drop to the lowest level in twenty-three years, was a special beneficiary of the new policy. However, the first of the reciprocal trade agreements with Cuba in 1934 was hardly an example of enlightened trade policy in that it did not offer Cuba most favored nation status; this meant that Cuba was not eligible to receive any lower tariffs the United States might later negotiate with other powers. On the other hand Cuba was granted a twenty percent reduction in American tariff rates in return for twenty percent to forty percent tariff reductions extended to American imports. Cuban nationalists, who sought to diversify the Cuban economy, were unhappy because the agreement perpetuated Cuba's vulnerable one-crop economy. However, the only practical way for Cuba to acquire dollars with which to purchase American manufactured goods was by exporting sugar to the United States.[9] Less one-sided were the trade agreements negotiated with Brazil (1935), Haiti (1935), Colombia (1935), Honduras (1935), Nicaragua (1936), Guatemala (1936), Costa Rica (1936), El Salvador (1937), and Ecuador (1938). Hull was certainly well aware that the Latin American trade agreements provided substantial benefits to American corporations, whose share of total Latin American trade increased to forty-five percent as compared with thirty-five percent in 1932. At the same time Latin America saw its exports to the United States soar by 114 percent from $329.4 million in 1933 to $705 million in 1937. From a material point of view the trade agreements of the Good Neighbor Policy were mutually beneficial even if they maintained the Caribbean as an economic sphere of the United States. The passage and implementation of the reciprocal trade agreements program established Hull as a master of bureaucratic infighting, as he had prevailed over Roosevelt's Foreign Trade Adviser George Peek, who advocated disposing of United States surpluses through barter agreements.[10]

Consistency, meaning the ability to declare a policy and stick to it, was characteristic of the New Deal's Good Neighbor Policy. By 1934, having learned a lesson from Welles's missteps in Cuba, the goals of Roosevelt's Latin American policy evolved to encompass the advancement of peace, the promotion of trade, and nonintervention in internal affairs. The objective of trade was addressed by Hull's reciprocal trade agreements program. Peace in the long-standing Chaco War came about in June 1935 when Bolivia and Uruguay agreed to a truce. The inability of both sides to continue the fighting explained the termination of hostilities, rather than futile peace efforts mounted by the United States and Argentina. Nevertheless, Roosevelt used the occasion of the Chaco War truce to propose to the president of Argentina, Augustino Justo, a conference at Buenos Aires for the purpose of avoiding further hemispheric conflicts.

First Roosevelt had to win reelection against the Republican candidate, Governor Alf Landon of Kansas. Foreign policy played only a minor role in the campaign. The Democrats, in a platform plank that left Hull "dumbfounded," endorsed an expansion of the Good Neighbor Policy, but offered only ambiguous support to the secretary's trade agreements program. In his campaign Roosevelt ignored both foreign policy issues and his Republican foe to focus instead on deriding Wall Street and "economic royalists." On November 3, Roosevelt won a decisive mandate for his domestic New Deal by trouncing Landon, who won only the seven electoral votes of Maine and Vermont.

Roosevelt's decision to attend the Buenos Aires conference came only after his reelection; probably he would have remained at home had he been defeated. Roosevelt told a press conference, on November 6, that he was contemplating combining a vacation with a visit to Buenos Aires, returning to Washington five weeks before his inauguration—which had been changed by constitutional amendment from March 4 to January 20. In the meantime Hull and Welles sailed for Argentina to undertake the discussion of an ambitious conference agenda emphasizing trade and consultative agreements designed to isolate the hemisphere from war. On his arrival, however, Hull found that the once cooperative attitude of Argentinean Foreign Minister Saavedra Lamas had been replaced by a chilly opposition to Pan-Americanism led by Washington. Saavedra Lamas, who had just received the Nobel Peace Prize and had been elected president of the League of Nations Assembly, stridently opposed any hemispheric collective security arrangement that might, in his view, undermine the League.

What made the difference, both for the success of the Buenos Aires conference and the image of the Good Neighbor Policy, was Roosevelt's decision to pay a personal visit to Latin America prior to his inauguration. Sailing from Charleston aboard the cruiser *Indianapolis*, Roosevelt first stopped at Rio de Janeiro on November 27 for a triumphal three-day visit. In Brazil Roosevelt's visit was regarded as the social event of the century: a national holiday was proclaimed, and the president was greeted by thousands of flag-waving school children. Roosevelt and President Getulio Vargas toured the city in an open limousine. For the occasion the residence of the Brazilian president was adorned with orchids.

Roosevelt's reception at Buenos Aires three days later was just as cordial. As Hull recalled: "Probably no distinguished visitor to Argentina ever received so great a welcome. I felt that both the Government and every individual citizen had made special efforts to make this an historic event." Roosevelt, who loved pageantry and campaigning, was in his element. He began his three days in the Argentinean capital by graciously accepting an honorary doctorate from the University of Buenos Aires. The high point of his visit was his speech, written by Adolph Berle, to the opening session of the conference. His theme, which was well received by the delegates, was that the Americas should remain at peace among themselves and should consult jointly if threatened by external acts of aggression. On his departure for Montevideo on December 2, Roosevelt cleverly waved a handkerchief woven in the national colors of Argentina to his audience. Even newspapers that were normally critical of the United States were silenced and endorsed Roosevelt as a "worthy successor of President Monroe!"[11]

The actual results achieved after Roosevelt's departure were unimpressive. Saavedra Lamas, largely for reasons of national pride, rejected Hull's proposal to establish a permanent consultative body to deal with threats to the peace of the western hemisphere. A watered-down version, which provided for voluntary consultation if threats to peace materialized, was passed. In principle the conference endorsed Hull's program of eliminating obstacles to trade and approved a proposal that originated with Welles for educational exchanges between nations of the hemisphere. On the topic of nonintervention, a subject that had caused great controversy during the Havana and Montevideo Pan American conferences, Roosevelt and Hull capitulated by signing a categorical pledge against nonintervention without reservations. If the solid achievements were a bit meager, the Buenos Aires conference was at least a psychological success and represented a further repudiation of Theodore Roosevelt's "big stick" policy in Latin America. It was also a step in the direction of making the "hands off" feature of the Monroe Doctrine a multilateral, rather than a unilateral, guarantee.

The most serious challenge to the Good Neighbor Policy came during the Buenos Aires Conference when the government of Mexican President Lázaro Cárdenas presented the Mexican Congress with a draft law, which was quickly passed, permitting the expropriation, with compensation, of foreign property. Both Acting Secretary of State R. Walton Moore and Hull were shocked, since they feared, with good reason, that the law presaged the confiscation of American investments. Surprisingly, Josephus Daniels, Roosevelt's ambassador to Mexico, consistently took the side of Mexico. Daniels was certainly no expert on Mexico. He had received the Mexico City appointment mainly because of his friendship with Roosevelt, who had been assistant secretary of the navy under Daniels during the Wilson administration. An incongruous aspect of Daniel's appointment was that he had been secretary of the navy in 1914 when United States marines seized Veracruz from Mexico, inflicting heavy casualties on the Mexican defenders.

American self-restraint was severely tested when Cárdenas, in June 1937, expropriated the unprofitable Mexican National Railways; the seizure was justified as necessary to avert the complete bankruptcy of the rail system. Far more shocking was Mexico's nationalization of the Mexican oil industry in March 1938; according to inflated American estimates the value of the confiscated property was $450 million. Daniels's reaction was that Cárdenas had made a mistake, but that his action was legal under the Mexican constitution, provided Mexico paid adequate compensation. The opposing viewpoint taken by the oil companies, Hull, and Welles was that the United States should adopt a get-tough policy such as that enacted by Britain, which broke relations with Mexico and imposed economic sanctions. Hull also persuaded Treasury Secretary Henry Morgenthau, Jr., to curtail purchases of Mexican silver, which caused the value of the peso to plummet. An unexpected result was that American investors in the Mexican silver industry bore the brunt of the blow.[12]

For the next three years Roosevelt's attitude toward the Mexican dilemma was one of ambivalence. On the one hand the president supported the unsuccessful efforts of Hull to settle the dispute through arbitration. Likewise he hoped that former National Recovery Administration executive Donald Richberg would be able to negotiate an amicable settlement. But two weeks of Richberg-Cárdenas talks at Mexico City and Saltillo (March 8–22, 1939) failed to break the impasse. Not until three weeks before the Pearl Harbor attack was the dispute finally resolved when Mexico agreed to submit the dispute to two experts, one from each side. In April 1942, the arbitrators awarded $29 million in compensation to the oil companies. Throughout, Roosevelt kept his faith, taking the view that the matter was more a political than an economic dispute. An incidental result of the oil settlement was that Mexico soon joined the United States in declaring war on the Axis. When forced to choose between the interests of oil companies and the Good Neighbor Policy, Roosevelt had no hesitation in taking the side of Josephus Daniels. Had Roosevelt intended to get tough with Mexico, he presumably could have torpedoed the Lima Pan American Conference, which opened in December 1938. Instead the president and Hull tactfully agreed to exclude from the agenda any discussion of the expropriation of foreign property.

The Lima Pan American Conference was held only two months after the infamous Munich Conference. German Chancellor Adolf Hitler inflicted a crushing moral defeat on Britain and France when the two western powers weakly accepted Hitler's annexation of the German-speaking part of Czechoslovakia. When Hull went to the Lima Conference, which opened on December 9, 1938, he was convinced that there was a real Nazi threat to the western hemisphere—not so much in terms of military intervention, but through various forms of subversion. It was Hull's goal for the conference to present a united front against any threat, either direct or indirect, from the Axis powers. Hull shrewdly stressed the bipartisan nature of the Good Neighbor Policy by naming Alf Landon, the unsuccessful Republican candidate in 1936, to the delegation.

At Lima Hull ran into an unexpected stone wall in the person of the new Argentinean foreign minister, Jose Maria Cantilo. The position of Argentina was that a collective security declaration was unnecessary, and Cantilo promptly departed for a vacation in Chile leaving Hull to face ten unhappy days that he remembered as "among the most difficult of my career."[13] Through cajoling, arm-twisting, and charm, Hull got his way and convinced the conference to endorse unanimously, on Christmas Eve 1938, the Declaration of Lima. In wording that was not far from what Hull had wanted, the signatories pledged to assist each other in the event of a direct or indirect foreign attack and to consult through meetings of the hemisphere's foreign ministers. Under the circumstances Hull did as well as could have been expected. Whether the Nazis were intimidated is less certain.

Because of the complications surrounding Hitler's invasion of Poland (September 1, 1939), Hull was not able to attend the next Pan American Conference, which opened on September 23, 1939 at Panama City. In Hull's place Roosevelt sent Welles with instructions to see the establishment of a presidential brainstorm: a neutrality zone about the western hemisphere from which all belligerent ships would be banned. Hull was less enthusiastic about the idea than the president, since such a zone was unprecedented and almost impossible to enforce. Nevertheless, after just eight days of discussion, the Declaration of Panama proclaimed a neutrality zone extending from 300 to 1,000 miles from the coast of the American continents and running from Nova Scotia around South America to the United States-Canadian border in the northwest. The concept that the belligerents would respect a paper "do not enter" zone or "chastity belt" about the western hemisphere proved naive when three British cruisers drove the damaged German pocket battleship *Graf von Spee* into Montevideo harbor on December 13, 1939. The incident ended four days later with the scuttling of the vessel and the suicide of its commander. The incident served to demonstrate that the western hemisphere was not immune to the European conflict.

Roosevelt's anti-Nazi policy intensified after Hitler overran western defenses in the spring of 1940. In particular, Roosevelt and Hull were worried that Hitler might occupy French or Dutch possessions in the western hemisphere, or that hostilities might break out between the British and the Vichy government of France—a collaborationist regime established in June 1940, which controlled two-fifths of France as well as the French fleet and colonies. Thus the Havana Pan American Conference, which opened on July 21, 1940, was designed to further counter the perceived German threat to the western hemisphere. Hull, who found himself on Cuban soil for the first time since 1898, was not enthusiastic about going since nine of the nations attending refused to send their foreign ministers. As usual the main conflict was with Argentina. Hull proposed the establishment of a collective trusteeship over territories threatened by foreign aggression, whereas the Argentinean delegate, Dr. Leopoldo Melo, preferred to limit action to a general endorsement of the principle that territory of the western hemisphere should not be transferred to a belligerent. Such a no-transfer statement had already been endorsed by Congress in June 1940. Hull went so far as to appeal over Melo's head to the president of Argentina, Roberto M. Ortiz, who was seriously ill. The tactic worked and the conference approved the Act of Havana, which permitted any American republic to administer a hemispheric colony in the event of an attack or subversive threat. But to placate Argentina, Chile, and Guatemala, the no-transfer principle was not to apply to the Falkland Islands, Antarctica, or British Honduras. In practice the Nazi threat to the western hemisphere fizzled once Hitler invaded the Soviet Union in June 1941, and the Act of Havana was never implemented.

Roosevelt's Good Neighbor Policy hardly transformed the hemisphere to one based on sentiment or brotherly love, as much of the unity achieved at Montevideo, Buenos Aires, Lima, Panama City, and Havana was superficial. Argentina, and to a lesser extent Brazil, consistently resisted a United States–dominated hemisphere. Essentially Roosevelt popularized a policy that had originated under Colby and was further developed by Harding, Coolidge, and Hoover, and by their secretaries of state Hughes, Kellogg, and Stimson. As was typical of Roosevelt's foreign policy in general, the Good Neighbor Policy was improvised on a day-to-day basis. By 1934 it had evolved into a policy of nonintervention, trade, and peace. It was a policy that was commendably free of the equivocation and lack of candor that was often characteristic of Roosevelt. About the only down side was that nonintervention meant the acceptance of dictators such as Somoza, Batista, and Trujillo, all of whom received state receptions in Washington between 1938 and 1939.

One of the most obvious benefits of the Good Neighbor Policy was that a majority of the Latin American republics (Chile and Argentina were the exceptions) either declared war on the Axis or broke relations. Politically Roosevelt was not bashful about claiming credit for the Good Neighbor Policy. In reality Hull and especially Welles deserved recognition for carrying out the details. However, much of the driving force behind the Good Neighbor Policy was lost when Welles unexpectedly left the State Department in 1943. For many years it was assumed his resignation as undersecretary of state was the result of personality and policy differences with Hull. Recent scholarship has demonstrated that Welles's downfall was actually the result of the exposure of his homosexuality; his enemies, notably Hull and Ambassador William C. Bullitt, were able to force his resignation.[14] The retirement of Welles meant that there was no one in the government with the expertise, the vigor, and the access to the White House to continue the most idealist and successful of New Deal foreign policies.

NOTES

1. Cordell Hull, *The Memoirs of Cordell Hull* (New York, 1948), Vol. 1, 311.

2. Hull, *Memoirs*, Vol. 1, 313.

3. Frederick W. Marks III, *Wind Over Sand: The Diplomacy of Franklin Roosevelt* (Athens, Georgia, 1988), 33; Bryce Wood, *The Making of the Good Neighbor Policy* (New York, 1961), 59–69; William E. Leuchtenburg, *Franklin D. Roosevelt and the New Deal, 1933–1940* (New York, 1963), 208.

4. Hull, *Memoirs*, Vol. 1, 319.

5. Lester D. Langley, *The United States and the Caribbean, 1900–1970* (Athens, Georgia, 1980), 31–38, 154–57.

6. Hull, *Memoirs*, Vol. 1, 345.

7. Langley, *United States and the Caribbean*, 153; Irwin F. Gellman, *Good Neighbor Diplomacy: United States Policies in Latin America, 1933–1945* (Baltimore, 1979), 35–36.

8. Ivan Musicant, *The Banana Wars: A History of United States Military Intervention in Latin America from the Spanish-American War to the Invasion of Panama* (New York, 1990), 355–61; William Kamman, *A Search for Stability: United States Diplomacy Toward Nicaragua, 1925–1933* (Notre Dame, Indiana, 1968), 143–216; Walter LaFeber, *The American Age: United States Foreign Policy at Home and Abroad since 1750* (New York, 1989), 358.

9. Langley, *United States and the Caribbean*, 148.

10. Donald Dozer, *Are We Good Neighbors? Three Decades of Inter-American Relations, 1930–1960* (Gainesville, Florida, 1959), 25–26.

11. Hull, *Memoirs*, Vol. 1, 497; speech by Roosevelt before the Inter-American Conference for the Maintenance of Peace, Buenos Aires, December 1, 1936, Edgar B. Nixon, editor, *Franklin D. Roosevelt and Foreign Affairs* (Cambridge, 1969), Vol. 3, 516–21; Dozer, *Are We Good Neighbors*, 31–32.

12. Josephus Daniels, *Shirt-Sleeve Diplomat* (Chapel Hill, 1947), 221–28; E. David Cronon, *Josephus Daniels in Mexico* (Madison, 1960), 193–200.

13. Hull, *Memoirs*, Vol. 1, 605.

14. Gellman, *Good Neighbor Diplomacy*, 176–79.

CHAPTER 8

Congressional Neutrality: Roosevelt, the British, and Bankers as Performing Circus Animals

Once the catastrophe of 1929 had struck, Herbert Hoover and the Republican Party were pilloried for failing to foresee the coming of the Great Depression—although no one else, certainly not the Democrats, had seen it coming either. Likewise, Franklin D. Roosevelt and the Democratic Party left themselves wide open to criticism for failing to anticipate the threat of fascism from Nazi Germany and Imperial Japan, even though Republican Cassandras warning of imminent peril to the nation were few and far between. Prior to 1939 Roosevelt did very little publicly to lead the nation away from isolationism and pacifism. The president's amazing power to inspire the confidence and devotion of the American people was, except for the Good Neighbor Policy, rarely applied to foreign affairs until the eve of World War II. That Roosevelt, unlike Hoover, avoided the opprobrium of history was due less to any last minute burst of preparedness on his part than to the prompt mobilization of American industry and the heroic sacrifices of the armed forces of the United States and its World War II allies. Had the Axis powers prevailed, Roosevelt might have been remembered with Nero as one of the most complacent leaders of all time.

The soaring idealism Roosevelt demonstrated after the outbreak of World War II, as reflected by such internationalist goals as the Atlantic Charter, the Four Freedoms, and the founding of the United Nations organization, was in apparent hibernation during the 1930s. Clumsy improvisation, political expediency, and aimless drift characterized the foreign policy of the Roosevelt who torpedoed the London Economic Conference and signed the Johnson Act. In one respect, however, Roosevelt's early diplomacy did reflect his Wilsonian heritage in that, like Wilson and his Republican successors, he persisted in an earnest and futile search for a naval disarmament formula. Reduction of armaments had been one of Wilson's Fourteen Points as well as a major theme of Republican foreign policy. Notwithstanding his role as assistant secretary of the navy under Wilson, Roosevelt shifted in the late 1920s to chiding the Republicans for excessive naval construction that was both expensive and obsolete. As late as June 1941, Roosevelt told a skeptical Assistant Secretary of State Adolf Berle, "Don't forget that the elimination of armaments is still the keystone—for the security of all little nations and for economic security."[1]

In the field of disarmament Roosevelt often gave the impression of accepting uncritically one of the basic assumptions of previous interwar administrations: that world leaders were essentially rational beings who intended to honor their pledged word. It followed that nonrecognition of aggression or the imposition of economic sanctions would teach wrongdoers the error of their ways without resorting to military measures. As a pragmatic Democratic statesman forced to balance the competing interests of internationalists, isolationists, pacifists, and the professional military establishment, Roosevelt was far too complicated to swallow such a simplistic view. More than likely his search for disarmament was partly based on principle, partly designed as a tactic for mollifying domestic isolationists and pacifists, and partly a shrewd strategy for blaming Japan (and getting naval appropriations bills from Congress) in the event of failure. But even after the disarmament process begun by Hughes in 1921 collapsed when Japan denounced the Washington agreements in 1934, Roosevelt displayed little sense of urgency. When asked by the press (December 12, 1934) whether the ongoing Senate investigation of the armament industry and the resulting discussion of neutrality legislation raised the need for compulsory military training and national preparedness, Roosevelt replied: "No. Really it would be of service if you all would leave out any suggestion of this being a question of preparedness. It is a question of permanent national legislation looking to an event which we hope will never happen, and I am bringing it up because there isn't any cloud on the horizon at the present time."[2] In reality dark storm clouds gathering in Germany and Japan might have suggested that a world based upon renunciatory pacts and the sanctity of disarmament treaties was rapidly crumbling.

In Germany Nazi Führer Adolf Hitler, a poorly educated Austrian with uniformed, chanting supporters, legally became chancellor five weeks before Roosevelt took office. Consistently Hitler's opponents at home and abroad underestimated his determination and his ability to move the German masses through the expert use of such media as films, press, and radio. Ruthlessly and efficiently Hitler moved to consolidate his grip. The mysterious Reichstag fire (February 27, 1933) was blamed on Communist revolutionaries and used as the pretext for calling new elections and intimidating the Reichstag into passing the Enabling Law, granting the Nazi government the power to enact laws and negotiate treaties. Within a year Hitler had established a dictatorship by placing Nazis in charge of the state governments, creating a secret police organization, murdering Ernst Rohm—his remaining rival in the Nazi Party—and banning all political parties except his own. His ultimate goals, which he had unambiguously spelled out in *Mein Kampf*, such as the need for *lebensraum* (living space) in eastern Europe and the extermination of the Jews and the expropriation of their property, seemed too creepy and grandiose to be taken seriously. His intention to achieve his goals by force could have been inferred from his decision (October 1933) to withdraw simultaneously from the League of Nations and the Geneva Disarmament Conference and to begin intensive rearmament. Skillfully, Hitler renounced the use of force and portrayed Germany as the innocent victim of the "Versailles Diktat."

Americans, civilian and military, also seriously underestimated the imperialistic ambitions and military threat of Japan. In part the explanation for the United States' complacency lay in the national habit of viewing Asians with paternalistic contempt. Even after the Russo-Japanese War and the Manchurian incident, it was common, even among government officials who should have known better, to dismiss the Japanese as polite, bowing practitioners of the Shinto tea ceremony who were devoted to the veneration of Mt. Fuji and the cultivation of cherry trees. A race of copiers who had been assigned inferior naval ratios at Washington and London, the Japanese were thought to have constructed top-heavy, unseaworthy ships. But Americans had no monopoly on national conceit or concepts of racial superiority. According to the official doctrine of the Japanese Ministry of Education, issued in August 1941, the "superb and lofty" mission of Japan was to enhance justice in all directions and place the universe under one roof through the leadership of the emperor, the source of all virtue. Under Japan's moral principles, it was explained, foreign exploitation of Asia would be ended and replaced by lasting peace and harmony.[3]

Steadily and surely during the interwar period the Japanese Navy had made impressive progress in developing new and superior battleships, aircraft carriers, carrier airplanes, submarines, and torpedoes. The American response, despite opposition from fiscal conservatives and pacifists, was a modest program of naval construction, concentrating on auxiliary vessels. By a lucky chance the United States Navy was the recipient of a $238 million windfall contained in the National Industrial Recovery Act passed in June 1933. Through the efforts of Representative Carl Vinson, chairman of the House Naval Affairs Committee, and Navy Secretary Claude Swanson, the construction of thirty-two cruisers, destroyers, and submarines was justified as a measure that would create jobs and aid in economic recovery. And in January 1934 Roosevelt cautiously supported the Vinson-Trammell bill authorizing, but not appropriating, funds to bring the navy up to treaty strength by 1936. Faced with strenuous criticism from peace societies, Roosevelt back-pedalled and offered assurances that his administration sincerely supported naval disarmament. "It is my personal hope," he added, "that the Naval Conference to be held in 1934 will extend all existing limitations and agree to further reductions."[4]

Plainly the Japanese Navy was not impressed, and by 1934 its planners had settled on an attrition/ambush strategy for defeating the American battleship fleet if, as expected, the Americans in a future war sought to defend the Philippines. The willingness of Tokyo to contest the United States Navy was strengthened by the fact that Japan had never lost a war, and in 1904–1905 had soundly defeated the nominally superior Russian Navy at Port Arthur and Tsushima Strait. As the United States fleet crossed the Pacific from Pearl Harbor, Japanese admirals assumed the American advantage of 10:7 would be reduced by submarine attacks and by torpedoes dropped from Mitsubishi bombers (the strategy that destroyed the British ships *Repulse* and *Prince of Wales* a few days after Pearl Harbor). In the final battle Japan's super dreadnoughts, firing long range naval artillery, supported by powerful new torpedoes, midget submarines, and carrier air strikes, would so decimate the United States Navy that Washington would capitulate and recognize Japan's paramount position in Asia.[5] The attrition/ambush strategy was modified in 1941 to commence with a surprise attack against the American battleships at Hawaii so as to delay American operations in the western Pacific indefinitely.

American naval war games in 1930 and 1932 confirmed that the defense of the Philippines was next to impossible, primarily because the American advantage of fourteen battleships to ten for Japan was deemed insufficient. And the navy opposed granting Japan naval parity at the forthcoming London Naval Conference of 1935, fearing concessions would lessen the ability of the navy to sail its capital ships across the Pacific in the event of a war with Japan. Roosevelt, however, well aware of the strident opposition by domestic pacifists and isolationists to armament expenditures, insisted on proposing a twenty percent cut in overall naval tonnage while leaving the Washington and London ratios on cruisers and battleships intact. If Japan refused to go along, Roosevelt felt the United States and Britain could reach a new parity agreement with an escalator clause permitting the signatories to ignore the agreement if they were threatened by Japanese construction. Few were shocked when, at the second London Naval Conference (December 1935–March 1936), Japan walked out after the western powers refused its demand for naval parity. In the process Japan reiterated a notice it had originally delivered to Britain and the United States on December 30, 1934, stating that it was abrogating the Five Power Treaty of 1921 limiting battleships. The remaining participants at London (the United States, Britain, France, and Italy) then signed a meaningless pledge to abide by the existing naval limitations. Now that Japan was freed from any treaty restraints, the naval race that culminated at Pearl Harbor was, in effect, off and running.

If the executive branch responded myopically to the rise of fascism, the reaction of congressional isolationists and pacifists was characterized by utter blindness. Between the wars isolationism and pacifism often went hand in glove, although it was common for isolationists to make a distinction between their opposition to foreign wars and their theoretical willingness to invoke the Monroe Doctrine in the unlikely event of a foreign invasion of the western hemisphere. In other words, those who would support the defense of the Americas only enjoyed the political luxury of being virtual pacifists. Nevertheless, the concept of isolation from foreign entanglements and commitments made a good deal more sense prior to Pearl Harbor than afterward. Those of isolationist/virtual pacifist persuasion advocated only political, not economic or cultural, isolation. A cardinal belief of isolationists and virtual pacifists was that World War I had been an aberration, and that they were holding true to a traditional and inexpensive policy that had served the nation well in the nineteenth century. Moreover, given the state of military technology, it could be argued that there existed no overt military threat to "Fortress America" in the western hemisphere. The elder statesmen of the movement during the New Deal years included two of the irreconcilables from the fight against the Versailles Treaty: Senators Hiram Johnson of California and William E. Borah of Idaho. Among their Senate colleagues they could count as supporters Senators Burton K. Wheeler of Montana, George W. Norris of Nebraska, Arthur Capper of Kansas, Gerald P. Nye of North Dakota, Henrik Shipstead of Minnesota, Robert M. La Follette, Jr., of Wisconsin, Bennett Champ Clark of Missouri, Arthur Vandenberg of Michigan, and Robert A. Taft of Ohio, who was elected in 1938. Representative leaders in the House included Bruce Barton and Hamilton Fish of New York, Joseph W. Martin, Jr., of Massachusetts, Louis Ludlow and Raymond Springer of Indiana, and John Vorys of Ohio. Governor Philip La Follette of Wisconsin and the aviator Colonel Charles A. Lindbergh represented the isolationist viewpoint outside the portals of Congress.

Prior to 1934 the forty-three-year-old Senator Gerald P. Nye of North Dakota, an eight-year veteran of the Senate, had been known as a progressive Republican who, like Landon of Kansas, saw the wisdom of cooperating with the New Deal, especially in agrarian affairs. In the spring of 1934 Nye inadvertently stumbled upon an issue that made him overnight an isolationist/pacifist leader of national stature as well as a thorn in the side of the Roosevelt administration. An investigation of the armament industry was an idea that originated not with Nye, but with Dorothy Detzer, who headed the Women's International League for Peace and Freedom. Ammunition for such an investigation was provided by a timely article published in *Fortune* magazine (March 1934), contending that the cynical aims of the "merchants of death" (the title of a sensational book by H.C. Englebrecht and F.C. Hanighen) were to prolong war and disturb peace.

At first Nye was reluctant to lead the investigation and only consented to do so in response to arm-twisting by Detzer and Nebraska Senator George Norris. Reputedly Nye was the only member of the Senate willing to take on such a project. Through a bizarre series of legislative blunders the Democratic leadership in the Senate permitted the legislation authorizing an investigation of the armament industry to pass on a voice vote; and when the seven-man special committee met, Vice President John Nance Garner unwisely left the selection of a chairman to the members, assuming that one of the four Democrats (James P. Pope of Idaho, Homer T. Bone of Washington, Bennett Champ Clark of Missouri, and Walter F. George of Georgia) would be selected, instead of one of the three Republicans (Nye, Arthur Vandenberg of Michigan, and W. Warren Barbour of New Jersey). Thus Roosevelt and Garner were surprised by Nye's selection. So was Hull, who recalled he would have opposed the investigation if he had "dreamed" an isolationist Republican would be named chairman. As it was, the special Senate investigation was permitted to slip through "virtually by default and without more than casual consideration."[6] The result was an investigative circus that grabbed headlines internationally and largely immobilized the Roosevelt administration as it pondered how to respond to the deterioration of the treaty structure erected at the beginning of the interwar period.

Largely responsible for the notoriety acquired by the Nye Committee was its expert, if irresponsible, staff headed by chief investigator Stephen Rauschenbusch (the son of the noted social gospel reformer Walter Rauschenbusch), attorney Alger Hiss (later accused during the McCarthy era of conducting espionage for the Soviets), and publicist John T. Flynn (a former writer for the liberal New Republic remembered for his poison-pen assaults on the New Deal such as While You Slept, The Country Squire in the White House, and The Roosevelt Myth). The initial stage of the hearings (September 4–21, 1934) focused on the activities of American companies that specialized in the production of weapons of mass destruction: submarine manufacturer Electric Boat Company; aircraft and engine manufacturers Curtis-Wright and Pratt and Whitney; and such producers of explosives as du Pont and Federal Laboratories. Beyond the obvious finding that manufacturers of armaments had aggressively sought to promote foreign sales, the Nye Committee found damning evidence that the bribery of foreign officials (as in the case of Argentina) had been a routine and accepted sales technique of the industry. Hull, who was deluged with protests from foreign governments denying the charges of bribe taking and influence peddling, met with Nye and received an admission that the publication of allegations did not constitute proof of guilt. Prior to the resumption of the hearings on December 4, 1934, Nye kept his name and the iniquity of armament manufacturers before the public through a nationwide speaking tour, an incidental result of which was to provide a welcome addition to his income. The startling revelations of the Nye Committee made good theater and, as even Roosevelt inadvertently admitted at a press conference, constituted a form of national "fun." (When a reporter asked whether the president favored appropriating more funds for the Nye committee, Roosevelt, to the amusement of the press, mistakenly thought the questioner meant "fun" rather than "funds".[7])

In a curious paradox, at a time when Roosevelt was at the height of his power in domestic politics, he could not find congressional support for the tamest of foreign policy initiatives. Normally in American politics, the party out of power regains seats in mid-term congressional elections. But in November 1934, despite depicting Roosevelt (in Sir Ronald Lindsay's words) as "The Big Bad Dictator," the Republicans managed to lose seats in both houses of Congress, leaving the Democrats in a commanding position. Subsequently Roosevelt, combining charm with the enforcement of party discipline, maneuvered through the Democratic Congress a "Second New Deal" that included such measures as Social Security, the Wagner Act (which guaranteed industrial labor the right to bargain collectively), and a bill raising income taxes on corporations and the wealthy. Given that there were sixty-eight Democrats in the Senate, and only fifty-nine votes needed for a two-thirds majority, it appeared to Roosevelt that the time was ripe to revisit the cause of United States membership in the World Court, an issue which had been derailed in 1926 by crippling isolationist reservations. Another favorable omen was that moderate Republicans, including Coolidge, Hoover, Hughes, and Elihu Root, had consistently supported participation in the World Court.

In this case Roosevelt suffered an embarrassing and unexpected reverse as he failed to take into account the determination and debating skill of his opponents. At first the administration's optimism seemed justified. By a decisive vote of 14 to 7 the Senate Foreign Relations Committee, on January 9, 1935, reported out a "Resolution of Adherence" to the World Court, with the proviso that the Court could not render an advisory opinion in any case regarded as objectionable by the United States. And a poll by the Women's World Court Committee found sixty-nine senators favorably disposed. Roosevelt followed with a mildly worded message advocating approval; in view of the favorable outlook a more vigorous executive effort seemed unnecessary and counterproductive. Even Senator Borah admitted that, with no more than ten Senate opponents, the Court proposal would pass easily. He told the Women's Committee that he insisted on a full debate but would not attempt to block a speedy vote with a filibuster.[8] In reality Borah had so lulled the Democratic leadership into complacency that it managed to snatch defeat from the jaws of victory.

Once the debate began the isolationists raised old fears and effectively mobilized public opinion. Senator Hiram Johnson returned to a theme he had sounded previously: that the "League of Nations Court" was an international ploy to entangle the United States in world affairs. Similar sentiments were advanced by Borah, who made the point that the World Court was a court of politics, not a court of law, and as such would inevitably drag the United States into European controversies. "To hell with Europe and the rest of those nations," added Senator Thomas Schall of Minnesota. The coup de grace came when the World Court was condemned by the Hearst press and by the Detroit radio priest Father Charles Coughlin. In response to Coughlin's pleas, so many telegrams descended upon Washington that Capitol employees were compelled to deliver them using wheelbarrows. In the final vote fifty-two senators approved membership in the World Court and thirty-six voted no, seven votes short of the required two-thirds majority.[9] Roosevelt, who hated to lose, was enraged by the unexpected turn of events. Probably one reason for his irritation was the realization that the defeat of the World Court proposal had given new energy and direction to the Nye committee investigation which, at the beginning of 1935, began to promote the bizarre concept that neutrality legislation could actually prevent the United States' entry into future wars.

In the second phase of its investigation the Nye committee concentrated upon exposing the role of the federal government in promoting traffic in arms and munitions. In his opinion, Nye told the press, "certain departments of our government are co-defendants with the munitions industry and its profiteers in this great trial."[10] The committee insisted that it was necessary for it to subpoena the files of New York bankers regarding private loans to the Allied governments prior to the United States' entry into the World War in April 1917. Both the French and British objected unsuccessfully. Sir Ronald Lindsay complained to the State Department that it was the intention of the Nye committee "to treat the British Government as a circus animal which would be made to perform for the spectators."[11] Actually it was the senator's intention to treat all those under investigation, foreign governments and bankers alike, as performing circus animals.

On the advice of Hull, who wished to contain the activities of the Nye committee "within reasonable limits," Roosevelt agreed to invite its members to the White House for an exchange of views. The point that Hull wished to emphasize, he wrote Roosevelt, was that a fishing expedition in banking records, combined with "unnecessary agitation in public hearings," would strain American relations with Britain and France at a time when Hitler and Mussolini were rearming. All seven members of the Nye committee appeared at the White House on March 19, 1935, and witnessed one of the more baffling performances in the history of the modern American presidency. Roosevelt's style of leadership has typically been described as displaying characteristics of a brave lion or a cunning fox; on this occasion the president, who appeared to rely on his considerable ability as an improviser and who could have been better prepared, was more a brainless ram than a lion or a fox.

Even Nye was stunned when the affable president capitulated unconditionally by enthusiastically endorsing a twelve-point plan for removing the profits from war by imposing prohibitory taxation. Instead of objecting to the proposal as too drastic, Roosevelt said that heavy taxation on armament-producing corporations and individuals should be applied during both peacetime and wartime. Turning to the topic of neutrality legislation, Roosevelt again surprised the Nye Committee by endorsing the concept of neutrality legislation and by offering assurances he was anxious to cooperate.[12] Inexplicably the president, somewhat like Wilson in 1919, had played into the hands of his isolationist opponents as the Nye committee promptly took up the topic of neutrality legislation, even though it properly belonged to the Foreign Relations Committee. Stephen Rauschenbusch, Nye's chief investigator, informed Hull that the committee was "hot on the trail" of a neutrality bill only because Roosevelt had "pushed" the subject at the White House meeting.[13] Carelessly the president had opened a Pandora's box. Roosevelt's defenders suggest that he had in mind a shrewd strategy of pushing the State Department to draft neutrality legislation acceptable to him while he ingratiated himself with the Nye committee through the medium of a red-carpet White House meeting. Subsequent developments suggest that Roosevelt had no visionary strategy at all and that he acted impulsively as he did two years later when he proposed packing the Supreme Court. In both instances—neutrality legislation and court packing—Roosevelt demonstrated that even a master politician could commit clumsy errors, as in both instances he managed to hand his critics a golden political issue.

Just as American and Japanese admirals were preparing in 1935 to refight the battle of Jutland, so were American isolationist/virtual pacifist politicians preparing to save the nation from involvement in a conflict that they believed would be similar, if not identical, in its origins to World War I. The possible outbreak of another European conflict was not just an abstract concern in 1935. Already the first clashes had occurred between Italian and Ethiopian troops along the disputed border between Italian Somaliland and Abyssinia. The strutting, pouting Italian dictator Benito Mussolini arrogantly demanded an indemnity from Ethiopia while shipping in reinforcements and gave every indication he intended to settle the dispute by force. Simultaneously Hitler defied the Versailles Treaty by introducing universal military training with the aim of enlisting an army of 500,000. Therefore, when Nye outlined a neutrality strategy to keep the United States out of war, he was reacting to Roosevelt's encouragement and to the threatening scene in Europe and Ethiopia. The senator's solution, spelled out in a speech at Lexington, Kentucky, was to require the president, at the start of hostilities, to ban loans and arms sales to belligerents and to prohibit travel by Americans on belligerent ships.

Despite the administration's best efforts to slow down the rush to a neutrality law, a competitive bidding war developed as Senators Nye and Clark introduced neutrality legislation in the Senate and as bills were introduced in the House by Representatives Maury Maverick of Texas, Frank Kloeb of Ohio, and Louis Ludlow of Indiana. Hull, now thoroughly upset, met with the Foreign Relations Committee, hoping to postpone the process. Hull feared the isolationists would tie the president's hands by notifying fascist states in advance that they could attack peaceful nations with impunity, knowing that the United States would embargo arms to both sides. Hull's strategy was to draft an innocuous neutrality bill giving the president discretionary authority to ban arms, loans, and travel (so as to distinguish between an aggressor and the victim). Hull hoped that his stalling would prevent the passage of any bill prior to the August congressional recess.

Weak leadership by Senate Foreign Relations Committee Chairman Pittman and loss of political nerve by Roosevelt, who feared for his domestic program, doomed the procrastination strategy. When asked by Hull and Roosevelt to introduce a discretionary arms embargo bill, Pittman agreed to do so without his personal endorsement. But Pittman warned the White House that the discretionary arms embargo would never pass the Foreign Relations Committee or the Senate. Off the record, Pittman heatedly told Roosevelt's press secretary, Stephen Early, "I tell you, Steve, the President is riding for a fall if he insists on designating the aggressor in accordance with the wishes of the League of Nations. He had better have nothing than to get licked, and I can assure you that is what he is facing."[14] Without a fight Roosevelt capitulated, on condition that the arms embargo was limited to six months. And Hull, who still hoped to kill the neutrality bill in the House, was routed. With only brief debate, the 1935 Neutrality Act sailed through both houses of Congress as only two senators (Peter G. Gary of Rhode Island and John H. Bankhead II of Alabama) dared oppose it.

In its final form, the act, reflecting its last minute scissors-and-paste nature, required the president in the event of war to ban the export of arms to belligerents and gave him discretionary authority to warn Americans taking passage on belligerent liners that they were traveling at their own risk. Loans were not mentioned, presumably because the Johnson Act already forbade loans to all European nations except Finland. Even Hull, noting that the arms embargo would expire on February 29, 1936, came to the reluctant conclusion that there was no alternative open to the president but to sign the bill. Roosevelt, who had assumed all along that the measure would be sidetracked, made a pragmatic decision to take the path of least resistance. A veto might well have been overridden and the repercussions could have damaged Roosevelt's domestic reform program and even his reelection chances. Roosevelt's signing of the 1935 Neutrality Act on August 31, 1935, demonstrated convincingly that the administration had lost control of foreign policy to the isolationists. Hiram Johnson, speaking for his coalition of isolationists and pacifists, declared that Congress had resolved "to keep out of European controversies, European wars, and European difficulties. So today is the triumph of the so-called isolationists and today marks the downfall, although we may not know it, of the internationalist."[15]

Roosevelt was vacationing aboard the heavy cruiser *Houston* (later sunk by Japan during the battle of the Java Sea) when Mussolini's infantry columns invaded Ethiopia on October 3, 1935. Outwardly the president took the news in stride and cultivated the image of a smiling fisherman who saw no need to interrupt his vacation in order to manage the crisis. Beneath his public calm Roosevelt was not so imperturbable. He feared that the Italian-Ethiopian conflict might escalate and that the congressional isolationists would accuse the administration of cooperating with the League of Nations. Designating the aggressor in accordance with the wishes of the League, as Pittman had put it, might destroy prospects for revising the Neutrality Act so as to give the executive discretion to distinguish between the aggressor and the victim. Thus the president bent over backwards to emphasize his independence from the League and, with an eye toward avoiding trouble with the isolationists, carried out the provisions of the Neutrality Act. At Roosevelt's insistence, the State Department issued a neutrality proclamation embargoing the sale of arms, but not raw materials, to either side. American citizens were informed that transactions with either side as well as travel on belligerent ships could be undertaken only at their own risk. Since Ethiopia had money for neither arms nor ships on which Americans could be endangered, Roosevelt's neutrality policy discreetly tilted toward Ethiopia.

A flaw in the moral embargo was soon evident as American exports of raw materials to Italy soared in the fall of 1935; shipments of oil, copper, scrap iron, and steel doubled. Roosevelt's response was to have Hull issue a statement condemning the exports as contrary to the spirit of neutrality. While protesting that he was impartial, Roosevelt alarmed the isolationists by lending support to League sanctions against Italy. But the League soon showed its spinelessness by taking six weeks to adopt economic sanctions, which failed to include the crucial item of oil. Britain's performance was especially disillusioning as London made no effort to close the Suez Canal to Italian troop movements. And the British foreign minister, Sir Samuel Hoare, together with French Foreign Minister Pierre Laval, proposed an abortive plan for ending the war by awarding half of Ethiopia to Mussolini. One of the chief results of the imbroglio over Ethiopia was to thoroughly alarm Roosevelt, who justifiably feared that Mussolini's unpunished aggression had established a precedent. But finding a workable strategy for combating the isolationist/virtual pacifist phalanx remained as elusive and baffling as ever.

The political momentum in foreign policy remained solidly on the side of the isolationists and pacifists even as Roosevelt began his enormously successful 1936 reelection campaign. Once again Roosevelt's chief antagonist was Senator Nye, who began the final phase of his special Senate investigation on January 7 by summoning before his committee the banker J.P. Morgan. A famous photograph showed Nye and Morgan warily eying each other from opposite sides of the hearing room table, each leaning forward upon the palms of his hands. Nye would not go so far as to say that President Wilson intervened in 1917 to save loans made by private bankers to the Allies; rather he argued that private loans were part of a pattern of unneutral conduct that made American intervention inevitable. Yet Nye committed a tactical error when he indiscreetly made the statement that President Wilson and Secretary of State Robert Lansing "falsified" when they denied knowledge of the secret treaties (in which the Allies had divided many of the possessions of Germany). The senator's statement provoked a storm of Democratic protest. Senators Tom Connally of Texas and Carter Glass of Virginia both bloodied their hands in table-pounding speeches denouncing Nye's attack on Wilson's integrity. According to Connally, the only fit place for Nye's remarks was "some checker-playing, back room of some low house." Glass characterized Nye's comments as "destitute of decency," and insisted he would oppose wasting another dollar upon the Nye committee.[16] However, the threat made by Glass to terminate funding proved moot since the committee was about to end its hearings. In subsequent months the committee issued a series of reports condemning the pernicious activities of bankers and advocating government ownership of the munitions industry and strict neutrality through mandatory legislation. Although its conspiratorial themes were too implausible to stand the test of time, the volumes of documentation gathered by the Nye committee proved a valuable resource to historians of World War I.

Consistently throughout the debate Roosevelt and Hull continued to favor granting the president as much discretionary authority concerning neutrality legislation as possible. Roosevelt, for example, wanted to be able to embargo raw materials such as oil, cotton, iron, steel, and copper, since such items had military applications. At the administration's urging, a revised, discretionary version of the neutrality act was introduced by Senator Pittman and Representative Samuel McReynolds. The opposing viewpoint, contained in a bill sponsored by Nye and Clark, required the president in the event of war to embargo not only arms and loans to belligerents, but even such civilian products as food, medical supplies, and clothing. With the 1935 Neutrality Act due to expire on February 29, 1936, both sides capitulated to expediency and agreed to the stopgap solution of extending the law until May 1, 1937. The only substantive change was to give the president slightly more discretion in deciding whether to invoke the law because he alone was given the authority to make the judgment call on the existence of a state of war. In effect Roosevelt and his adversaries had agreed to postpone further neutrality battles until after the conclusion of the presidential campaign.

Neither major party chose to exploit foreign policy in the 1936 campaign. Carelessly the Platform Committee at the Democratic Convention adopted a foreign policy plank written by Roosevelt's close friend William C. Bullitt. New York Senator Robert Wagner, the committee's chairman, strangely failed to consult Hull or even review a platform draft he had sent the White House. Hull, so he recalled, was "dumbfounded" even though it was not the first or the last time that Roosevelt had ignored his secretary of state and sought the advice of his intimates.[17] With one exception the content of the platform statement pleased Hull because it praised the Good Neighbor Policy and his efforts to stimulate trade though reciprocal trade agreements. But, in an apparent effort to appeal to the isolationist/virtual pacifist mood, the platform committed the party to observe "true neutrality," to "take the profits out of war," and "to guard against being drawn—by political commitments, international banking, or private trading—into any war which may develop anywhere."[18] Senator Nye would have been hard of political hearing had he failed to recognize the overtures being made to solicit his endorsement. However, after several months of flirting with the administration, Nye, on October 1, announced that he had decided not to participate in the presidential campaign.

Repeatedly during the 1936 campaign Roosevelt bent over backwards to appeal to the isolationist/virtual pacifist vote. Perhaps subconsciously he was prompted by Wilson's 1916 reelection slogan, "He kept us out of war." In March Roosevelt, as jovial as ever, received the "People's Mandate to End War Committee" at the White House. The goals of the People's Mandate, which was headed by President Mary Woolley of Mount Holyoke College, were to reduce arms through a "world treaty" and to bring about world peace through mutual acceptance of the Kellogg-Briand Pact and the rule of law. One million signatures had been gathered by the organization on a petition advocating an end to war. Amiably and disarmingly Roosevelt related that he had considered making a European radio appeal for peace, only to discover that few Europeans owned radios designed to receive long distance broadcasts. Notwithstanding his personal commitment to peace, Roosevelt reminded his audience that since the Monroe Doctrine of 1823 the United States had pledged to protect the Americas from foreign intervention or colonization. He illustrated the need for improved coastal defenses by telling how the navy during the Spanish-American War had assured the alarmed residents of Portland, Maine, that they were safe from Spanish shelling by sending newly painted but obsolete Civil War ironclads to their "defense." Eventually, he conceded in answer to a question that the cost of all defense expenditures had to be borne by the taxpayers.[19]

Peace was also on Roosevelt's mind when he delivered a campaign speech at Chautauqua, New York, on August 14. Drafted by William C. Bullitt, the address emphasized America's commitment to the Good Neighbor concept and to the advancement of world peace through disarmament and by discouraging "war profits" gained from trade with belligerents. "I hate war," Roosevelt told his listeners, suggesting that "safe sailing" depended upon continuing in office his administration's experienced statesmanship. Roosevelt would admit to being "more concerned and less cheerful about international world problems than about our immediate domestic prospects," but for the time being he was sanguine.[20] As he had told the People's Mandate Committee on March 12, "I am not worried about our foreign affairs, not the least bit. At present all we can do is show by [peaceful] example."[21]

In reality, Roosevelt had good reason to be seriously worried about America's foreign relations as only five days before his remarks to the People's Mandate Committee, on March 7, 1936, Hitler had sent his army into the Rheinland, an area permanently demilitarized by the Versailles Treaty. Furthermore, civil war in Spain broke out in mid-July when the Spanish army in Spanish Morocco under General Francisco Franco revolted against Spain's loyalist government. As Hitler and Mussolini sent arms and volunteers to aid Franco, and the Soviet Union urged a common front against fascism, the Spanish conflict had the potential to escalate into a much broader war. Moreover, the civil war in Spain illustrated the fallacy of trying to keep the nation out of war through legislation. Because the neutrality act had not anticipated a civil war, much less one with international implications, the mandatory arms embargo did not apply. Although the State Department lacked the power to forbid American sales to either side, Hull announced a moral embargo upon the reasoning that the Montevideo Conference had committed the United States to nonintervention everywhere in the world. An equally important consideration was that a moral embargo on arms would avoid antagonizing the isolationist/virtual pacifist vote.

Except for courting the peace movement, Roosevelt gave primary billing in 1936 to the New Deal's efforts to alleviate the impact of the depression upon farmers and workers. Tearing a page from the campaign book of his uncle Theodore Roosevelt, who had once assailed "malefactors of great wealth," Franklin D. Roosevelt stereotyped the Republicans as "economic royalists." That description hardly fit the Republican nominee, Governor Alf Landon of Kansas, a former member of Theodore Roosevelt's Bull Moose Party, who had balanced the budget in Kansas and often cooperated with the New Deal. In contrast to the aristocratic style of Roosevelt, Landon projected a down-to-earth, plain-folks manner of expression, but his radio addresses seemed colorless in comparison with the polished, beautifully phrased and well-delivered oratory of the president. A case in point was Landon's address on foreign affairs in which he promised to return to a high tariff and to restore morale in the Foreign Service by appointing a competent secretary of state and rewarding departmental merit. According to the brutal assessment of Sir Ronald Lindsay, the speech was "not illuminating reading, and inevitably reminds one of the story which was current earlier in the campaign that when an interlocutor asked Mr. Landon what his views were on the international situation, he replied that he thought 'those International boys' were getting too much of the business, and that Deere and the others (referring to the well-known manufacturers of harvesters) ought to have a bigger share of it."[22] Another weakness in the Landon campaign was a lack of unified Republican support for a return to a high tariff. Lindsay was told by Henry L. Stimson that he was so "disgusted" by the Republican attitude on tariffs that "he was not going to lift a finger for the election of Mr. Landon."[23] Other prominent Republicans such as Ogden Mills and Frank Knox, the latter prior to his becoming Landon's running mate, had also advocated lowering tariffs as a means for developing American foreign trade.

Probably only the *Literary Digest*, which had predicted a Republican landslide, was surprised that Roosevelt won reelection. Everyone was surprised that Landon carried only Maine and Vermont. The final disappointment belonged to Father Charles Coughlin who withdrew from broadcasting when his third party candidate, Representative William Lemke of North Dakota, carried fewer than a million votes instead of the nine million promised by the Detroit radio priest. Basking in the aftermath of his election mandate, Roosevelt embarked on his triumphal trip to Buenos Aires where he was hailed (much as Wilson had been in 1919) as a messiah. On his return to Washington, the president turned to the preparation of his second inaugural address (scheduled by the newly ratified Twentieth Amendment to be delivered on January 20 instead of the traditional date of March 4) basking in the knowledge that his party enjoyed unprecedented control of Congress. With a margin of 328 to 107 in the House and 77 to 19 in the Senate, the president appeared as a master politician who possessed the votes to get his way in both domestic and foreign policy.

Surprisingly, despite his commanding new majorities, Roosevelt was unable to transfer his landslide victory over Landon into either an expanded domestic New Deal or a more activist foreign policy. In retrospect, much of the blame for the resulting domestic and foreign policy debacle of 1937 can be attributed to overconfidence and poor judgment on the part of Roosevelt himself. First, disregarding the advice of the acting secretary of state, the president meekly surrendered on the issue of applying a discretionary arms ban to the Spanish Civil War. Both Assistant Secretary of State R. Walton Moore (Hull was returning from Buenos Aires) and Senator

Pittman urged Roosevelt to seek an amendment to the Neutrality Act giving the president discretionary authority to apply an arms embargo to the Spanish conflict. Instead, the president embraced a mandatory ban on arms sales to both sides and, with Roosevelt's endorsement, the measure sailed routinely through both houses of Congress; only a solitary member of the Farmer-Labor Party voted in the negative. Theoretically the arms ban to Spain was only an emergency measure that was unrelated to general neutrality legislation. However, Roosevelt's capitulation on a discretionary arms ban in the case of Spain sent a signal that he was unlikely to fight on the issue when Congress debated a permanent neutrality law to replace the 1936 measure, which expired on May 1, 1937. Hull later defended the arms ban as an effort to cooperate with British and French efforts to limit the war to the Iberian peninsula. An additional justification for the measure offered by the administration was to prevent the delivery of aircraft to the Spanish Loyalists by an aggressive New Jersey exporter who had discovered that the Neutrality Act did not apply to a civil war.

More than likely Roosevelt's support of a mandatory ban on arms sales to Spain had less to do with the threat of war in Europe than with a desire to avoid controversy with Congress at a time when he was about to spring upon the nation one of the most outlandish proposals in United States political history: the court packing plan, which he announced on February 5, 1937. Angered at the "nine old men" of the Supreme Court for having invalidated his farm and national recovery policies, Roosevelt proposed that the president be permitted to add an additional justice for each member of the court reaching the age of seventy and not retiring. The packing plan, which purported to improve judicial efficiency, would have permitted Roosevelt to enlarge the Supreme Court from nine justices to fifteen.

Ostensibly Roosevelt's controversy with the Supreme Court was unrelated to foreign policy. But in several respects Roosevelt's handling of the issue foreshadowed his later conduct of foreign policy in that he consulted with no one before taking action and he presented with great tenacity arguments that were not entirely candid. At first, given Roosevelt's majorities in Congress, he seemed likely to prevail. Soon substantial opposition developed within both parties. Roosevelt's critics argued that basic democratic institutions should not be altered so easily and that packing the court was too similar to the techniques used by European dictators in seizing power. Somewhat like Wilson's handling of the Versailles Treaty, Roosevelt insisted that it must be his plan, all or nothing; and he rejected a plausible opportunity to withdraw gracefully, claiming his objectives had been achieved when Justice Willis Van Devanter announced his retirement. Roosevelt's plan was further undercut when Justice Owen Roberts shifted his ideological alignment and the Court validated the National Labor Relations Act and the Social Security Act ("the switch in time that saved nine"). Thus as Congress took up permanent neutrality legislation in the spring of 1937, Roosevelt's prestige and ability to lead were in serious jeopardy.

With Roosevelt and Hull watching from the sidelines, the shaping of a permanent neutrality bill became (with one exception) a dreary repeat of previous debates on the topic. The State Department did not even prepare a neutrality bill for submission to Congress, feeling that the odds of securing discretionary authority would be better if the administration worked through Senator Pittman. Nor did Hull testify before the House and Senate Foreign Relations Committees. Instead the administration's desire for greater presidential flexibility was argued by Assistant Secretary of State R. Walton Moore, who told Pittman's committee "the more legislation you put on the statute books which tends to tie the hands of the Government the more definitely you advertise to war-minded nations what they can count upon when a war occurs."[24] But Pittman, as usual, proved a weak reed to lean upon, and the strategy miscarried. The senator's Peace Act of 1937 repeated the main features of the previous neutrality acts: if war broke out the president was required to ban loans and arms to either side. He was also required to prohibit travel by Americans on belligerent ships, whereas the 1935 Neutrality Act had left such a ban up to the discretion of the president.

The main departure from earlier neutrality legislation was that Pittman borrowed an idea that had originated with the financier Bernard Baruch. Writing in *Current History*, Baruch argued that restricting the flow of civilian goods to belligerents would invite inevitable retaliation. His imaginative and simple solution was the "cash and carry" formula, which held that "we will sell to any belligerent anything except lethal weapons, but the terms are cash on the barrel head and come and get it."[25] Among the general public the formula found broad acceptance as it promised both trade and peace. Moreover, cash and carry favored wealthy nations that possessed sea power and were able to purchase American products and transport them across the Atlantic. In other words, Baruch's formula decidedly favored Britain and France.

Members of the Nye committee (the "mandatory bloc") opposed cash and carry, contending the formula gave too much discretion to the president and, by tilting toward Britain and France, failed the test of true neutrality. Nye argued that the president should have no discretion to determine which commodities were to be included under cash and carry and that the prohibition on loans, arms, and travel should go into effect automatically and not when the executive determined that a state of war existed. Had Nye had his way, he would have banned, without exception, all trade with belligerents. The final act, passed only forty-eight hours before the expiration of the old law, was the rushed product of a conference committee which reconciled the slightly differing versions of the House and Senate neutrality bills. The "permanent" Neutrality Act required that when the president determined that a state of war (including a civil war) existed, he must ban arms, loans, and travel to either side; he also was required to forbid the arming of American merchant ships trading in civilian goods with belligerents. Finally, the measure gave the president discretionary authority to place trade in civilian goods on a cash and carry basis for a two-year trial period. On the advice of Hull, Roosevelt decided to sign the bill, which had to be flown by seaplane to the naval vessel on which the president was enjoying a fishing trip in the Gulf of Mexico. Just hours before the old law expired on May 1, 1937, Roosevelt signed the measure into law. A last gasp of the rule of law movement that had dominated American diplomacy during the interwar period, the Neutrality Act of 1937 proved just as futile and shortsighted as the disarmament treaties and the anti-war pact that had gone before and tarnished the reputations of all connected with it.

NOTES

1. Robert W. Love, Jr., "FDR as Commander in Chief," in Robert W. Love, Jr., editor, *Pearl Harbor Revisited* (New York, 1995), 182.

2. Presidential press conference, December 12, 1934, Edgar B. Nixon, *Franklin D. Roosevelt and Foreign Affairs* (Cambridge, 1969), Vol. 2, 311.

3. Marleen Kassel, "Japanese Wartime Rhetoric in the Traditional Philosophical Context," in Love, *Pearl Harbor Revisited*, 62–64.

4. Robert Dallek, *Franklin D. Roosevelt and American Foreign Policy, 1932–1945* (New York, 1979), 76.

5. Stephen E. Pelz, *Race to Pearl Harbor: The Failure of the Second London Naval Conference and the Onset of World War II* (Cambridge, 1974), 34–39.

6. Cordell Hull, *The Memoirs of Cordell Hull* (New York, 1948), Vol. 1, 398.

7. Presidential press conference, December 12, 1934, Nixon, *Franklin D. Roosevelt and Foreign Affairs*, Vol. 2, 313.

8. Elizabeth Eastman, Chairman, Women's World Court Committee, to Roosevelt, January 11, 1935, Nixon, *Franklin D. Roosevelt and Foreign Affairs*, Vol. 2, 353–57.

9. William E. Leuchtenburg, *Franklin D. Roosevelt and the New Deal, 1933–1940* (New York, 1963), 216–17.

10. Wayne S. Cole, *Senator Gerald P. Nye and American Foreign Relations* (Minneapolis, 1962), 82–83.

11. Memorandum of conversation between Joseph C. Green and Lindsay, April 20, 1935, General Records of the Department of State, File No. 811.113, Senate Investigation/252, RG 59, National Archives.

12. Wayne S. Cole, *Roosevelt and the Isolationists, 1932–1945* (Lincoln, 1983), 153–55.

13. Hull, *Memoirs*, Vol. 1, 405.

14. Pittman to Early, August 19, 1935, Nixon, *Franklin D. Roosevelt and Foreign Affairs*, Vol. 2, 607–9.

15. Robert A. Divine, *The Illusion of Neutrality: Franklin D. Roosevelt and the Struggle over the Arms Embargo* (Chicago, 1962), 115.

16. Cole, *Senator Gerald P. Nye*, 88–90.

17. Hull, *Memoirs*, Vol. 1, 485–86.

18. Foreign policy plank from the 1936 Democratic Party Platform, June 25, 1936, Nixon, *Franklin D. Roosevelt and Foreign Affairs*, Vol. 3, 336–37.

19. Roosevelt to the People's Mandate to End War Committee, March 12, 1936, Nixon, *Franklin D. Roosevelt and Foreign Affairs*, Vol. 3, 248–52.

20. Speech by Roosevelt, Chautauqua, New York, August 14, 1936, Nixon, *Franklin D. Roosevelt and Foreign Affairs*, Vol. 3, 377–84.

21. Roosevelt to the People's Mandate to End War Committee, March 12, 1936, Nixon, *Franklin D. Roosevelt and Foreign Affairs*, Vol. 3, 250.

22. Lindsay to Anthony Eden, October 26, 1936, FO414/273/A8732, Public Record Office (PRO).

23. Lindsay to Anthony Eden, November 9, 1936, FO414/273/A9110, PRO.

24. Divine, *Illusion of Neutrality*, 176.

25. Divine, *Illusion of Neutrality*, 165–66.

CHAPTER 9

The Shifting of the
Foreign Policy Momentum

July 22, 1937, was the lowest point of Roosevelt's New Deal. It was on that date that the Senate, at the climax of a six-month battle, handed Roosevelt a major defeat by soundly killing his court-packing plan. It was true that the setback did not directly involve foreign policy, but the clash produced bitter and lasting recriminations, since Roosevelt never forgave those who voted against him. For their part his critics saw the court plan as clear evidence that Roosevelt harbored dictatorial ambitions. The resulting mutual distrust was a liability the administration could ill afford because Roosevelt was soon pushed by events into speaking out against the national mood of isolationism and virtual pacifism. But even as he sought to regain control of foreign policy, the president, as before, was improvising and experimenting on a day-to-day basis, rather than working from a polished blueprint.

The incident that raised new alarm bells in Washington came on July 7, 1937, when Chinese and Japanese troops clashed at the Marco Polo Bridge near Peiping. Initial accounts suggested that the incident (in which both sides accused the other of firing first) was not sufficiently grave to be the *casus belli* of a major conflict. Japan's charming ambassador to the United States, Hiroshi Saito—who was a master of American slang and so westernized as to be able to distinguish between an infield hit and a Texas leaguer—assured Hull that a peaceful settlement was in sight. Just when it seemed the crisis had passed, fighting broke out again on July 25. Within three days Japanese troops had seized both Peiping and Tientsin. Next the fighting spread to Shanghai, where enormous civilian casualties were incurred by shelling from Japanese warships and inaccurate bombing by inexperienced Chinese pilots. One American sailor died and eighteen were injured when the cruiser *Augusta* was bombed, and two American sailors aboard the steamer *President Hoover* were killed by misaimed Chinese bombs. When the Japanese attacked Nanking in September, Ambassador Nelson Johnson took refuge on the gunboat *Luzon*. Despite the outbreak of hostilities, neither side broke diplomatic relations or declared war, nor did Roosevelt, realizing that China alone would be hurt by a ban on American loans and arms sales, invoke the Neutrality Act. Officially the conflict was only an incident—one that lasted until Japan surrendered unconditionally in August 1945.

The immediate American response to the China incident was predictably legalistic and ineffective: appeals to the belligerents to cease and desist, protests to Tokyo against assaulting civilians, the offer of American good offices (mediation) to arrange a peaceful solution, and the endorsement of resolutions of the League of Nations Assembly condemning Japan's actions as contrary to the Nine Power Treaty and the Kellogg-Briand Pact. Sensing the need for a more vigorous executive response to the Far Eastern crisis, Cordell Hull and Norman H. Davis urged Roosevelt to speak out against isolation during the course of scheduled western tour to which the president agreed.

Working from a draft prepared by Davis, Roosevelt prepared his "Quarantine" address, which was delivered on October 5, 1937, at the dedication of a Chicago bridge constructed by the Public Works Administration. Much of his speech could have been uttered by any of the interwar presidents; he condemned international anarchy and made the noncontroversial observation that the United States of America stood for the sanctity of treaties and the maintenance of international morality. Only slightly more adventurous was his statement that no country could successfully isolate itself from the spread of "world lawlessness." What caught the public's attention were the revisions inserted by Roosevelt. He compared the growth of lawlessness to the spread of an infectious microbe and added, "When an epidemic of physical disease starts to spread, the community approves and joins in a quarantine of the patients in order to protect the health of the community against the spread of the disease." He concluded by calling for unspecified "positive endeavors to preserve peace." No specifics were supplied explaining how peace was to be preserved or aggressors quarantined.[1]

Was Roosevelt boldly advocating a "get tough with Japan" policy? Every indication is that that was not his intention in 1937. In the face of determined isolationist criticism (Representative Hamilton Fish muttered threats of impeachment, and the *Chicago Tribune* warned against foreign meddling), Roosevelt, ignoring the fact that most reactions were positive, backed away from any suggestion of toughness. The next day Roosevelt met the press on the front porch of the family home at Hyde Park and pointedly denied he was thinking of imposing economic sanctions against aggressor nations. "Look," he said, " 'sanctions' is a terrible word to use. They are out of the window." He also denied there was any conflict between his quarantine speech and neutrality. One of his most revealing remarks was that he was "looking for a program," which suggested he had no specific course of action in mind.[2]

That Roosevelt was still searching in an abstract way for a response to the threat of "lawlessness" was illustrated by his embrace of an idealistic peace plan suggested by Sumner Welles. Welles, who was congenial with the president, probably knew that before the 1936 campaign Roosevelt had floated the idea of summoning the world's leaders to a conference aboard an American battleship where, in an atmosphere of detachment, they would rationally resolve their differences and set the world on the path of peace. At the time Roosevelt decided to abandon the idea, knowing it would be criticized as empty election year bombast. Welles's idea, presented to Roosevelt in two memoranda, was for Roosevelt to call a world conference at Washington to meet (like the 1921 Washington Conference) on Armistice Day for the purpose of agreeing upon "the basic principles which should be observed in international relations."[3] Hull, who disliked Welles personally and professionally, was furious. "Before I knew it," Hull recalled, "I found the President completely embracing this project."[4] Only after Hull strenuously objected, on the ground that a conference would surely fail and make the United States the laughing stock of the world, did Roosevelt defer to his secretary of state and agree to drop the conference project—for the time being. Still the idea reappeared for a final time in early 1938 when Roosevelt sounded out British Prime Minister Neville Chamberlain about calling an international peace conference. Chamberlain's lack of interest caused the president to abandon Welles's brainstorm once and for all.

Had Roosevelt been contemplating the application of a quarantine against aggressors, a likely vehicle could have been the conference of signers of the Nine Power Treaty (minus Japan), which was held at Brussels, November 3–24, 1937. Norman Davis headed the American delegation, and he took as advisers the State Department's Far Eastern expert Stanley K. Hornbeck and Jay Pierrepont Moffat, head of the European Division. Since Japan refused to participate and because there was no consensus for imposing sanctions, there was not much to do except to deplore Japan's conduct. The closest approach to getting tough with Japan was a suggestion by Davis to ask Congress to suspend the Neutrality Act as it pertained to the war in China. "This," reasoned Davis, "would startle and worry Japan, encourage the Chinese and have a dynamic effect upon world opinion."[5] Both the State Department and the White House were unenthusiastic, believing such a request would stir up a hornets' nest of opposition from isolationists and pacifists. Thus the conclusion of the Brussels Conference left Roosevelt confronting a public and congressional opinion that was as fragmented as ever and still improvising how to respond to the forces of lawlessness.

In 1898, 1941, and 1964, the United States entered major conflicts in response to outraged public opinion following attacks or imagined attacks on American naval vessels. Yet in December 1937, the sinking of the gunboat *Panay* by Japanese naval aircraft on the Yangtze River twenty-eight miles upstream from Nanking occasioned public demands for withdrawal rather than intervention. Both the United States and Britain maintained Yangtze River patrols for protecting their commerce and citizens. The *Panay* was one of five shallow-draft gunboats constructed expressly for patrol purposes. It displaced 450 tons and was armed with two three-inch guns and ten .30-calibre machine guns. According to its commander, James J. Hughes, the *Panay* was repeatedly attacked by Japanese naval planes in broad daylight while it convoyed three tankers belonging to the Standard Oil Company. The bombing of the ship, which was plainly marked with large horizontal flags, was very likely deliberate. Two American sailors and an Italian journalist were killed, and eight other sailors were seriously wounded. Thirty-two sailors suffered minor injuries, as did J. Hall Paxton, the second secretary of the American Embassy. Several of the injuries occurred when Japanese planes strafed lifeboats conveying survivors to the shore. Paxton was able to make his way to a nearby village, where he engaged porters who carried the wounded to the nearest hospital. Still it was three days after the incident before the survivors were evacuated by the *Oahu* to Shanghai. On their arrival, correspondents filed detailed accounts of the outrage as well as graphic accounts of Japan's "Rape of Nanking."[6]

Briefly a first class war scare flared. An angry Roosevelt directed Treasury Secretary Henry Morgenthau, Jr., to investigate whether he could seize Japanese assets (the answer was that the Trading with the Enemy Act gave the president sufficient legal power). And Roosevelt told his cabinet that he was considering economic sanctions and a long range naval blockade. Even Hull lost his customary poise and lashed out at the Japanese invaders as "wild, runaway, half-insane men."[7] Within a few day tempers had cooled a good deal since Japan met the conditions demanded by Roosevelt, including an apology and a $2.2 million indemnity. Furthermore, public opinion remained calm. In contrast to his belligerent response in 1898, an aged William Randolph Hearst appeared to agree with the verdict of the *Christian Science Monitor*: "The gunboat *Panay* is not the battleship *Maine*." Senator Henrik Shipstead inquired, "What are they doing there anyway?"[8] Borah added that he was unwilling to go to war "because a boat was sunk which happened to be traveling in a dangerous zone."[9] The *Panay* clash, instead of producing a tougher policy toward Japan, provided ammunition to isolationists and pacifists who advocated an amendment to the Constitution requiring a national referendum before war could be declared.

Representative Louis Ludlow of Indiana first introduced his war referendum amendment in 1935, but until the *Panay* crisis it had been bottled up in the House Judiciary Committee because Ludlow was 13 votes short of the 218 needed for a discharge petition. Within two days of the *Panay* sinking, the required signatures were gathered and a vote on the amendment was scheduled for January 10, 1938. An impressive collection of isolationists, pacifists, and feminists, as well as *Good Housekeeping* magazine, rallied behind the measure. Supporters argued that ordinary people, who were called on to die during war, should have a direct vote on American involvement. Hull, who regarded the Ludlow Amendment as "a disastrous move toward the most rigid form of isolationism," led the attack by drafting a letter signed by Roosevelt stating the amendment would "cripple the President in his conduct of foreign relations."[10] Unexpected support for the administration came from Alf Landon and Frank Knox, the Republican presidential and vice presidential candidates in 1936. Michigan Senator Arthur Vandenberg, normally an isolationist, argued that the Ludlow Amendment made as much sense as requiring the holding of a town meeting before permitting the fire department to put out a fire. And both the American Legion and the Veterans of Foreign Wars agreed that a national referendum on war was impractical and would invite aggressors to violate American rights. On the eve of the vote, James A. Farley, the chairman of the Democratic National Committee, personally contacted all Democratic representatives. In the final vote the administration prevailed, but by the perilously close vote of 209 to 188. From Hull's perspective, the episode was a striking demonstration of isolationist strength inasmuch as defeating the Ludlow Amendment had required an all-out effort by the administration. At the same time the vote illustrated that the strength of the isolationists was somewhat overrated as they could not muster a majority of the House for a discharge petition, much less the two-thirds majority of both houses of Congress required for the passage of a constitutional amendment. Only dimly seen at the time, the defeat of the Ludlow Amendment was a turning point in the administration's struggle against isolationism and pacifism.

The defeat of the Ludlow Amendment averted an embarrassing public reverse for New Deal foreign policy but made no real contribution to the development of a coherent response to the China Incident or the growing military power of Nazi Germany. As before, Roosevelt was reluctant to focus systematically on the details of foreign policy. Domestic rather than foreign problems still had a higher priority in 1938 for Roosevelt: the economic reverse that had begun the previous fall (Congress approved a $3.75 billion public works bill); the government reorganization bill (which was narrowly defeated amid charges Roosevelt was plotting to establish a dictatorship); and the Fair Labor Standards Act (establishing a maximum work week of forty-four hours a week for a twenty-five-cents-an-hour minimum wage). Furthermore, Roosevelt made determined efforts to purge conservative Democrats who had refused to support his court packing plan, but in the fall elections the purge failed and the Republicans rebounded by gaining eighty-one seats in the House and six in the Senate.

One modest development stemming from the crisis over China was the start of the first tentative steps for improving Anglo-American relations. As late as 1938 the dominant theme in relations between Roosevelt and Prime Minister Neville Chamberlain was distrust. Washington had not appreciated Britain's cavalier default of its war debt, and Roosevelt was not forgiven in Britain for having torpedoed the London Economic Conference. Chamberlain was highly skeptical that Roosevelt could be counted upon in a crisis, noting "it is always best and safest to count on nothing from the Americans but words."[11] Yet in January 1938, United States Navy Captain Royal Ingersoll traveled to London for staff discussions with British naval planners regarding the size of their respective Far Eastern naval forces as well as general strategy in the event of war with Japan. American naval maneuvers in the spring of 1935 had demonstrated that the United States badly needed allies in a possible Far Eastern naval conflict. In a hypothetical fleet problem the navy sought to implement its Plan Orange for the defense of the Philippines only to experience heavy losses from Japanese submarines and destroyers and finally to suffer the humiliation of having the American "T" crossed by the enemy's battle line. A new plan known as Rainbow Two was developed by Admiral Harry Yarnell that stressed defending the East Indies and establishing a blockade to deny Japan access to vital war materials. Presumably Japan's ability to make war would peter out. Tentatively it was agreed that the United States would dispatch ten and Britain nine battleships to Singapore. But a year later, as tension in Europe deepened, the British reduced their commitment to seven or eight battleships and in March 1939 to just two.

Anglo-American naval cooperation was also facilitated by the program of naval construction begun by the United States in 1938. In a special message to Congress, Roosevelt appealed for additional ships to defend the western hemisphere and the Panama Canal. Japan, which had denounced the Washington limitations, was the obvious target of Roosevelt's request. On paper the second Vinson Act, which overwhelmingly passed Congress on May 17, 1938, permitted the construction of three new Iowa class battleships armed with sixteen-inch guns, two additional aircraft carriers, nine new cruisers, twenty-three new destroyers, and nine additional submarines. But in the appropriation phase of the legislation only one new battleship was authorized. Unknown to American intelligence, Japan was secretly constructing two super battleships of 63,700 tons carrying eighteen-inch guns (the *Yamato* and the *Musashi*). Also, Japan countered the 1938 Vinson Act with a comparable "Replenishment" program in 1939, while, contrary to the recommendations of a naval board headed by Admiral A.J. Hepburn, the administration decided for fiscal reasons not to improve the defenses of Guam or Corregidor.

In the summer of 1938 Anglo-American social relations received a boost when Roosevelt learned through Canadian Prime Minister Mackenzie King that King George VI and Queen Elizabeth were contemplating a tour of Canada in the early summer of 1939. Political considerations were ignored in the initial planning, and the British ambassador, Sir Ronald Lindsay, was not even asked for an opinion as to the advisability of the trip. The primary purpose of the tour—the first visit by a reigning British monarch to North America—was to serve social and imperial purposes and to introduce George VI, who had become king in 1936 following the sensational abdication of his brother. Roosevelt, on August 25, 1938, enthusiastically invited the royal couple to extend their visit from Canada to the United States. The president's invitation tactfully preceded the formal announcement of the royal visit, thereby avoiding any implication that the trip was contrived to influence American opinion. Neither London nor Washington foresaw that the world crisis of 1939 would introduce political implications that were not intended when the visit was first proposed.

Political rather than economic motives were also behind the Anglo-American trade agreement of 1938. When Sir Ronald Lindsay was asked by Foreign Secretary Anthony Eden in March 1937 to recommend how to retain American goodwill in the event of a major European crisis, the ambassador strongly advised a favorable response to Hull's overtures for a trade agreement. Should Britain reject an agreement because of minor economic disputes comprehensible only to experts, London would be guilty of "a first-class political crime." "America," concluded Lindsay, "is still extraordinarily youthful and sensitive. She resembles a young lady just launched into society and [is] highly susceptible to a little deference from an older man."[12]

The negotiation proved especially arduous because Hull and Lindsay lacked personal rapport. Lindsay found it difficult to listen to Hull's repetitive and boring monologues "without allowing one's mind to wander to other topics."[13] For his part, Hull considered Lindsay "difficult to deal with" and always unappreciative of Hull's viewpoint.[14] In the fall of 1938 the talks reached the crucial stage, bringing Lindsay "personally to that state of bitterness and exasperation which usually results from dealing with [the] United States Government." Hull, he complained, was unreasonable in his demands and insisted upon putting Britain "through the mangle of American politics."[15] Suddenly, after Hull and Roosevelt relaxed the American terms, all the obstacles were swept away. To Hull the agreement was the capstone of his campaign to remove the causes of war by expanding trade. To Lindsay the significance of the agreement was that it had strengthened Anglo-American political ties.

The same lack of rapport that existed between Hull and Lindsay also characterized relations between Roosevelt and Chamberlain. The new prime minister, who took office in May 1937, favored improved Anglo-American relations in principle, but placed a higher premium on reaching an understanding with the European dictators than with Washington. Likewise, Roosevelt held Chamberlain, whom he had never met, at arm's length, especially after Chamberlain turned down an offer to visit the United States in the summer of 1937 and then had disappointed Roosevelt by rejecting Welles's peace plan in early 1938. But Roosevelt did not raise a public confrontation when Chamberlain embarked on his appeasement policy toward Germany, although Roosevelt did mildly protest after Chamberlain recognized Mussolini's conquest of Ethiopia. When Hitler, in March 1938, massed troops on the border of Austria and forced the resignation of the Austrian chancellor in favor of a Nazi, Roosevelt responded to the *Anschluss* with silence.

Having annexed Austria, Hitler expanded his drive for *lebensraum* by demanding that Czechoslovakia turn the Sudetenland over to Germany. Again Roosevelt stood aside as the crisis over Czechoslovakia threatened to plunge the world into a second world war. Indirectly Washington encouraged Chamberlain, who twice flew to Germany to meet with Hitler, to avoid hostilities. Roosevelt told Lindsay that "if the policy now embarked on proved successful he would be the first to cheer."[16] Thinking out loud, Roosevelt suggested that if war could not be averted, the French and British should fight a defensive conflict stressing blockade tactics. He also thought he might be able to avoid an arms embargo if, as in the case of the China incident, the war was undeclared. Or the Allies could always ship American arms to Canada for transhipment. In the abstract the Czechoslovak crisis caused Roosevelt to consider how the United States might assist the French and British short of sending troops. But when Roosevelt learned that Chamberlain had accepted Hitler's invitation to attend a four-power conference at Munich to discuss the Sudetenland issue, his reaction was to send Chamberlain a cheery cable reading simply: "Good Man."[17] As the Munich Conference reached a critical phase, Roosevelt and his aides drafted a final appeal to Hitler urging a peaceful settlement. Roosevelt's sense of relief, when Britain and France capitulated and accepted Hitler's annexation of the Sudetenland, was reflected in his admission to William Phillips, "I want you to know that I am not one bit upset over the final result."[18]

The initial euphoria faded rapidly. Almost immediately it became evident that Munich, beyond buying Britain and France a breathing spell, had settled nothing. Hitler's appetite for *lebensraum* and his anti-semitism were just as violent as ever. In reality, Britain and France (and by association the United States) had suffered a crushing moral defeat. The horror of the Nazi regime was vividly brought home to Americans by an officially inspired pogrom carried out throughout Germany in retaliation for the murder of a German diplomat in Paris by a Jewish refugee from Poland. On the night of November 9 (Kristallnacht) Nazis smashed Jewish property and synagogues in an intimidating reign of terror. Roosevelt's reaction was to issue a forceful condemnation, which he added to a bland statement drafted by the State Department, "I myself could scarcely believe that such things could occur in a twentieth century civilization."[19] And as a further gesture of protest he recalled Ambassador Hugh Wilson from Berlin, to which Hitler responded by summoning home Ambassador Hans Dieckhoff from Washington. In the aftermath of Munich, official Washington for the first time perceived that Hitler's warlike intentions, as spelled out in *Mein Kampf*, were not just a figment of the imagination.

By the fall of 1938, as the momentum of the domestic New Deal was blocked by a powerful coalition of conservative Democrats and Republicans, Roosevelt showed signs of resolving the foreign policy drift that had characterized his foreign policy from the first day of his presidency. The new strategy that emerged from the White House blended together the strengthening of national defense, especially air power, with attempts to repeal the mandatory arms embargo that prevented the president from distinguishing between an aggressor and the victim. Simultaneously Roosevelt urged the British to take a more militant stand against Hitler. "Our British friends must begin to fish or cut bait," he wrote. "The dictator threat from Europe is a good deal closer to the United States and the American continent than it was before."[20] After years of suffering one defeat after another at the hands of isolationists and pacifists, Roosevelt (with an assist from Nazi Germany and Japan) formulated a strategy that outflanked the opposition, held forth the hope of avoiding armed involvement in war, and eventually rallied public opinion behind his leadership. Typically Roosevelt played his cards close to his vest and, in explaining his policy and its risks, he often displayed the devious side of his personality as well as a tendency to avoid telling the whole truth and nothing but the truth.

Roosevelt's concern with America's glaring deficiencies in air power coincided with Munich. The president's anxiety was well founded as first class fighter planes such as the Curtiss P-40 and the Grumman Wildcat were still under development; only in heavy bombers did American manufacturers have a head start. From Ambassador to France William C. Bullitt, Roosevelt received a detailed account of the inferiority of French as well as American aviation. One of Bullitt's sources was Colonel Charles A. Lindbergh, who had just completed a detailed red-carpet tour of Nazi aircraft plants, the high point of which was the presentation of the highest Nazi aviation medal by Air Marshall Hermann Göring. Roosevelt's response was to propose a $500 million increase in defense expenditures, much of which would go to increase aircraft production from 2,600 to 15,000 planes annually.

By December, faced with strong objections from the army, Roosevelt was convinced such rapid expansion would lead to the production of obsolete aircraft that would be useless without pilots and training and repair personnel. Thus he accepted a balanced compromise target of just 3,000 planes annually, supported by adequate training and repair installations. In line with the new emphasis on developing air power, Roosevelt also gave approval for a visiting French military mission to test and order advanced planes developed by the Curtiss and Douglas aviation companies. Roosevelt told his Treasury secretary, Henry Morgenthau, Jr., the Maginot Line was America's first line of defense and that the sale of the planes would benefit France and the development of the American aircraft industry. The plan almost backfired when, on January 23, 1939, a prototype Douglas bomber carrying a member of the French military mission crashed at Los Angeles. Isolationist critics then accused Roosevelt of divulging military secrets and entangling the nation in foreign affairs. Seeking to defuse the controversy, Roosevelt took the bold step of inviting the Senate Military Affairs Committee to the White House (January 31, 1939) where he outlined the need to expand rearmament to prevent "by peaceful means" the domination of the world by Germany, Italy, and Japan.[21] Afterwards Roosevelt was furious when an anonymous senator, possibly Nye, told the press the president had said that America's frontier was on the Rhine, an interpretation that was not wholly inaccurate even though the phrase quoted was not one that Roosevelt had used specifically.

A logical problem with Roosevelt's strategy of selling aircraft to Britain and France was that such sales would be automatically prohibited under the Neutrality Act should war break out in Europe. Therefore, Roosevelt's dilemma was how to repeal the mandatory arms embargo in the face of certain isolationist/virtual pacifist protests prior to the outbreak of a second world war. Hoping to avoid the fiasco of another court packing battle, Roosevelt sought to build legislative support for repeal by conferring before Christmas 1938 with Senator Pittman, but found him reluctant to take action. Two weeks later, in his State of the Union address (January 4, 1939), Roosevelt warned of the danger posed by aggressor nations. And he called attention to the likelihood that "our neutrality laws may operate unevenly and unfairly—may actually give aid to an aggressor and deny it to the victim. The instinct of self-preservation should warn us that we ought not to let that happen anymore."[22] Although Roosevelt did not specifically mention it, a plausible reason for a new neutrality bill was that the cash-and-carry provision of the 1937 Neutrality Act was set to expire on May 1, 1939. A few days later, following his return from Lima, Hull contacted Pittman and offered to prepare a new neutrality bill that either repealed the arms embargo entirely or gave the president discretionary authority to impose an arms embargo. Pittman took the position that the chance of revising the arms embargo would be much better if he introduced legislation independently of the administration.

Perhaps nothing that Roosevelt and Hull could have done in 1939 would have persuaded Congress to modify the Neutrality Act prior to the outbreak of hostilities. What is certain is that Pittman, who still hoped to do something for western silver, was a weak reed. The Nevada senator, after consulting with R. Walton Moore, sponsored a new Peace Act of 1939 that repealed the arms embargo but left the other features of the Neutrality Act intact. In the meantime Roosevelt concluded that the entire 1937 Neutrality Act should be repealed and Senators William King of Utah and J. Hamilton Lewis of Illinois introduced separate repeal bills acceptable to the administration. Another variation came from Senator Elbert Thomas of Utah whose bill authorized the president to impose an arms embargo against treaty violating nations. Instead of pressing his own bill, Pittman served as a mediator, holding lengthy and inconclusive hearings that led nowhere.

In desperation Hull turned to Acting House Foreign Affairs Chairman Sol Bloom who introduced an arms repeal measure which he managed to get through the House Foreign Affairs Committee on a straight party-line vote. Hull gave the legislation top priority, but admitted the prospects for its passage by the full House were unpredictable. (Comparing the House of Representatives to a herd of sheep, Hull told of the board of education member who asked a student: "If there are sixteen sheep in a field and one jumps the fence, how many are left?" When told there would be none left, the board member concluded the student knew nothing about arithmetic only to be met with the rejoinder, "You don't know anything about sheep."[23] Reflecting his country origins, Hull told congressmen they were "making the mistakes of their lives" if they thought the conflict with Hitler was just "another goddam piddling dispute over a boundary line."[24]

What Hull had in mind was Hitler's dramatic seizure in mid-March of the remainder of Czechoslovakia in blatant violation of the assurances he had given at Munich. The Czechoslovak government, faced with a choice between annihilation or incorporation into Hitler's Reich, chose the latter. Lithuania was the next to capitulate to a Nazi ultimatum, ceding the port of Memel, an action that suggested Poland was the next on Hitler's list. And in the first week of April, Mussolini invaded impoverished Albania, and the Loyalist government in Spain collapsed as Franco triumphantly entered Madrid. Roosevelt now conceived the idea of addressing an appeal to the European dictators not to engage in new aggression and to attend a disarmament conference arranged by Roosevelt. Specifically the president requested assurances that Hitler and Mussolini would not attack for a ten-year period thirty-one specific nations including Poland. From the viewpoint of his isolationist/virtual pacifist opponents, Roosevelt's appeal backfired as Hitler delivered a clever and sarcastic rebuttal that had the Nazi members of the Reichstag rolling in the aisles. All thirty-one states, he claimed, had given him assurances that they had nothing to fear from Germany, and he suggested Roosevelt was sanctimonious in proposing a conference when the United States had refused to join the League of Nations. Senator Hiram Johnson's impression was that "Roosevelt put his chin out and got a resounding whack"; Senator Nye's verdict was, "He asked for it."[25]

The public relations setback at the hands of Hitler was soon overshadowed by a resounding triumph in public relations—both for Roosevelt and for Britain—in the form of the British royal visit to the United States (June 7–11, 1939). Accidental circumstances focused more attention upon the visit than could possibly have come from an official publicity campaign. First came the war scare caused by Hitler's annexation of Moravia and Bohemia, which led to rumors that the trip would have to be postponed. Then the royal voyage across the Atlantic was delayed for two days by fog, ice, and the threat of icebergs. Their belated arrival threw into disarray and rendered inaccurate the dates on many of the buildings and monuments dedicated by the monarchs. American interest was whetted as the royal couple embarked upon a three-week train tour of Canada in which they received Indians and the Dionne quintuplets, toured an Ontario mine, and were glimpsed by an estimated six million of the eleven million citizens of Canada. From the moment the king and queen entered the United States at Niagara Falls on the evening of June 7, the visit, in Lindsay's words, "went with a roar."[26] Traveling by train to Washington, the sovereigns were greeted at Union Station in ninety-four-degree heat by Roosevelt and his wife Eleanor and escorted to the White House in a military parade, in which one army tank caught fire. In their first full day in the capital the king and queen were warmly received in the rotunda of the capital by 74 senators and 357 members of the House of Representatives. Reporters, detecting a note of irony in the ceremony, noted that the decor included paintings of the British surrenders at Saratoga and Yorktown, while to one side of the king stood a statue of Thomas Jefferson holding the Declaration of Independence.

From Washington the royal train proceeded to New York where the visitors were met at the Battery by Mayor Fiorello La Guardia and Governor Herbert Lehman, both of New York. Three and a half million cheering spectators, some of whom cried out "Hello King!" lined the streets as the procession proceeded to the World's Fair on Long Island. The New York itinerary concluded with a final stop at Columbia University (founded in 1754 as King's College) where the sovereigns signed the visitors' book and examined the school's charter. However, the presentation of an honorary degree was omitted because, according to Lindsay, the king "hated" them, although the ambassador facetiously claimed that Queen Elizabeth was very anxious to receive one. An eighty-mile drive to the Roosevelt home at Hyde Park (where Roosevelt waited in the family library disagreeing with his mother over whether the king would prefer tea or cocktails) completed the day's travels, an hour and a half behind schedule. Needless to say, when the fatigued king did arrive at the library, the president and the cocktails prevailed. The final day of the visit (Sunday, June 11) was occupied by church services at the local Episcopal Church, followed by a picnic at which the king consumed a hot dog, baked beans, and strawberry shortcake, and drank several glasses of the local beer from Poughkeepsie.

Both Washington and London viewed the royal visit as beneficial to strengthening Anglo-American relations. Former Secretary of State Henry L. Stimson wrote to Lindsay: "They have carried away the hearts of our people, and the trip will have a quiet, solid influence towards a good understanding on both sides of the Atlantic which can hardly be overestimated." Secretary of State Cordell Hull agreed, recalling that the royal visit "was very effective in improving and solidifying" relations with Britain. Just as enthusiastic was Lindsay, who characterized the visit as a masterful appeal to American emotions that had immensely strengthened Britain's "hidden reserves." Although the visit produced no formal political commitments (which were never intended anyway), the British had good reason to be cheered by the personal expressions of support offered by Roosevelt. In an early morning conversation at Hyde Park between the king, the president, and the Canadian prime minister, Roosevelt spoke of the likelihood of war and discussed America's interest in banning the impending conflict from the western hemisphere. If Britain could make Halifax available to the navy, said Roosevelt, American ships could assist Britain in keeping the Atlantic free of Nazi vessels. The general tone of Roosevelt's remarks, noted Canadian Prime Minister Mackenzie King, "was to the effect that every possible assistance short of actual participation in the war could be given." During a private conversation with the king, Roosevelt expressed an interest in acquiring access to additional British bases on Trinidad and Bermuda. The United States Navy could then patrol the Atlantic from Cape Cod to Brazil for as far as a thousand miles out to sea. American ships and planes could locate any approaching enemy fleet and prevent Nazi submarines from threatening British convoys. Throughout the discussion the president's tone was decidedly martial. He stated that if he spotted a Nazi U-boat he would sink it at once and wait for the consequences, and he expressed the opinion that if the Nazis bombed London the United States "would come in."[27]

Within a few weeks it became evident that Roosevelt was speaking only for himself and not for Congress. In the House the crucial vote on the Bloom resolution, repealing the mandatory arms embargo, miscarried. During a late night session Ohio Representative John Vorys attached a crippling amendment requiring the president in the event of war to embargo arms and ammunition to belligerents. Only aircraft were exempted—on the reasoning that they had civilian applications. Many Democratic members of the House were absent when Vorys's amendment came to a vote, apparently failing by a show of hands. However, when Representative Hamilton Fish demanded an accurate count by tellers, the Vorys Amendment passed by a vote of 159 to 157. "Once in," Hull lamented, "it was impossible to take it out."[28] A total of 61 Democrats, apparently convinced a vote against the Vorys Amendment would be political suicide, then joined 150 Republicans and 3 Independents to endorse the Bloom resolution, now emasculated by the addition of an embargo on arms, excepting aircraft only.

Roosevelt, who had stood in the background during the House debate, was plainly angered that he had suffered another legislative setback. Worse yet, as revealed by reports from American embassies across Europe, the debate hurt British and French morale by demonstrating that they would have no opportunity to purchase American military equipment if war broke out with Germany. Roosevelt and Hull next turned to the Senate Foreign Relations Committee where they sought the approval of Pittman's bill deleting the arms embargo. Once again Pittman's leadership proved disappointing to the administration. First he demanded a higher support price for silver to benefit western miners. And, after Roosevelt had capitulated, Pittman failed to deliver the votes as the Senate Foreign Relations Committee voted 12 to 11 to postpone action on neutrality legislation until the next session of Congress, which would not meet until January 1940. In his fury, Roosevelt drafted a blunt message to Congress, reminiscent of his "bombshell" message dispatched to the London Economic Conference, in which he planned to condemn those who misrepresented his efforts to revise the Neutrality Act as men deserving "only the utmost contempt and pity of the American people."[29] On second thought, Roosevelt accepted Hull's advice to send Congress a more polite protest (July 14, 1939).

In effect the administration was asking the Senate to disown the Foreign Relations Committee and revise the Neutrality Act through independent legislative action. Presumably the next step would have been to reconcile a new Senate bill with the Bloom bill to produce a revised neutrality act acceptable to the administration. It was a long-shot strategy and it failed miserably. On Hull's advice Roosevelt called the Senate leaders of both parties to the White House on the evening of July 18. Roosevelt began by summarizing his view that a second world war was near at hand (which proved true) and that the repeal of the arms embargo would deter Hitler from further aggressive acts (which was questionable as there is no evidence Hitler took America into his political or military thinking at all). Almost immediately Borah (termed the "Dowager Senator" by Lindsay) interrupted with the authoritative statement that his private sources in Europe, which were more reliable than State Department channels, had assured him there would be no war in Europe in the near future. "Cordell," asked Roosevelt, "what do you think about the possibility of danger lying ahead?"[30] Barely able to keep his composure, Hull answered that the State Department was swamped with warnings that the outbreak of war was imminent. Vice President John Nance Garner, who was well aware that thirty-four senators had pledged to filibuster any revision of the Neutrality Act to death, did a quick head count of the senators and concluded: "Well, Captain, we may as well face the facts. You haven't got the votes and that's all there is to it."[31] Although Roosevelt concealed his anger over what Hull termed a "Neutrality Disaster," he never forgave those who had blocked the revision of the arms embargo. The loss of the initial skirmish made Roosevelt more determined than ever to win the war and to seize foreign policy leadership away from the isolationist/virtual pacifist coalition. As he had told King George VI, his policy was to offer all possible assistance to Britain and France short of active participation. Even before war was declared, Roosevelt had taken a giant step toward switching from "Dr. New Deal" to "Dr. Win the War."

Contrary to Senator Borah's superior sources of information, Hitler refused to validate the senator's no-war-in-Europe prediction. On August 23 Hitler and Stalin took the world by surprise by signing a ten-year nonaggression treaty. A secret protocol divided Eastern Europe into respective German and Soviet spheres of influence with Stalin receiving a free hand in Finland, the Baltic states, and eastern Poland. Roosevelt's response was to address a last minute appeal to the king of Italy, the president of Poland, and to Hitler urging the leaders to refrain from hostilities. Supposedly Assistant Secretary of State Adolph Berle cynically compared the action to sending one's mother-in-law a valentine out of season. Hitler, whose military plans were highly advanced, was not deterred in the slightest by appeals to morality or reason. Nor was he influenced one way or the other by the efforts of Roosevelt and Hull to permit the sale of munitions to Britain and France, and he was decidedly not impressed by America's puny army, which ranked just behind Portugal and ahead of Bulgaria in nineteenth place among world armies. Even less impressive was America's ranking of forty-fifth in the percentage of the population under arms. The Nazi invasion of Poland on September 1 was followed two days later by the British and French declarations of war against Germany. Now that war had actually broken out, the strength of the isolationist/virtual pacifist coalition was never the same again. Roosevelt quickly sensed that the momentum had suddenly shifted in his favor, but even as he advocated assistance short of war to Britain and France, the government, in its civilian and military operations, often operated in a sluggish, peacetime atmosphere of business as usual.

NOTES

1. Speech by Roosevelt, Chicago, October 5, 1937, Donald B. Schewe, editor, *Franklin D. Roosevelt and Foreign Affairs* (New York, 1995), Second Series, Vol. 7, 10–21.

2. Presidential press conference, October 6, 1937, Schewe, *Franklin D. Roosevelt and Foreign Affairs*, Second Series, Vol. 7, 33–37.

3. Welles to Roosevelt, October 6, 1937, and Welles to Roosevelt, October 9, 1937, Schewe, *Franklin D. Roosevelt and Foreign Affairs*, Second Series, Vol. 7, 29–32, 57–58.

4. Cordell Hull, *The Memoirs of Cordell Hull* (New York, 1948), Vol. 1, 546.

5. Robert A. Divine, *The Illusion of Neutrality* (Chicago, 1962), 214.

6. Admiral William Leahy to Roosevelt, December 17, 1937, and Lieutenant Commander James J. Hughes to Secretary of the Navy Claude Swanson, December ?, 1937, Schewe, *Franklin D. Roosevelt and Foreign Affairs*, Second Series, Vol. 7, 412–13, 472–87.

7. Dorothy Borg, *The United States and the Far Eastern Crisis of 1933–1938* (Cambridge, 1964), 492.

8. William E. Leuchtenburg, *Franklin D. Roosevelt and the New Deal 1932–1940*, 229.

9. Wayne Cole, *Roosevelt and the Isolationists, 1932–1945*, (Lincoln, Nebraska, 1983), 252.

10. Hull, *Memoirs*, Vol. 1, 563.

11. Stephen Pelz, *Race to Pearl Harbor*, (Cambridge, 1974), 193–94.

12. Thomas E. Hachey, editor, "Winning Friends and Influencing Policy: British Strategy to Woo America in 1937," *Wisconsin Magazine of History* (Winter 1971–1972), 124.

13. Lindsay to Viscount Halifax, August 16, 1938, FO 414/275/A6602, Public Record Office (PRO).

14. Hull, *Memoirs*, Vol. 1, 380.

15. Lindsay to Halifax, October 8, 1938, FO414/275/A7645, PRO.

16. David Reynolds, *The Creation of the Anglo-American Alliance, 1937–1941: A Study in Competitive Cooperation* (Chapel Hill, 1981), 35.

17. Robert A. Divine, *The Reluctant Belligerent: American Entry into World War II* (New York, 1965), 54.

18. Arnold A. Offner, *American Appeasement: United States Foreign Policy and Germany, 1933–1938* (Cambridge, Mass., 1969), 266–68.

19. Presidential press conference, November 15, 1938, Schewe, *Franklin D. Roosevelt and Foreign Affairs*, Second Series, Vol. 12, 84.

20. Roosevelt to Herbert C. Pell, November 12, 1938, Schewe, *Franklin D. Roosevelt and Foreign Affairs*, Second Series, vol. 12, 60.

21. Cole, *Roosevelt and the Isolationists*, 305.

22. Divine, *Illusion of Neutrality*, 234.

23. Hull, *Memoirs*, Vol. 1, 645–46.

24. Robert Dallek, *Franklin D. Roosevelt and American Foreign Policy, 1932–1945* (New York, 1979), 187.

25. Dallek, *Franklin D. Roosevelt and American Foreign Policy*, 187; James MacGregor Burns, *Roosevelt: The Lion and the Fox* (New York, 1956), 391–92.

26. Lindsay to Halifax, June 20, 1939, FO414/276/A4443, PRO.

27. Benjamin D. Rhodes, "The British Royal Visit of 1939 and the 'Psychological Approach' to the United States," *Diplomatic History* 2 (Spring 1978), 210–11.

28. Hull, *Memoirs*, Vol. 1, 646.

29. Divine, *Illusion of Neutrality*, 278.

30. Hull, *Memoirs*, Vol. 1, 650.

31. Dallek, *Franklin D. Roosevelt and American Foreign Policy*, 192.

?

CHAPTER 10

Aid to Britain Short of War

Prior to entering both world wars the United States had been technically neutral for more than two years. From August 1914 to April 1917 the Wilson administration, composed of men who (with the exception of William Jennings Bryan) were decidedly pro-Allied, paid lip service to neutrality while munitions manufacturers and bankers sold arms and made loans to Britain and France. Again the United States was technically neutral from September 1939 to December 1941. But Roosevelt hardly hid his sympathy for the Allies and his loathing for Hitler. Whereas Wilson had called on Americans to be impartial in thought as well as action, Roosevelt stressed that a neutral could not "close his mind or his conscience."[1]

The Nazis' invasion and lightning defeat of Poland fundamentally altered the power equation between Roosevelt and his isolationist/virtual pacifist foes. Prior to September 1939, Roosevelt had suffered one setback after another in foreign policy—the World Court proposal; the 1935, 1936, and 1937 Neutrality Acts; as well as his inability in mid-1939 to convince Congress to drop the mandatory arms embargo. Now the momentum shifted as public opinion moved decisively away from the fortress America concept. As expressed by a Gallup Poll taken after the invasion of Poland, eighty-four percent favored the Allies, fourteen percent had no opinion, and only two percent supported Hitler. After the Quarantine Speech, Roosevelt had agonized to Samuel Rosenman, "It's a terrible thing to look over your shoulder when you are trying to lead—and to find no one there."[2] After the outbreak of war, Roosevelt—who was certainly contemplating running for a third term—seized the moment and became more assertive in advocating American assistance to Hitler's enemies. And although his opponents did not easily concede defeat, they failed to prevail on any major issue once the European war had been declared. When Roosevelt cautiously went on the foreign policy offensive, he no longer had to fear there would be no one there to follow.

To comply with the letter of the Neutrality Act, Roosevelt—within a few days of the outbreak of hostilities—issued proclamations imposing a ban on arms sales to belligerents and restricting travel on belligerent ships. Now, he concluded, was the time to call a special session of Congress to consider a neutrality law overhaul. As he wrote Neville Chamberlain on September 11, "I hope and believe that we shall repeal the embargo next month and this is definitely a part of the Administration's policy."[3] Roosevelt and Hull did not take victory on the arms repeal issue for granted. Not only was there the prospect of a diehard defense of the existing act by its supporters, but a Gallup Poll showed that fifty percent of Americans wanted to retain the existing arms embargo even though they favored the Allies over the Nazis. Carefully the administration prepared for the special session of Congress by inviting to the White House a bipartisan group of politicians who supported repeal, including Roosevelt's 1936 Republican opponents Alf Landon and Frank Knox. Roosevelt's theme was that the cause of peace would be better served by a flexible neutrality policy rather than by a rigid one.

Addressing the joint session of Congress on September 21, Roosevelt bluntly said of the Neutrality Act: "I regret that Congress passed that Act. I regret equally that I signed it." It was his conviction, said Roosevelt, that by repealing the arms embargo "the United States will more probably remain at peace than if the law remains as it stands today."[4] He made no specific reference to the obvious fact that repeal of the arms embargo would benefit Britain and France, and he avoided any insinuation that America's frontier was on the Rhine. Wary and distrustful of his opponents and fearful of a Senate filibuster, Roosevelt was less than forthright in explaining why he wished the arms embargo repealed. To tell the whole truth and nothing but the truth, as he had come close to doing during his reception of the Senate Military Affairs Committee in January, might well have played into the hands of the isolationist/virtual pacifist leadership. That Roosevelt's oblique strategy worked was suggested by a Gallup Poll taken after his speech, showing that sixty-two percent favored repeal of the arms embargo.

The logistics of the debate were similar to the previous neutrality battles of the period. The isolationists and virtual pacifists were as well organized and determined as ever. Father Coughlin and Colonel Charles A. Lindbergh took to the airwaves, and their appeals produced a torrent of mail to congressmen. But after a few weeks the mail barrage diminished when Roosevelt's opponents ran short of funds. Furthermore, several defectors appeared in the isolationist/virtual pacifist ranks including Senators George W. Norris of Nebraska, Robert A. Taft of Ohio, Warren Austin of Maine, and W. Warren Barbour of New Jersey. As before Roosevelt and Hull trusted to Senator Pittman to shepherd a revised bill through the Senate.

To Hull's irritation he was telephoned by Pittman who "said rather arrogantly that he hoped his committee would not be embarrassed by indiscreet utterances from the Executive 'end of the avenue.' "[5] Once again Pittman disappointed the administration by presenting a poorly drafted bill that forbade American ships from trading with belligerents except for Canada. But Hull and Roosevelt had little choice but to accept Pittman's revision of the Bloom bill since it had the virtue of eliminating the mandatory arms embargo.

After a month of debate Roosevelt's opponents were too feeble to delay a vote through a filibuster. Thus the Senate on October 26 repealed the arms embargo 63 to 30, and the House of Representatives followed suit 243 to 181. A final conference bill easily passed on November 3, and Roosevelt signed the measure two days later with two pens that he presented to Senator Pittman and Representative Bloom. Now it was legal for the Allies to purchase American munitions on a cash-and-carry basis. The revised act also continued the previous prohibition on loans to belligerents and travel by Americans on belligerent ships, and it forbade American ships from entering the war zone. Roosevelt, smiling broadly, contended that the repeal of the arms embargo had "restored the historic position of the neutrality of the United States."[6] As long as the Allies had sufficient cash to buy American goods, the revised Neutrality Act afforded them the ability to improve their defenses. Actually only the French took advantage of the opportunity. For the time being Britain held back, seeking to conserve its dollar reserves.

The "storm cellar" neutrality embodied in the revised Neutrality Act was the first in a series of cautious stopgap solutions improvised in response to the outbreak of World War II. But, as illustrated by the timid American response to Stalin's Winter War against Finland, which broke out on November 30, 1939, the repeal of the arms embargo did not immediately inaugurate a bold departure in New Deal foreign policy. One reason Finland held a special place in America's affections was that the Baltic nation was the only World War I debtor still making semi-annual payments to the United States Treasury. And Americans admired the courage displayed by "brave little Finland" in holding the Red Army at bay for months in Karelia.

Roosevelt responded sympathetically to "this dreadful rape of Finland," but as had been the case with the 1934 debt agreement, his benevolence did not extend to the taking of unnecessary political risks. As Soviet-Finnish relations worsened, Roosevelt appealed to the Soviet Union to respect the boundaries and independence of Finland. Subsequently Roosevelt called upon both sides to renounce aerial attacks on civilians, and he requested American aircraft manufacturers to withhold the sale of their products to "nations obviously guilty of such unprovoked bombing."[7] Another expression of American friendship was to place Finland's debt payment of December 15, 1939, in a special Treasury account. At a press conference Roosevelt speculated that Congress might authorize Finland to use the funds for relief purposes. The idea proved stillborn when Finland was forced to make peace in March 1940, and the Treasury quietly credited the December 15 payment to Finland's war debt account. Despite overwhelming sentimental support for Finland the actual assistance furnished by the United States was quite meager, including a $10 million Reconstruction Finance Corporation loan for the purchase of surplus agricultural products and a moratorium on Finland's 1940 debt payments—although, in deference to the latent strength of congressional isolationists, Finland was required to pay three percent interest for the privilege.

Along the Western Front, World War II was uneventful from September 1939 to April 1940. Although correspondents spoke truthfully of a phony war or a *sitzkrieg*, all concerned were aware that massive military operations were likely once weather conditions became favorable. Like Wilson, who had sent Colonel House to Europe in 1915 and 1916 on mediation ventures, Roosevelt explored possible peace moves in 1940. Undersecretary of State Sumner Welles and Jay Pierrepont Moffat were dispatched on a fact-finding mission to London, Paris, Rome, and Berlin in February and March with instructions to ascertain prospects for peace. Hull, who suspected that Welles had used his friendship with the president to arrange the trip, was unhappy because he feared the mission would complicate his life by producing wild rumors. Predictably, the mission failed. Welles, on his return, reported: "I do not believe there is the slightest chance of any successful negotiation at this time for a durable peace."[8] Although the Welles mission went nowhere, Roosevelt took satisfaction from having made the effort and, by conspicuously advocating peace, he gained a political advantage in his continuing battle with isolationists and virtual pacifists.

No one in the United States predicted the worst case scenario that unfolded between April and June 1940. The first disaster was Hitler's easy conquest of Denmark and Norway. Then on May 10 the Nazis attacked Holland and Belgium—the same day that Neville Chamberlain was replaced as British prime minister by Winston Churchill. In accordance with a well-rehearsed contingency plan, the Allies met the German invasion by sending a million men into Belgium. The fatal flaw in Allied strategy was that the Ardennes forest, the pivot of the Allied advance, was left lightly fortified. Hitler's *blitzkrieg* ripped open a fifty-mile gap in the French defenses and pinned the British against the sea. Miraculously the British succeeded in evacuating their army of some 300,000 at Dunkirk, but for all practical purposes Hitler now controlled Europe. The fall of France was formalized when Hitler imposed an armistice on June 22; he insisted that the signing ceremony be held in the same railroad car in which Marshall Foch had signed the armistice on November 11, 1918.

The collapse of France, more than any other event, undermined the influence of isolationism in the United States. The ease of Hitler's triumph raised serious doubts about the ability of Britain to survive as well as doubts as to America's invulnerability to attack. For Roosevelt the Allied defeat, though regrettable, provided vindication of a sort in that it exposed the shortsightedness of isolationist thinking and it made it easier to secure defense appropriations. Moreover, the world crisis provided all the justification Roosevelt needed to seek an unprecedented third presidential term. Even before the French surrender, Roosevelt called on Congress to expand defense spending from the $2 billion he had originally requested to $3 billion. Half was to go for enlarging and equipping the nation's decrepit army, and the balance was to build army and navy air power to 50,000 planes. Roosevelt warned that the oceans were no longer sure shields against attack, although in making his point, he exaggerated the ease with which German planes could fly from West Africa, the Azores, and Greenland to mid-America. Practically in a panic Congress complied and voted $320 million more for defense spending than Roosevelt had requested. Another $1 billion was approved in June, and in July, following the French surrender, Congress voted an additional $5 billion appropriation. Included in the build-up were funds for 250 new ships, including 7 battleships, 19 aircraft carriers, 60 cruisers, 150 destroyers, and 150 submarines. In 1940 Congress appropriated $10.5 billion for defense, more than the entire federal budget the year before.

With momentum running against isolationism and virtual pacifism, Roosevelt went on the offensive. In a fighting speech to the graduating class at the University of Virginia, Roosevelt unambiguously characterized isolation as a delusion. Referring to Mussolini's belated declaration of war against an already defeated France, Roosevelt ad libbed the comment, "On this tenth day of June, 1940, the hand that held the dagger has struck it into the back of its neighbor." He spoke of "extending to the opponents of force the material resources of this nation." He further pledged that the United States would proceed "full speed ahead" to prepare for "every emergency and every defense."[9] Roosevelt's determination to support beleaguered Britain was further illustrated by the appointment of two leading Republicans to the cabinet. As secretary of war he named Henry L. Stimson, and as secretary of the navy he appointed Frank Knox. Stimson, now seventy-two years old, had headed the War Department once before (under Taft). Under Coolidge he had undertaken a successful diplomatic mission to Nicaragua, and as Hoover's secretary of state he had taken the lead in condemning Japan's annexation of Manchuria. Knox, the publisher of the *Chicago Daily News*, had been Alf Landon's running mate in 1936. Both men had publicly endorsed extensive aid to Britain. Stimson favored the outright repeal of the Neutrality Act and the convoying of supplies to Britain, while Knox favored a million-man army and the development of modern aircraft, which could be supplied to the British. At the same time Roosevelt established close links to a national committee organized by William Allen White, the progressive Republican editor from Emporia, Kansas. Often called just the White Committee, its official name—the Committee to Defend America by Aiding the Allies—simply and imaginatively summarized Roosevelt's new foreign policy emphasis. But as Roosevelt spoke out forthrightly against the Nazis, traces of his characteristic method of presenting only part of the story could be glimpsed in the appointment to his cabinet of two prominent Republicans on the eve of a presidential campaign and in his refusal to reveal his own intentions regarding the Democratic nomination. As the Democrats met at Chicago, Roosevelt's furtive mind was pondering how to respond to an urgent request from Churchill for American destroyers to combat the submarine.

Roosevelt's nomination for a third term as the Democratic candidate appeared to be a completely spontaneous event. Actually, by veiling his intentions until the last minute, Roosevelt had discouraged potential adversaries from coming forth. Moreover, Vice President John Nance Garner and Hull, two potential successors, were ruled out by age; Harry Hopkins was too controversial; William O. Douglas had been removed from contention by his appointment to the Supreme Court; and Henry Wallace was slated to become the new vice president. Cleverly Roosevelt had engineered Democratic succession politics so that he was the only logical candidate to succeed himself in 1940. In Wendell Willkie of Indiana, the long-shot candidate of the Republicans, Roosevelt faced a campaigner who projected a tousled image of energy and magnetism. However, as a recent convert to the Republican Party, Willkie was viewed with some skepticism by conservative and isolationist Republicans. As expressed by Indiana Senator James Watson, Willkie was akin to a reformed prostitute who wanted to lead the choir immediately after joining the church.

Outwardly foreign policy was not an issue in the 1940 campaign. On the question of assistance to Britain the platforms of the two parties were in agreement; both pledged aid to peoples fighting for liberty who were under attack. Both opposed American involvement in foreign wars. The Republicans categorically promised not to send Americans into battle; the Democrats followed suit, adding the proviso that they would refrain from involvement in war "except in case of attack."[10] Both candidates supported rebuilding the army through a draft. In reality foreign policy dominated the campaign while the Battle of Britain raged in the form of Nazi air raids and submarine attacks launched from French soil and as Americans debated the question of what form American assistance to Britain should take.

The idea of exchanging American destroyers for British bases in the western hemisphere did not originate with Roosevelt but with the White Committee. Since May 15, when Churchill asked for destroyers, Roosevelt had been procrastinating while he tried to decide how to respond. The obvious problem facing Roosevelt was that the executive lacked authority to give away government property to a foreign government. However, asking Congress for authority to comply with Churchill's request would likely provoke determined isolationist resistance and possibly invite a filibuster. Journalist Joseph Alsop, a member of the White Committee's Century Group, hit upon a simple and imaginative solution: the destroyers should be offered in exchange for British naval and air bases in British possessions in the western hemisphere. On August 2 Roosevelt reviewed the idea with his cabinet, and there was general agreement that the idea should be pursued. Hull, who had just returned from Havana, questioned whether acquiring British bases would violate the nontransfer principle, but Roosevelt suggested that leasing British bases would be a workable solution. And Postmaster General James Farley recommended securing the agreement of Willkie so as to remove the deal from partisan politics. It was also the consensus that congressional criticism would be greatly lessened if Churchill would publicly give assurances that the British fleet would never be surrendered.

Considering the urgency of Britain's needs, it is surprising that arranging the fine print of the agreement required the better part of three months. William Allen White took up the delicate matter of consulting Willkie. Understandably the Republican candidate was extremely reluctant to endorse an agreement that existed only in vague generalities, especially when he had not had a chance to consult Republican congressional leaders. Although Willkie refused an advance commitment, he did issue a statement saying that his view of America's vital interests had not changed, implying that he would not use a destroyer-for-bases swap as a campaign issue. On the British side there were also problems. Churchill had second thoughts about an arrangement that was clearly one-sided, since Roosevelt wanted the lease of seven or eight bases, rather than the three bases contemplated by Churchill. The prime minister also objected to offering a public assurance concerning the fate of the Royal Navy as being defeatist and as likely to have a harmful effect on British morale.

During the month of August most of the obstacles were removed. Attorney General Robert Jackson held that the navy could certify that the destroyers were not essential to the defense of the United States. And Jackson, at Roosevelt's request, ruled that the president possessed sufficient authority to formalize the trade through an executive agreement which, unlike a treaty, did not require the approval of the Senate. The actual drafting was entrusted to the British ambassador Lord Lothian, Knox, and Hull. In its final form the agreement leased bases in Newfoundland and Bermuda to the United States "freely and without consideration" for a period of ninety-nine years.[11] Six other bases were leased (in the Bahamas, Jamaica, Antigua, St. Lucia, Trinidad, and British Guiana) in exchange for the fifty destroyers. Churchill agreed to repeat in an exchange of notes his previous assurances that the fleet would never be surrendered. On September 3 the agreement was signed by Hull and Lothian and announced to the public.

Most of the material advantages were on the side of the United States. In return for valuable bases, Britain received little of immediate value: only nine of the destroyers were fit for immediate use, and only thirty were in service by the end of May 1941. Furthermore, due to a proofreading error by Lothian, the final agreement only promised Britain destroyers and not other military equipment requested by the British and approved by Roosevelt: twenty motor torpedo boats, five heavy bombers, five PBY flying boats, and 250,000 rifles together with 30 million rounds of ammunition. Once the omission was detected it was too late, Roosevelt concluded, to reopen the question. Not until the passage of the Lend-Lease Act the following spring did Britain receive the desired items, with the exception of the rifles, which were shipped at the end of September. On the other hand Roosevelt never received the public assurances promised by Churchill in regard to the fleet, since the British artfully contended there was no need to reiterate what the prime minister had already stated in Parliament. When viewed in detail the destroyers-for-bases deal appears less a Machiavellian scheme than another hastily improvised stopgap New Deal foreign policy.

Without the assistance of the *blitzkrieg*, the destroyers-for-bases deal would not have been possible, and the same can be said of the Selective Service Act passed on September 16. The idea of peacetime conscription, like the destroyers deal, did not originate with Roosevelt, but with preparedness advocates such as New York attorney Grenville Clark and Secretary of War Henry L. Stimson. Roosevelt's endorsement of "selective training" in his acceptance speech (July 19) gave the draft concept political momentum. When Willkie in his acceptance speech (August 1) enthusiastically gave his blessing, the passage of Selective Service was assured.

The unnatural alliance of Willkie and Roosevelt on behalf of the destroyer deal and Selective Service dismayed isolationist senators who raised numerous objections, some of which were perfectly valid, to both measures. David I. Walsh, Arthur Vandenberg, and Gerald Nye noted that the destroyers deal, contrary to the opinion of Attorney General Jackson, violated the spirit of the Neutrality Act and weakened American coastal defenses. Another objection that was true enough was that furnishing destroyers to Britain through an executive agreement had denied the public and Congress an opportunity for a meaningful debate. Selective Service, which passed by almost 2 to 1 in both houses of Congress, was also assailed by virtual pacifists and isolationists as unnecessary, provocative, and un-American. The loudest and most effective criticism of Roosevelt's aid short of war policy came from the America First Committee, which was officially formed in September 1940. Well organized and financed, the America First Committee included among its leaders Generals Robert E. Wood and Hugh Johnson,

George Peek, Alice Roosevelt Longworth, Henry H. Regnery, Philip La Follette, Senators Burton K. Wheeler and Gerald Nye, and Colonel Charles A. Lindbergh. The basic principles of the America First Committee stressed building an impregnable defense to deter aggression and opposing aid short of war as weakening America's defense at home and as threatening to involve the nation in war abroad. Theoretically the America First Committee did not take a stand on the destroyers deal or selective service. However, since most of the members were bitter opponents of Roosevelt and the third term, it is unlikely that few if any of the members approved anything favored by Roosevelt.

The issue of defense was where Willkie and America First were most in agreement. The Republican platform supported "the prompt, orderly and realistic building of our national defense," and Minnesota Governor Harold Stassen, without admitting any past shortsightedness on the part of his fellow Republicans, criticized Roosevelt for being "tragically unprepared."[12] In the closing weeks of the campaign the civility earlier demonstrated by both candidates evaporated. On the advice of Representative Joseph W. Martin, Jr. (whom Roosevelt had assailed for his obstructionist isolationism, along with New York Representatives Bruce Barton and Hamilton Fish), Willkie attacked Roosevelt as a warmonger. Roosevelt's reelection, charged Willkie, meant war no later than April 1941. At Boston in a speech hurriedly prepared aboard his campaign train, Roosevelt made a categorical pledge that he later regretted: "And while I am talking to you mothers and fathers I give you one more assurance. I have said this before, but I shall say it again and again and again. Your boys are not going to be sent into any foreign wars." Playwright Robert Sherwood, one of Roosevelt's speech writers, recalled that Roosevelt was annoyed when Samuel Rosenman suggested adding the qualification "except in case of attack." In hindsight, Sherwood saw that he, as well as Roosevelt, had erred in yielding to "the hysterical demands for sweeping reassurance."[13] Like Sherwood, Roosevelt probably burned inwardly when he recalled the words "again and again and again." Whether the last minute breakdown of bipartisanship had much effect on the election is doubtful; Roosevelt comfortably won a third term with a margin of 449 to 82 in the electoral college and about 27 million popular votes to 22 million for Willkie. Since both candidates supported aid to Britain short of war, the campaign can be viewed as a repudiation of isolationism. Left dangling was just how American aid to Britain was to be implemented beyond the existing policy of selling American military products on a cash-and-carry basis.

The general idea behind lend-lease originated with Roosevelt, who three days after the election told Interior Secretary Harold Ickes that the time was coming when Britain would need loans or credits. But how was America to outflank the Johnson Act and the Neutrality Act? Roosevelt's answer to Ickes was that the government could lease Britain military equipment such as ships. The immediate initiative for action came in the form of an indiscreet remark to the press by the new British ambassador, Lord Lothian, on his return from London on November 23. Probably Lothian did not actually make the statement often attributed to him, "Well boys, Britain's broke, it's your money we want."[14] But Lothian did say that within six months Britain would have difficulty paying for munitions. Roosevelt was initially annoyed by Lothian's remarks on finance because he did not believe Britain faced an immediate financial crisis. Still Lothian's press conference forced the administration to come to grips with the specifics of how—short of war—Britain was to be aided.

Roosevelt resolved his British aid dilemma in an unlikely setting. On December 2 the president left Washington for a two-week vacation and tour of the bases leased from Britain. Harry Hopkins, the White House physician, and three correspondents accompanied Roosevelt aboard the cruiser *Tuscaloosa*. Most of the voyage was devoted to fishing, entertaining British officials (including the Duke of Windsor, who was the governor of the Bahamas), smoking, sunning, and watching the latest movies. Periodically navy seaplanes delivered mail—including, on December 9, a lengthy epistle from Churchill. Only reluctantly, responding to urging from Lothian, did Churchill agree to write Roosevelt detailing the "mortal danger" faced by Britain from Nazi submarines. He asked Roosevelt for three million tons of shipping, including more destroyers, 7,000 combat aircraft, and 7,000 training aircraft; and he suggested that soon Britain would be short of ready cash to pay for American military equipment. "We ask for an unexampled effort believing it can be done," he concluded.[15]

According to Harry Hopkins (the president's former relief director and closest adviser), Roosevelt's carefree and nonchalant manner of vacationing was his way of "refueling" while he contemplated how to respond to Churchill. "Then one evening," Hopkins recalled, "he suddenly came out with it—the whole program. He didn't seem to have any clear idea how it could be done legally. But there wasn't a doubt in his mind that he'd find a way to do it."[16] The day after his return to Washington, Roosevelt told his Treasury secretary, in what Morgenthau called one of Roosevelt's "brilliant flashes": "I have been thinking very hard about what we should do for England. It seems to me the thing to do is to get away from a dollar sign. I don't want to put the thing in terms of dollars or loans." At a press conference later that same day (December 17) Roosevelt floated the lend-lease idea, blending together generous amounts of charm, corn, and oversimplification. Roosevelt compared Britain's situation to seeing one's neighbor's house catch on fire. In such a case no one would ask the neighbor to pay for help. Instead, a good neighbor would lend his garden hose and when the fire was extinguished expect to have the hose returned, assuming it was undamaged. Referring to the mess that had followed

America's World War I loans to Britain, Roosevelt said his goal was to get rid of the "silly foolish old dollar sign."[17]

Roosevelt rallied public support with a skillfully prepared and well-delivered fireside chat (December 29) in which he characterized isolationism and appeasement as delusions. "We cannot escape danger, or the fear of danger," he said, "by crawling into bed and pulling the covers over our heads." The phrase that was the most memorable was supplied by Hopkins: "We must be the great arsenal of democracy. For us this is an emergency as serious as war itself. We must apply ourselves to our task with the same resolution, the same sense of urgency, the same spirit of patriotism and sacrifice as we would show were we at war."[18] At the White House telegrams and mail ran one hundred to one in favor of the "arsenal of democracy" fireside chat. Almost as successful was Roosevelt's State of the Union address (January 6, 1941) in which he again blasted "enforced isolation" and asked for authority to manufacture munitions to be furnished to nations defending themselves from aggression. Roosevelt concluded with a moving call for a world founded upon "four freedoms"—freedom of speech and expression, freedom of worship, freedom from want, and freedom from fear. Political momentum was firmly on Roosevelt's side, and had he looked over his shoulder he would have seen many eager to follow.

Typically, Roosevelt played only a small role in working out the legislative details. With Morgenthau cracking the whip, two Treasury Department lawyers composed the legislation so as to give Roosevelt a "blank check" format. The resulting legislation gave Roosevelt his way since it permitted him "to sell, transfer title to, exchange, lease, lend or otherwise dispose of any defense article to any country whose defense the President deems vital to the defense of the United States."[19] For public consumption Roosevelt adopted the Olympian strategy of remaining high above the fray and leaving the details to Democratic legislative leaders. Operating far behind the scene, however, Roosevelt directed the passage of the Lend-Lease Act complete to the smallest of details. The official title, suggested by Justice Felix Frankfurter, "An Act to Further Promote the Defense of the United States," had a Rooseveltian ring to it.[20] And so did the unusual number assigned the bill by the enrolling clerk of the House of Representatives: H.R. 1776. The Parliamentarian of the House suggested the number to provide political cover to House Majority Leader John McCormack of Boston, whose district was heavily Irish in composition.

Lend-Lease was the last stand of the isolationists and virtual pacifists. Although they eventually went down to defeat, they did not succumb without a bitter fight in which they scored numerous debating points. Roosevelt was particularly incensed by Senator Burton K. Wheeler's colorful accusation that "Lend-Lease is the New Deal's triple A foreign policy; it will plow under every fourth American boy." At a press conference Roosevelt referred to Wheeler's remark as "the most untruthful, the most dastardly, unpatriotic thing that has been said in public life in my generation."[21] In speeches and congressional testimony critics called Lend-Lease a fascist bill and a declaration of war against Germany (Hamilton Fish, Gerald Nye, Bennett Champ Clark, Robert La Follette, Jr.), a "blank check book with the power to write away our manpower, our laws and our liberties"[22] (General Robert Wood), a power grab by the executive paving the way for a future dictatorship (William R. Castle, Jr., Hanford MacNider, Father Charles Coughlin, and Charles A. Beard), and a futile policy since a British victory over Germany was not possible (Colonel Charles A. Lindbergh). For the most part Roosevelt kept in the background, with the exception that at his January 10 news conference, he denied that Lend-Lease repealed either the Johnson Act or the Neutrality Act, and he also denied any desire on his part for additional presidential powers. In congressional hearings Hull, Morgenthau, Knox, and Stimson defended Lend-Lease as vital to American security in the face of a real fascist threat. In answer to the dictatorship charge defenders either avoided the question or, in the case of Speaker of the House Sam Rayburn, contended that the act added little to the powers already possessed by the president as commander in chief of the armed forces. A common theme of defenders was that American security and British security were linked and that the British navy was essential to the defense of the western hemisphere. Lend-Lease, said its advocates, was an act of self-defense and was designed to avoid involvement in the European conflict.

Once again Roosevelt's opponents were unable to mount a filibuster or attach crippling reservations. Thus the Lend-Lease Act passed by substantial majorities, and Roosevelt signed the measure into law on March 11, 1941. The passage of what Hull called "one of the most revolutionary legislative actions in American history" was a brilliant example of Roosevelt's ability to direct an inspirational public crusade.[23] His handling of Lend-Lease also contained traces of his devious tendency to avoid telling the whole truth and nothing but the truth. In downplaying the risk of war, in denying he was subverting the Johnson Act and the Neutrality Act, and in rejecting suggestions that United States Navy convoys would be required to ensure that lend-lease supplies reached their destination, Roosevelt and his spokesmen presented a partial and reassuring picture that was not entirely forthcoming.

In effect the Lend-Lease Act made the United States an unofficial ally of Britain. Still, to the discomfort of the British and interventionists such as Stimson, Roosevelt made no immediate effort to follow up his advantage. Caution and indecision characterized Roosevelt's policy of aid to Britain short of war after Lend-Lease. The apparent explanation for Roosevelt's drift and vacillation was his conviction that American opinion, while it favored Lend-Lease in principle, was not prepared to support the risk of convoying supplies to Britain. So, instead of sanctioning navy convoys of lend-lease supplies, Roosevelt would only accept an extension of patrols into the mid-Atlantic. American naval ships were not to fire at German submarines, but only to warn the British of their presence. Quietly Roosevelt did approve clandestine high level "American-British Conversations" between military experts, which led to the ABC-1 contingency plan to be followed in the event the United States entered the war. (Its gist was that the primary effort of the Allies should be the defeat of Germany, while a defensive strategy should be followed against Japan.) Simultaneously Roosevelt signed an executive agreement with the Danish Embassy which placed Greenland, a Danish possession, under American control. The action was justified as a measure to defend the western hemisphere from Hitler.

Hitler's immediate interest was not the Americas, but the Balkans. In April the Nazis seized Greece, driving the British to Crete, which had to be evacuated two months later. In the Mediterranean, General Erwin Rommel drove the British back into Egypt. Almost as embarrassing to the British was the dramatic voyage of the German battleship *Bismarck*, accompanied by the cruiser *Prinz Eugen*, into the Atlantic. When the cruiser *Hood* and the battleship *Prince of Wales* tried to intercept the raiders, Britain suffered an embarrassing defeat. Both German ships scored direct hits on the *Hood*, which blew up with the loss of all but 3 of a crew of 1,400 men. On May 29 the British managed to sink the *Bismarck*, but the *Prinz Eugen* took refuge at Brest. To the chagrin of British admirals, the ship escaped on February 11, 1942, by sailing in broad daylight up the English Channel to Norway. (In the summer of 1946 the *Prinz Eugen*, having survived the war, became one of the target ships for the Bikini atomic bomb tests).

Two days before the sinking of the *Bismarck*, Roosevelt—just recovered from a persistent cold—delivered, for Pan American Day, a ringing speech warning of the menace posed by Hitler to the western hemisphere. He pledged to deliver crucial supplies to Britain, stating, "it can be done; it must be done; and it will be done." He concluded by dramatically proclaiming that "an unlimited national emergency exists and requires the strengthening of our defense to the extreme limit of our national power and authority."[24] But Roosevelt's tough talk was not followed with tough action. He told a press conference he was not contemplating convoying of lend-lease supplies and had no intention of issuing an executive order implementing a national emergency. The sinking by a German submarine of the American freighter *Robin Moor* in the South Atlantic on May 21 could have produced a crisis. The freighter, carrying general cargo from Copenhagen to Cape Town, was torpedoed after the submarine captain ordered the crew into lifeboats hundreds of miles from land. But no lives were lost and Washington did not learn of the incident until June 11. Roosevelt, by executive order, retaliated by seizing Germany and Italian assets, and for good measure he impounded Soviet assets as well, since Stalin seem a virtual ally of Hitler.

That latter seizure was soon reversed, for on June 22, 1941, Hitler surprised the world by invading Russia—picking the same day Napoleon had chosen to attack Russia in 1812. Hitler's decision proved the turning point of World War II, since Hitler's legions were eventually consumed by Russia's vastness and harsh climate. Unexpectedly Britain received a new ally, while Roosevelt's response was to release $40 million in frozen Russian funds and to send Harry Hopkins to Moscow to assess the Russians' chances of survival. Cautiously Roosevelt had launched what his critics later called the "Be Good to Russia" policy. Caution also characterized Roosevelt's decision (July 7, 1941) to send 4,000 United States marines to Iceland to replace 20,000 British troops. The action was justified as necessary for the defense of Atlantic sea lanes and the protection of Greenland. In fact Roosevelt was hard pressed to locate even 4,000 surplus troops since the Selective Service Act restricted draftees to service for one year within the western hemisphere only. On the advice of Stimson, Knox, and Army Chief of Staff George C. Marshall, Roosevelt decided to ask Congress to extend the period of service to cover the national emergency and to remove the restriction to the western hemisphere. After a two-week debate, Roosevelt won only a partial victory when the Senate (August 7) approved an eighteen-month extension of service, but retained the western hemisphere restriction. On August 12 the House concurred by the slimmest of margins, 203 to 202.

In the meantime Roosevelt managed to escape from the heat and frustration of Washington for what was disguised as a fishing trip aboard the yacht *Potomac*. Departing from New London, Connecticut, Roosevelt soon transferred to the heavy cruiser *Augusta* to meet Winston Churchill, who arrived at Placentia Bay, Newfoundland, aboard the battleship *Prince of Wales*. From August 9 to 12, the two leaders, as well as such top military and diplomatic personnel as Army Chief of Staff George C. Marshall and Undersecretary of State Sumner Welles, discussed a range of subjects, including how to assist the Soviet Union and how to respond to Japanese aggression in Southeast Asia. Churchill, who underestimated Japan even more seriously than American leaders did, favored sending Japan a formal note of warning, but Roosevelt preferred the milder course of continuing diplomatic discussions at Washington through the State Department and the Japanese Embassy. Socializing and male bonding occupied much of the leaders' time. Roosevelt forgave Churchill for having forgotten their first meeting in 1918 when Roosevelt had been merely the assistant secretary of the navy. For Roosevelt one of the highlights was a moving ecumenical church service held aboard Churchill's flagship. Anglican and Episcopal clergymen presided, and the service concluded with hymn-singing by British sailors—many of whom, including their captain, later perished when the *Prince of Wales* was sunk by Japanese aircraft on December 10, 1941.

As had been the case during his meeting in 1939 with George VI, the president engaged in tough anti-Nazi talk. On his return to London, Churchill told the cabinet: "The President had said he would wage war, but not declare it, and that he would become more and more provocative. If the Germans did not like it they could attack American forces."[25] From the secluded retreat of Newfoundland ("Riviera" was the code name of the meeting) Roosevelt had approved in principle navy convoys of British and neutral ships from Newfoundland to the vicinity of Iceland. Churchill's impression was that it was Roosevelt's intention to create an incident that would justify American entry into the war.

The incident that Roosevelt chose to exploit was the indecisive clash between the destroyer *Greer* and a German submarine on September 4. According to Roosevelt's version, presented a week later to a national radio audience, "the German submarine fired first upon this American destroyer without warning, and with deliberate design to sink her." Roosevelt called the submarine's action "piracy" and part of Hitler's design "toward creating a permanent world system based on force, on terror, and on murder." He termed Nazi submarines "rattlesnakes of the Atlantic" and proclaimed, "The time for active defense is now."[26] Finally he announced that the Navy would provide convoy protection for lend-lease supplies between North America and Iceland.

Roosevelt's public explanation left out several key elements of the *Greer* drama. He failed to mention that the *Greer* and a British patrol plane had shadowed the German submarine for hours before the submarine fired two torpedoes that missed their target. The *Greer*, which may well have been mistaken by the submarine for a British destroyer, responded with depth charges with unknown effect. Roosevelt's *Greer* speech, with its selective use of facts, was not an inadvertent case of his failing to tell the whole truth and nothing but the truth; rather it was a deliberate distortion.

Now that American ships were patrolling the Atlantic, Roosevelt found that the Neutrality Act was a major inconvenience because, as he told Churchill, the act was "crippling our means of helping you." His objective was to eliminate Section VI of the Neutrality Act, which forbade the arming of American ships. Again, Roosevelt used clashes between American destroyers and German submarines to get his way. On October 17 the destroyer *Kearny* was torpedoed while escorting a British convoy 400 miles south of Iceland. The ship managed to limp into port with the loss of eleven dead. On October 27 (Navy Day) Roosevelt delivered a stirring address saying that America did not intend to ignore the attack on the *Kearny*. "Our determination not to take it lying down," he stated, "has been expressed in the order to the American Navy to shoot on sight. These orders stand."[27] The president's most questionable tactic in his fight to revise the Neutrality Act was his announcement that he possessed a secret (and highly dubious)

Nazi map to divide South America and part of Central America into five vassal states. Another secret Nazi document planned the abolition of all existing religions: *Mein Kampf* would replace the Bible, and in place of the Christian cross the Nazis would substitute the swastika and the naked sword. Even so it was not until after the sinking of the destroyer *Reuben James*, with the loss of 115 sailors, that the Senate narrowly (50 to 37) supported neutrality revision. The favorable vote in the House was even closer (212 to 194).

Aid to Britain short of war became Roosevelt's method for outflanking the 1937 Neutrality Act, which he genuinely regretted having signed, since the act came back to frustrate him. Alternating between forthrightness, charm, and deviousness, Roosevelt plunged ahead: orchestrating the British royal visit, signing the destroyers deal, running for a third term, abolishing the mandatory arms embargo, conceiving the Lend-Lease Act, occupying Greenland and Iceland, and then convoying lend-lease supplies. Acting as his own secretary of state, Roosevelt felt his way on a day-to-day basis. Roosevelt's plan, to the extent he had one, was to continue convoying, to extend lend-lease aid to the Soviet Union, and to await further developments—which it was assumed would be in the North Atlantic or on the mainland of Asia.

NOTES

1. Robert A. Divine, *The Illusion of Neutrality* (Chicago, 1962), 288.

2. James MacGregor Burns, *Roosevelt: The Lion and the Fox* (New York, 1956), 318–19.

3. Divine, *Illusion of Neutrality*, 289–90.

4. Wayne S. Cole, *Roosevelt and the Isolationists, 1932–1945* (Lincoln, 1983), 323–24.

5. Cordell Hull, *The Memoirs of Cordell Hull* (New York, 1948), Vol. 1, 693.

6. Divine, *Illusion of Neutrality*, 331.

7. Benjamin D. Rhodes, "The Origins of Finnish-American Friendship, 1919–1941," *Mid-America* 54 (January 1972), 3–19.

8. William L. Langer and S. Everett Gleason, *The Challenge to Isolation: The World Crisis of 1937–1940* (New York, 1952), 374.

9. Langer and Gleason, *Challenge to Isolation*, 515–17.

10. Langer and Gleason, *Challenge to Isolation*, 672.

11. Langer and Gleason, *Challenge to Isolation*, 768.

12. Langer and Gleason, *Challenge to Isolation*, 669.

13. Robert E. Sherwood, *Roosevelt and Hopkins: An Intimate History* (New York, 1948), 201.

14. David Reynolds, *Lord Lothian and Anglo-American Relations, 1939–1940* (Philadelphia, 1983), 48–49.

15. William L. Langer and S. Everett Gleason, *The Undeclared War, 1940–1941* (New York, 1953), 232–33.

16. Sherwood, *Roosevelt and Hopkins*, 224.

17. Langer and Gleason, *Undeclared War*, 238–39.

18. Sherwood, *Roosevelt and Hopkins*, 226.

19. Robert Dallek, *Franklin D. Roosevelt and American Foreign Policy, 1932–1945* (New York, 1979), 258.

20. Dallek, *Franklin D. Roosevelt and American Foreign Policy*, 259.

21. Warren F. Kimball, *The Most Unsordid Act: Lend-Lease, 1939–1941* (Baltimore, 1969), 154.

22. Cole, *Roosevelt and the Isolationists*, 418.

23. Hull, *Memoirs*, Vol. 2, 925.

24. Dallek, *Franklin D. Roosevelt and American Foreign Policy*, 266.

25. Reynolds, *The Creation of the Anglo-American Alliance, 1937–1941* (Chapel Hill, 1981), 214–15.

26. Langer and Gleason, *Undeclared War*, 743–46.

27. Langer and Gleason, *Undeclared War*, 757.

CHAPTER 11

Japan and the United States Miscalculate

The tragedy that began with the Pearl Harbor attack and culminated in Japan's destruction and unconditional surrender in August 1945, had a long historical genesis. In a sense the United States and Japan had been on a long-term collision course since the McKinley administration when the United States embarked on a vaguely defined policy of protecting China from foreign dismemberment while simultaneously seeking equal commercial opportunity. Despite the ambiguity of the Open Door Policy, subsequent presidents, especially Wilson, Harding, and Hoover, felt an obligation to defend China's rights as a neutral. Under Wilson the United States objected to Japan's notorious Twenty-one Demands in 1915 and to Japan's acquisition of Shantung at the Peace Conference; Harding's administration contributed the Nine Power Treaty during the Washington Conference; and Hoover condemned Japan's forcible annexation of Manchuria. Against the objections of Raymond Moley, Roosevelt embraced the legal/moralistic Far Eastern policy of his predecessors. Given that tradition it was inconceivable that Roosevelt could have ignored the China incident and the sinking of the *Panay*.

If, as the Far Eastern crisis deepened, American policy was often marked by inflexibility and moral superiority, Japan's unstable and frequently changing government was responsible for a naval race in the Pacific; for fostering hateful attitudes of racial superiority toward Asians, Europeans, and Americans; and for yielding to a fierce warrior mentality by recklessly starting a conflict against an opponent possessing twice its population and nine times its industrial output. Yosuke Matsuoka, Japan's foreign minister, no doubt had a point when he said the western powers taught Japan the game of stud poker but, having won all the chips, pronounced the game immoral and took up contract bridge instead. However, after Prince Fumimaro Konoye, in the winter of December 1938, announced to nationwide acclaim the goal of the Greater East Asia Co-Prosperity Sphere, the Roosevelt administration—given the open door tradition followed since McKinley—had little choice but to offer strenuous opposition. Theoretically, of course, hostilities could have been averted had Japan abandoned the new order, but such a course of action was never even remotely considered since, according to Japanese logic, retreat would have constituted a humiliating loss of face. By the same token, war presumably could have been averted had Roosevelt and Hull acquiesced in the Greater East Asia Co-Prosperity Sphere. But any accommodation on Japan's terms was just as impossible since, from America's way of thinking, such a course would have amounted to a crushing moral defeat. That diplomacy failed to avert the conflict is hardly surprising when it is considered that both sides were locked into positions they would not and could not change.

Miscalculation by both sides was the order of the day: American civilian leaders, with few exceptions, erroneously believed economic sanctions would cause Japan to cease and desist, and the United States Navy seriously underestimated the skill and daring of their Japanese counterparts. That Japan, with a million men bogged down in China, would dare go to war with the United States was a proposition not worthy of serious consideration. Likewise Japanese leaders were deluded in thinking the United States would quickly capitulate and sue for peace. Japan's war hawks also failed to take into account that in a protracted conflict the odds decisively favored the United States. Once the United States military recovered from its amateurish and embarrassing performance at the outset of the conflict, Japan found itself badly overextended and confronted with overwhelming numbers of superior ships, long-range bombers, fighter aircraft, and heavy artillery, manned by sailors, aviators, soldiers, and marines who fought with a ferocity that belied the Japanese propaganda image of westerners as effeminate and cowardly.

In the two years prior to Pearl Harbor, American policymakers were preoccupied above all with the European crisis. Neither Roosevelt nor Hull claimed any particular expertise about the Far East. Typically Roosevelt, who was often hazy about policy details, focused on the big picture and sought to blend the conflicting views of subordinates into a consensus. Hull's role in the Far Eastern crisis was consistently one of caution; he retreated to enunciating basic moral principles while discreetly opposing a tough stand toward Japan. Often portrayed as a weak handwringer, Hull's timidity appears less open to criticism when viewed in the context of the disastrous reverses suffered by the United States and its allies in the opening months of the war in the Pacific. In retrospect, Hull had a point when he told of the unarmed Tennesseean who unwisely confronted a highwayman. "I leave it you," he told his listeners, "how that conversation ended."[1] Or, reverting to his occasional role of a Tennessee frontiersman, Hull summed up the Axis threat to a weak America by quoting a prophetic, if crude, bit of backwoods folklore: "When you're in a pissin' contest with a skunk, make sure you got plenty of piss."[2]

A harder line toward Japan was advocated by the chief of the State Department's Far Eastern Division, Stanley K. Hornbeck. A Colorado native with a Ph.D. from the University of Wisconsin, where he studied under the Far Eastern specialist Paul Reinsch, Hornbeck was appalled by Japan's wanton aggression in China. His anger was intensified by Japan's 1938 fall offensive in the vicinity of Hong Kong and by the capture of Canton and Hankow. The continued Japanese advance seemed to demonstrate that China's "lure in deep" strategy was not working. Also shocking was the proclamation in November by Prime Minister Prince Konoye of a New Order in Asia. Hornbeck's response was to advocate the adoption of a "diplomatic war plan" to halt Japanese aggression; this would take the form of assistance to China, economic sanctions against Japan (including the abrogation of the 1911 United States–Japanese commercial treaty), trade embargoes, and the threat of naval force to show Japan that "we mean business."[3]

Furthermore, Hornbeck supported a complicated but imaginative plan for aiding nationalist China that was being promoted by Secretary of the Treasury Henry Morgenthau, Jr. Known as the tung oil project, the Morgenthau proposal suggested that the Export-Import Bank loan China $25 million to be used for completing the 650-mile road then under construction from Rangoon, Burma to the nationalist capital of Chungking. The loan could also be used for purchasing trucks, spare parts, and gasoline. Exports to the United States of tung oil, a component of paint and varnish, would repay the loan. Morgenthau appealed to Roosevelt to endorse the project, despite Hull's reservations, because, he wrote the president, "It is the future peace and present honor of the United States that are in question. It is the future of democracy, the future of civilization that are at stake."[4] Hull emphatically disagreed. His view was that the tung oil project would do little to aid China, which had sufficient resources to keep fighting for at least a year. The most important objection, from Hull's point of view, was that the loan would be regarded by Japan not as a mere commercial transaction, but as a hostile act that would invite Japanese retaliation. Although he was reluctant to see Japan occupy China, Hull favored delay in launching a get tough policy. Provoking Japan, Hull advised Roosevelt, "would result in a serious possibility of this country being ultimately drawn into the war."[5]

This time Hull was the loser in the bureaucratic skirmishing. Morgenthau and Hornbeck, joined by Sumner Welles, took advantage of Hull's attendance at the Lima conference to press their views on the White House. On his return to Washington from Warm Springs, Georgia, on December 14, Roosevelt gave his approval. Thereupon the Export-Import Bank extended China a $25 million credit to be repaid with proceeds from tung oil sales.

Cleverly Morgenthau anticipated and outmaneuvered Senator Arthur Vandenberg by pointing out to the Michigan isolationist that his state stood to profit from the transaction. Subsequently 1,300 American trucks made in Michigan were delivered to Burma without protest from Vandenberg. Probably Hull was not too disappointed by Roosevelt's approval of the tung oil project since the amount of the credit ($25 million) was small even for 1938. However, on the basis of the tung oil project, China was able to arrange another $75 million in international credits. The loan raised Chinese morale, sent a small signal to Japan, and set a precedent for a tougher American Far Eastern policy. But for the time being the hardliners in the administration failed to get the comprehensive program of sanctions they sought against Japan.

In the interim the administration returned to Hull's policy of avoiding provocation. An example was Hull's mild reaction when Japan occupied Hainan Island off the coast of French Indo-China in February. The acquisition made a convenient staging area for Japanese military adventures in the region. Again Hull filed a mild, legalistic protest when Japan occupied the Spratly Islands adjacent to the Philippines. A further manifestation of the conciliatory mood was Roosevelt's decision in March 1939 to extend a symbolic olive branch to Japan through returning the ashes of former ambassador Hiroshi Saito aboard the cruiser *Astoria*. The popular, peripatetic Saito had been forced to resign in October due to the lung cancer that caused his death in February. Joseph Ballantine, assistant chief of the Far Eastern Division, conceived the idea of returning Saito's ashes in the hope that the gesture would have a moderating effect on Japanese policy. Hornbeck, now promoted to the post of political adviser to Hull, took a neutral position, and Roosevelt, who loved naval displays, gave his blessing to the month-long journey.

When the *Astoria* entered Tokyo Bay on April 17 much of the initial American enthusiasm for the visit had cooled. Two days earlier, Roosevelt, reversing a decision made in June 1938, had ordered a redeployment of American ships from the Atlantic to the Pacific. The action was taken at the urging of Britain, which was preoccupied with the Czechoslovakian crisis and unable to meet its naval commitments to the defense of Southeast Asia. Both Hornbeck and Ambassador to Japan Joseph Grew tried to tone down any suggestion that the visit of the *Astoria* implied American approval of Japan's foreign policy. Hornbeck, dropping his veil of neutrality, forbade the *Astoria* from accepting any unusual gifts or entertainments and discouraged any thought of a return goodwill visit to the United States by former prime minister Konoye. Grew, normally sympathetic to Japan, convinced officials to cancel a planned patriotic rally at a Tokyo soccer stadium and to move a scaled down demonstration to a college auditorium instead. To the casual observer the transfer of Saito's ashes went without a hitch. Marine pallbearers and a navy honor guard of 120 men contributed to the pageantry of Saito's state funeral. Captain William Kelly Turner, nicknamed "Turn-to-Turner" by his crew, received an audience with the emperor, and the *Astoria's* sailors were given a tour of Tokyo and the vicinity. The visit concluded with a three-hour farewell banquet served by the *Astoria's* crew to a blue ribbon assemblage of guests. Unnoticed by the public, Turner had installed a camera with a powerful telephoto lens atop a mast to photograph the shipyard where Japan's super battleships were secretly under construction. As the *Astoria* departed, the strategy miscarried when two coal-burning tugboats appeared and laid down a smoke screen, obscuring the photographic target. The sentimental journey of the *Astoria*, while it did no particular harm, failed to allay American suspicions of Japan's motives and integrity.[6]

That was made clear when Prime Minister Hiranuma, who held office from January to August 1939, offered a poorly thought out peace plan in May to Eugene Dooman, who was in charge of the Tokyo embassy while Grew was en route to the United States. The prime minister's suggestion was to call an international conference to be attended by the United States and the major European and Asian powers. As Hiranuma visualized it, such a meeting would lead to concessions in the form of payments from the "have" to the "have not" nations. Hull gave the half-baked overture short shrift as he suspected the prime minister was actually thinking less of peace than avoiding the outbreak of war over the Czech crisis while the China incident remained unresolved. For Japan to advocate peace while simultaneously bombing Chungking and driving the British from Tientsin was an incongruous proposition. Hull's response was to quietly pigeonhole the peace overture by mailing rather than telegraphing a rejection letter to Tokyo.

As war clouds gathered over Europe in the summer of 1939, the idea of economic sanctions against Japan, already proposed by Hornbeck, received serious discussion for the first time among members of Congress and the public at large. The appeal of sanctions was largely based upon the popular assumption that an embargo of war materials would punish Japan while avoiding hostilities. For over a year American armament manufacturers had complied with a moral embargo on selling bombs, ammunition, and torpedoes to Japan. However, the moral ban did not apply to American oil or scrap iron sold to Japan and used against China. Former secretary of state Henry L. Stimson, then a private citizen, organized the highly effective American Committee for Non-Participation in Japanese Aggression, which aimed to prevent the sale to Japan of raw materials that were likely to be used against Japan's victims. Subsequently numerous bills requiring trade sanctions were introduced by members of Congress including Senator Pittman. Hull, with good reason, opposed a legislative embargo because he feared such an action would backfire and provoke Japan into hostilities. A solution appeared in the form of a resolution introduced by Senator Vandenberg, which proposed to terminate, after six months' notice, the United States-Japanese Commercial Treaty of 1911. Hull decided to accept the Vandenberg resolution to gain time and to avoid the spectacle of an acrimonious Senate debate. Roosevelt concurred and on July 26, 1939, the administration announced its intention to terminate the treaty. Although the action was only symbolic, the cancellation of the commercial treaty served as a warning to Japan and foreshadowed the imposition of tougher sanctions a year later.

What was Roosevelt's position on sanctions? Privately the president subscribed to the popular delusion that trade embargoes would deter further Japanese expansion. Despite the lack of even a shred of evidence that sanctions had ever worked in the past, the conventional wisdom of the day received support not only from Roosevelt but from such top administration officials as Hornbeck, Morgenthau, Interior Secretary Harold Ickes, and former secretary of state Henry L. Stimson. When Ambassador to Japan Joseph Grew warned Roosevelt that sanctions might goad Japan into seizing the Dutch East Indies, the president shocked the ambassador by offhandedly remarking, "Then we could easily intercept her fleet."[7] However, Roosevelt's tough talk was not matched by tough action. In September Roosevelt accepted a mild Treasury recommendation to restrict, through a voluntary appeal to American businessmen, the export of eleven critical raw materials including rubber, tin, and quinine. Presumably Roosevelt could have asked Congress for mandatory authority to ban the sale of crucial raw materials to Japan except that Congress was meeting in special session debating—successfully from Roosevelt's perspective—the repeal of the mandatory arms embargo.

The leading opponent of economic sanctions was Ambassador Grew. A product of Boston society, prestigious schools (Groton and Harvard), and a veteran of the foreign service, Grew was a believer in the power of diplomacy. That was a strength in that he, practically alone (except for Hull), saw that Japan was likely to respond to an American get tough policy with drastic action. Grew's weakness was that he ardently believed an accommodation was possible in which Japan would accept some limitation of the Greater East Asia Co-Prosperity Sphere. Grew made a commendable effort to understand Japan's needs and psychology, but he was too optimistic. After lengthy conversations with Japan's foreign minister, Admiral Kichisaburo Nomura (who became ambassador to the United States in 1941 and held months of lengthy, fruitless talks with Hull), Grew asked Washington to accept an opening of the Yangtze River to American commerce as far upstream as Nanking in return for the negotiation of a new commercial treaty. Neither Roosevelt, Hull, nor Hornbeck was impressed as they believed the concession offered by Nomura was insignificant. Thus in

January 1940, the commercial treaty expired, although there was no consensus in Washington as to what should be the next step. Trade with Japan was not affected because the State Department, on a technicality, ruled it was not legally necessary to impose high Hawley-Smoot Tariff duties. Hull, who wanted to keep Japan guessing and to continue trade without sanctions, prevailed for the time being. Roosevelt, in approving Hull's policy, made it clear that his forbearance on sanctions was "temporary" and that he reserved the right to change his mind if no resolution of disputes with Japan was forthcoming.[8]

Until the spring of 1940 Hull's cautious policy of continuing trade with Japan while threatening sanctions seemed to be working. A case could be made that the stalemate in China was bleeding Japan white and that soon Japan would see the light of reason. A mildly encouraging development was the formation in mid-January of the second new Japanese government in six months under Admiral Mitsumasa Yonai, an opponent of signing an alliance with the Axis powers. Grew optimistically recorded: "A new and healthy attitude and point of view are gradually emerging which may be capable of achieving a great deal, if not rebuffed by us."[9] Hope that the Yonai government would alter Japanese foreign policy quickly faded when Tokyo established a puppet government at Nanking and expanded attacks against Chungking. Roosevelt's mild response was to approve another small loan of $20 million to Chiang Kai-shek through the Export-Import Bank.

What totally altered the Far Eastern scene was an event in Europe that neither Tokyo nor Washington had anticipated: the devastating success of the Nazi *blitzkrieg*. Hitler's lightning conquest of Denmark, Norway, Holland, Belgium, and France wrecked not only the European balance of power but the Asian balance of power as well. Suddenly, with Europe in turmoil, Japan found itself in a position to exploit the Far Eastern power vacuum and achieve the Greater East Asia Co-Prosperity Sphere. The Yonai government promptly demanded assurances from the Dutch authorities that Japan would receive access to all the aluminum produced by the Dutch East Indies and one million metric tons of oil—double what Japan had previously imported. French Indo-China, now under the control of a collaborationist regime at Vichy, France, was another obvious target. Japan demanded the right to station military observers in the Hanoi area to make sure that rail shipments to Chungking were halted. The French, who were well aware that Japan would use force if they refused, complied on June 20. Next, Japan demanded that the British, who were still in shock from the defeat of their expeditionary force in France and fearful of an imminent Nazi invasion of the British Isles, close the Burma road. Under duress London in early July agreed to a closure of three months. With Chiang Kai-shek isolated, the achievement of the new order in Asia seemed in sight. As expressed by Foreign Minister Hachiro Arita, the uniting of the nations of East Asia and the South Seas "in a single sphere . . . is a natural conclusion." Under the benevolent influence of Japan "the peoples within that region will secure their co-existence and co-prosperity as well as the stability of their sphere."[10] Only two major Far Eastern powers remained after the fall of France. More than ever the national interests of the United States and Japan clashed.

Still, the immediate focus of Washington remained on Europe first. Now that France was defeated, Roosevelt was understandably concerned about the fates of the British and French empires as well as the British and French fleets. Just before the Nazis launched their *blitzkrieg*, the Pacific fleet sailed from San Diego to conduct maneuvers near the Hawaiian Islands. Roosevelt, who loved naval displays as much as his uncle Theodore Roosevelt had, then committed a serious error in judgment by ordering the fleet, against the wishes of the navy, to remain at Pearl Harbor. Theoretically the presence of the fleet in the middle of the Pacific would restrain further Japanese expansion; in reality the American ships became a tempting target. Admiral James O. Richardson, the commander of the Pacific fleet, plausibly argued that Pearl Harbor was not equipped to properly service the fleet. Returning the fleet to San Diego, its permanent base, would be the most effective way to maintain the navy in battle-ready condition and deter Japan, he argued. Richardson's objection to the Pearl Harbor move, and to an amateurish Roosevelt contingency plan for blockading the Japanese fleet in the event of an assault on Burma, led to his being relieved of his command half way through his tour of duty.

In Congress the response to the fall of France and the continued crisis in the Pacific was the approval of a massive rearmament program. A two-ocean navy was authorized that would leave Japan with only fifty percent of American naval strength by 1943 and only thirty percent by 1944. Specifically Congress approved building 6 *Iowa*-class battleships of 45,000 tons, 5 *Montana*-class super battleships of 58,000 tons (which, on second thought, were not constructed), 6 *Alaska*-class heavy cruisers of 27,000 tons, 11 *Essex*-class aircraft carriers of 27,000 tons, 40 light cruisers, 115 destroyers, and 67 submarines. The realization that the American naval program would overwhelm Japan produced a sense of desperation among Japanese admirals. By 1941 or 1942 Japan expected to complete its own construction program, which would include new heavy cruisers, two modern aircraft carriers, and the two formidable *Yamato*-class battleships. The cold statistics suggested that Japan stood a better chance of winning an early naval war with the United States rather than waiting until the American construction program became operational. Anticipating the completion of Japan's naval program in the spring of 1941, Admiral Kondo Nobutake told a September 14, 1940, conference of government and military leaders: "When that is done, we have prospects of achieving victory, if we fight an early, decisive battle." However, as time went on the advantage would shift decisively to the United States, creating a naval gap that Japan could not hope to overtake. Thus, in the view of the Japanese navy, "If we go to war, today would be best." That opinion was echoed by the navy minister who contended, "At present we have adequate chances of victory if we meet the Americans in an early decisive battle."[11]

The decision of the Roosevelt administration to move beyond mere warnings to Japan to the first economic sanctions came in July. Neither Roosevelt (who was about to accept the Democratic nomination for a third term) nor Hull (who was occupied with the Havana Conference) initiated the change in policy. Instead, the decision to get tougher came as the result of congressional pressure, public opinion, and agitation by cabinet members Morgenthau, Stimson, and Ickes. British Ambassador Lord Lothian also pushed for sanctions, noting that the United States was shipping aviation gasoline to the nation that had intimidated Britain into closing the Burma Road. The National Defense Act, signed by Roosevelt on July 2, contained a provision that gave administration hardliners an opening. At the suggestion of the War Department, Section VI of the bill gave the president the power to "prohibit or curtail" the export of military equipment, munitions, and raw materials judged necessary for America's national defense. Thus the existing moral embargo on selling military supplies to Japan was replaced by legislation that enabled the executive, if he so desired, to impose far reaching sanctions. Yet the mild executive order signed by Roosevelt on July 2, while it restricted the sale of arms, ammunition, aluminum, and magnesium, did not mention exports to Japan of scrap iron or oil, the items most necessary to Japan's military operations.

The passage of the National Defense Act produced a strenuous tug-of-war within the administration. The debate covered familiar ground, and the positions of the participants were well rehearsed. On one side stood Morgenthau, Stimson, and Ickes, who passionately believed the time had arrived to deter Japanese aggression through an embargo of strategic materials. Their logic seemed unassailable: without oil, scrap iron, and aviation gasoline, Japan's war machine would grind to a halt. In Morgenthau's view comprehensive economic sanctions "might give us peace in three to six months."[12] On the other side, Hull continued to oppose sanctions as being unlikely to alter Japanese policy. What was more probable, he thought, was that sanctions would provoke the untrustworthy Japanese into seizing the East Indies to fuel their expansion. Furthermore, Hull wanted no confrontation with Japan until the European war scene became more favorable and the United States' rearmament effort became effective. Hull's critics took advantage of his departure for Havana to present a comprehensive embargo proposal to Roosevelt: the Dutch would dynamite their oil fields in the East Indies, the British would bomb Nazi synthetic oil plants, Venezuela and Colombia would guarantee Britain adequate supplies of oil, and the United States would then halt all oil exports for reasons of national defense. Morgenthau, the author of the plan, conceived it before word arrived that the Yonai government had fallen and had been replaced by a more militant and pro-Axis cabinet headed by former prime minister Prince Konoye with the aggressive Yosuke Matsuoka as foreign minister and General Hideki Tojo as war minister. At first glance Roosevelt liked the idea of doing something instead of waiting passively for the knock of destiny. When the subject turned to the effect of an oil embargo on the Far East, Welles advanced Hull's arguments and stressed that a war in the Pacific might soon follow the cutoff of oil sales to Japan. Probably remembering that the Democratic platform opposed involvement in foreign wars except in case of attack, Roosevelt ended the discussion without making a decision.

Roosevelt had a reputation, which was frequently exaggerated, of agreeing with the last person to speak with him. If that was not exactly what happened on this occasion, the president's leadership on the question of an oil embargo was marked by ambiguity. The first to approach Roosevelt were Morgenthau and Stimson, who criticized Welles's position, which they characterized as weak and immoral appeasement. According to Morgenthau, Welles had delivered a "beautiful Chamberlain talk" and had, in effect, promised that Japan would behave itself and "kiss our big toe."[13] While Roosevelt was at Hyde Park, Morgenthau presented him with the draft of a presidential proclamation banning the export of petroleum and all grades of scrap iron. Stimson's contribution was to forward to the president a military report from California saying that the Japanese were placing so many orders for the purchase of high-grade aviation gasoline that soon insufficient supplies would be left for American aviators. On July 22, without consulting the State Department, Roosevelt signed the document.

When Welles, by telephone, protested, Roosevelt promptly backtracked and agreed to revise the embargo proclamation. An inconclusive cabinet discussion on July 26 ended with Roosevelt telling Welles and Morgenthau to "go off in a corner" and reach a consensus.[14] As a result Morgenthau made a strategic decision to yield, and the embargo order was rewritten to ban only the sale of aviation gasoline and lubricants and number one grade scrap iron. By sending a modest signal to Japan, Roosevelt had achieved a balance between competing administration factions, and he had avoided an action that could have been criticized as a violation of the Democratic platform by his opponent in the presidential election. The downside to the limited embargo was that it had no observable deterrent value. Much of the ineffectiveness of the sanctions was attributable to a loophole in the embargo order. Only the sale of high octane gasoline was forbidden, but Japan was not blocked from purchasing medium-octane fuels, which were just as suitable for Japanese planes. The iron determination of Japan's "moderate" government to establish a new order in Asia, in defiance of sanctions, was not well understood by Washington hardliners. With stockpiles of scrap iron and petroleum in excess of a year's supply, Japan could afford to ignore sanctions, at least over the short run.

In terms of vacillation and a tendency to agree with the most recent visitor, Roosevelt could not hold a candle to Prince Konoye. During his previous stint as prime minister the Japanese Army had invaded China, and Konoye's attitude had been typically ambiguous. That characteristic reappeared again as the dominant theme of his second term in office (July 1940–October 1941). A typically vague and contradictory policy paper adopted by the new government on July 26 endorsed the expansionist goals of the Greater East Asia Co-Prosperity Sphere in Indo-China and the Dutch East Indies, and called for a "firm attitude" toward the United States but an avoidance of hostilities. A further goal was to achieve an alliance with Germany and Italy. Thus Ambassador Grew was unusually perceptive when he recorded in his diary: "At first sight the Konoye Government gives every indication of going hell-bent toward the Axis and the establishment of a New Order in East Asia, and of riding rough-shod over the rights and interest, and the principles and policies, of the United States and Great Britain."[15]

The accuracy of Grew's analysis was soon borne out as the Konoye government pressured the Dutch and the Vichy government of France for new concessions. Under duress the French capitulated to an ultimatum delivered by Matsuoka and agreed to permit Japan to occupy bases in Tonkin province in northern Indo-China. Vichy was forced to recognize "the preponderant interests of Japan in the Far East in the economic as well as the political domain."[16] Theoretically Vichy still retained sovereignty over the region. At the same time Japan notified the Dutch of its intention to send a mission of high ranking officials to the East Indies to discuss political and economic relations, which meant guaranteeing that Japan could purchase large quantities of oil. For the time being Hull, returned from Havana, held out against retaliating through a further economic tightening. Roosevelt had just concluded the destroyer deal with Britain and was campaigning for a third term on promises of noninvolvement in foreign wars. From Hull's viewpoint imposing tough sanctions while the outcome of the battle of Britain and the result of the election were unknown would be reckless both from the perspective of domestic politics and foreign policy. Hull was also worried that Japan might respond against tougher sanctions on oil by attacking Singapore or the East Indies, bypassing the Philippines and leaving the administration on the horns of a dilemma.

None of the American policy makers realized that they were about to receive a secret weapon in the game of diplomatic poker that would enable them to see the cards of their Japanese diplomatic counterparts. Colonel William F. Friedman of the Army Signal Corps had succeeded in breaking Japan's Purple Code enabling Washington to eavesdrop on communications between Tokyo and Japanese diplomats. The top secret system of intercepting, decoding, and translating Japanese radio messages was appropriately code named "Magic." The ungentlemanly Roosevelt administration, reversing Stimson's policy when he served under Hoover as secretary of state, had decided that there was nothing immoral about reading the mail of others.

Even before the completion of the election campaign, Roosevelt decided to tighten the economic screws on shipments of scrap iron to Japan. The president's thinking was heavily influenced by Ambassador Grew's "green light" message of September 12 in which he reversed his opposition to sanctions. The status quo in the Pacific, Grew advised, could no longer be maintained by piling up paper protests. Instead, without defining the term, he suggested a "show of force."[17] Over the next week Grew reported that Japan intended to sign some form of alliance with Germany and Italy. At the same time Washington learned that Japan had increased its demands for Dutch oil and that Japan was about to take over northern Indo-China. On September 25 the White House announced that the administration had expanded economic sanctions against Japan to include all grades of scrap iron and steel. Two days later Japan signed the Tripartite Pact with Germany and Italy.

The treaty, the work of Matsuoka, was exceptionally vague. It merely stated that Japan recognized the leadership of Germany and Italy in establishing a new order in Europe, while Germany and Italy reciprocated in recognizing Japan's new order in Asia. The definition of the term "new order" was left up in the air. The key provision, from the American point of view, was Article III in which the signatories agreed to assist each other if either was "attacked by a power at present not involved in the European War or in the Sino-Japanese Conflict." It did not require much imagination to perceive which nation the Axis powers had in mind. Hull tried to put the best possible face upon the bad news by contending the alliance did not alter what had been an existing fact for years. One unforeseen advantage that inadvertently came from the pact was that it led Germany and Italy to declare war upon the United States after Pearl Harbor. On December 8, 1941, Roosevelt only requested a declaration of war against Japan. Had Germany and Italy not literally fulfilled their treaty obligations under the Tripartite Pact, the United States would have had no obvious reason for going to war with Japan's Axis partners or joining the strange Allied wartime coalition formed by Churchill and Stalin.

The announcement of the Tripartite Pact, instead of igniting a crisis in relations with Japan, was actually followed by a lull that lasted precariously for the better part of ten months. Any improvement in United States–Japanese relations during that time was illusory, but not until July 1941 did a drastic decline occur. In the meantime Japan awaited the result of the battle of Britain and completed military preparations for a push into Southeast Asia. And Washington, once the bitter election campaign was over, focused first of all on the European conflict and upon Churchill's urgent need for American aid. The Far East was not forgotten, but it consistently had a lower priority than did Europe, and the region received less personal attention from Roosevelt than from Hull. Doggedly, making use of an insider's knowledge of Washington's ways, Hull maneuvered skillfully against hardliners for control of Far Eastern policy. Bearing in mind the overextended condition of the Pacific fleet, Hull successfully argued that the United States should avoid a confrontation with Japan. He would consent to an increase in aid to China and to a tightening of the trade embargo, provided that oil—America's ultimate economic weapon—was not affected.

Roosevelt's reelection coincided with Japan's announcement that a new ambassador was being sent to the United States—retired admiral and former foreign minister Kichisaburo Nomura. Simultaneously Roosevelt received plaintive messages from the demoralized Chinese at Chungking practically begging for large scale American aid against Japan, including 500 planes in the next three months and American pilots to fly them. Working through Morgenthau and Welles, Roosevelt extended a $100 million loan to Chiang Kai-shek on November 30, telling Morgenthau the credit was "a matter of life or death." Morgenthau was also behind an amateurish plan that received Roosevelt's enthusiastic support: to provide Chungking with heavy bombers for attacking Japan. "Wonderful," remarked the president. And even Hull chimed in, "If we could only find some way to have them drop some bombs on Tokyo."[18] When it became clear there were no bombers, flight crews, or mechanics to spare, and when Stimson and General George C. Marshall characterized the idea as "half-baked," the plan to bomb Tokyo expired before getting started.

Hull had never been sold on the Morgenthau/Stimson/Hornbeck policy of tightening economic sanctions in the expectation Japan would be convinced to reverse course. As a consensus politician, Hull did not object when the trade embargo was tightened in December by the addition of pig iron, iron ore, and steel to the list of products Americans were forbidden to sell Japan. With Hull's reluctant support the list was further expanded in January by the addition of copper, brass, bronze, zinc, nickel, and potash. And it was at the end of January that Hull received from Grew a bizarre report stating that Japan was preparing a military response to America's get tough policy. Relying on information from a Peruvian diplomat as well as Japanese sources, Grew reported that "a surprise mass attack" was being planned by Japan against American naval and air installations at Pearl Harbor.[19] Grew's cable of January 27, 1941, was the first of many warnings received by the United States, but the report was regarded as so fantastic as not to be taken seriously. Far more plausible was a rumor reported a week later by the American Embassy at London that Japan was planning an imminent mass attack against the remainder of French Indo-China, Singapore, and the Dutch East Indies. For three weeks Washington, which was fearful that a Far Eastern war would jeopardize the passage of the Lend-Lease Act, was in a state of high tension until the report was proved to be untrue.

Was there no way out of the diplomatic deadlock in the Pacific? Incredibly, or so it seemed, a solution appeared out of the clear blue sky in the strange form of two Catholic priests: Bishop James W. Walsh and Father James M. Drought, both of whom were members of the Catholic Foreign Mission Society based at Maryknoll, New York. The two priests had just returned from a visit to Japan where they had conferred with such highly placed officials as Matsuoka and Konoye. Apparently unaware of the Logan Act, passed in 1798 to prohibit private citizens from engaging in diplomacy, the priests hoped to present to the Roosevelt administration a Japanese peace overture that was so secret and controversial that the Konoye government dared not reveal it in public. Postmaster General Frank Walker, a prominent Catholic, arranged a fifteen-minute interview for the priests on January 23, 1941, with Roosevelt and Hull.

In fact the meeting lasted for two hours because Roosevelt and Hull were fascinated by what they heard. According to Drought and Walsh, Japan was exhausted by the war in China and disillusioned by the Tripartite Pact, and was therefore anxious to reach an immediate accommodation with the United States. Furthermore, Japan was willing to withdraw from China in return for American economic assistance and the recognition of Japan's special interests in Asia. Any agreement would have to be reached outside the glare of publicity, but the Maryknoll fathers believed a diplomatic settlement would erode the influence of Japan's militarists and guarantee peace in Asia. Both Roosevelt and Hull were skeptical, but decided to initiate discussions with the new Japanese ambassador on the outside chance the priests were right. Walsh and Drought were encouraged to remain in contact with their Japanese sources.

The result was the preparation by Walsh and the banker Ikawa Tadao of a preliminary draft agreement that summarized Walsh's ideas for a settlement, including a requirement that Japan would withdraw unconditionally from China. Subsequently Colonel Iwakuro Hideo, a military adviser to Ambassador Nomura, revised the document to make any evacuation from China contingent upon the signing of a Sino-Japanese peace settlement. Japan remained free to employ the troops evacuated in any way it saw fit. Furthermore, the United States would be required to revoke its economic sanctions and resume normal trade. In return Japan would agree to limit its obligation under the Tripartite Pact to an event in which the United States aggressively attacked Germany or Italy, but Japan was free to define what was meant by an aggressive attack. Known as the Draft Understanding, it became the starting point for the secret negotiations begun by Hull with Nomura.

Hull first made the acquaintance of Nomura on March 12, and his first impression was favorable. Nomura, Hull recalled, was "tall, robust, in fine health, with an open face, differing considerably in physique from the average Japanese."[20] Among his greatest shortcomings were his hesitant command of the English language, his lack of instructions, and his insistence on negotiating without the aid of a translator. Two days later Hull introduced Nomura to Roosevelt who, remembering their initial meeting two decades before, disarmingly said he would address him as Admiral, not as Ambassador. He urged Nomura to talk candidly as he would to any friend. In that spirit Roosevelt expressed concern over the recent deterioration in relations and suggested that Nomura sit down with Hull and discuss how to resolve the impasse in the Pacific.

The resulting Hull-Nomura talks were inspired by well-intentioned but wildly optimistic clerics. But from the beginning they were doomed by Nomura's basic lack of credibility with his own government—which, strangely, he failed to keep fully informed of major proposals offered by Hull. Nomura frequently withheld basic information from Hull also, but through Magic code intercepts Hull was able to read Nomura's communications nonetheless. In August Nomura indiscreetly revealed to the press that Prime Minister Konoye had sent a message to the president touching off a wave of press speculation about a possible Roosevelt-Konoye meeting. Once Nomura offered Hull personal proposals without securing the approval of his government, which promptly repudiated him. On another occasion, Nomura was so disorganized that he managed to hand Hull the wrong set of documents and had to return later to retrieve them. In his *Memoirs* Hull generously credited Nomura with "having been honestly sincere in trying to avoid war between his country and mine."[21] But the former admiral's apparent sincerity hardly compensated for his lack of basic diplomatic skills and instincts.

On March 8 Hull and Nomura, meeting at Hull's Washington apartment, began a series of secret meetings that proved to be among the most bizarre in the history of American foreign relations. At the outset a pattern was established whereby Joseph Ballantine of the State Department's Foreign Affairs Division would arrive at 7:45 P.M. to brief Hull. Then at 8:30 P.M. Nomura would appear and remain for about two hours. One limiting factor, Hull recalled, was that "Nomura's command of English was so marginal that I frequently doubted whether he understood the points I was making. I took care to speak slowly and often to repeat and reemphasize some of my sentences."[22] Soon Ballantine, who was fluent in Japanese, began attending the meetings to facilitate Nomura's comprehension. Another limiting factor was that Nomura had no instructions from Tokyo. In retrospect, the panglossian hope of the Maryknoll fathers that Japan was ready to reach a realistic accommodation with the United States was simply unfounded.

On April 14 Hull sought to move the talks forward by asking Nomura to introduce the Draft Understanding as a basis for negotiations with the understanding that both sides could suggest modifications. Nomura, according to Hull's account, answered that he was familiar with the Draft Understanding, that he would be willing to present it as a basis for negotiation, and that he believed the Konoye government would receive the document favorably. Hull followed up two days later, just as he learned that Japan and the Soviet Union had signed a nonaggression treaty, by handing Nomura a list of four principles (a condensed version of his six pillars for peace) that were essential to a Japanese-American settlement: "(1) Respect for the territorial integrity and the sovereignty of each and all nations; (2) Support of the principle of noninterference in the internal affairs of other countries; (3) Support of the principle of equality, including equality of commercial opportunity; (4) Nondisturbance of the status quo in the Pacific except as the status quo may be altered by peaceful means."[23]

Even before the negotiations started, Hull told Roosevelt that "there was not one chance of success in a hundred" he would be able to reach an agreement.[24] Hull understood that the odds were poor that Japan would accept his principles, which required the abandonment of the Greater East Asia Co-Prosperity Sphere, including the evacuation of China but not (as subsequent negotiations revealed) Manchukuo. Hull's ambitious goal was to strengthen those opposed to Matsuoka and to regenerate Japan; he regarded any half-way accommodation that sacrificed the Open Door policy as too similar to a Munich-like appeasement and as politically and morally unacceptable in the United States. Hull's slim chances of reaching an agreement were not at all helped by the bumbling of Nomura, who gave Tokyo the mistaken impression the Draft Understanding was an official American proposal instead of the unofficial work of clerics and their Japanese advisers. He also failed to make it clear to Tokyo that the acceptance of Hull's four principles was a *sine qua non* of any negotiated settlement. Thus while Hull waited for a response to his four principles a basic element of misunderstanding had been created.

Konoye's reply, which took a month to arrive, dashed cold water on Hull's slim hopes for an accommodation. Written in obscure prose, it was described by Hull's State Department colleagues as "scheming" for it required Chiang Kai-shek to make peace with Japan on Japan's terms and required the United States to halt aid to Chungking.[25] The Tripartite Pact remained intact and Japan omitted any mention of maintaining the status quo in the Pacific by peaceful means. A day before Hitler's invasion of the Soviet Union (June 21, 1941), Hull brought months of fruitless diplomacy to a head by sending Tokyo a note reiterating his four principles and demanding an annulment of the Tripartite Pact. The June 21 note was accompanied by an "oral statement" indirectly demanding the resignation of

Matsuoka as foreign minister. Hull's dramatic tactic actually backfired, since Tokyo (because of Nomura's ineptness) interpreted the note as a significant toughening of the American position as stated in the Draft Understanding, whereas Hull all along had regarded that document as merely an unofficial starting point for discussions, not an irrevocable commitment. Japan's hardliners were furious at what they regarded as Hull's interference in Japan's internal affairs. Matsuoka himself contended: "Hull's statement is outrageous. . . . I was truly amazed that he [Nomura] would listen without protest to a demand that Japan, a great world power, change her government."[26] Although Hull readily agreed to withdraw his "oral statement" when Japan protested, the misunderstanding strengthened Japan's hardliners and was a contributing factor in Japan's decision to go to war. Military opportunism also played a role. In May, responding to British pleas, Roosevelt agreed to divert a quarter of the Pacific fleet to the Atlantic, presenting Japan with a heaven-sent opportunity to defeat the scattered American and British Pacific naval forces in a decisive battle. Japan's admirals saw that the longer they waited, the odds—due to America's naval construction program—would become more and more unfavorable. The temptation to achieve the Greater East Asia Co-Prosperity Sphere by force was irresistible.

Between June 25 and July 2 Japanese leaders reached decisions that made a confrontation with the United States likely if not certain. Senior members of the army, the navy, and the cabinet agreed on June 25 to demand from the Vichy government of France naval, air, and army bases in southern Indo-China. Presumably the French, who had no hope of resisting, would agree. But, according to the minutes of June 25 Liaison Conference, "In case the French Government or the French Indo-China authorities do not comply with our demands, we shall obtain our objective by force of arms."[27] The policy of expanding southward to establish the Greater East Asia Co-Prosperity Sphere was confirmed by the Imperial Conference of July 2. The seizure of southern Indo-China including Thailand was approved with the notation, "we will not be deterred by the possibility of being involved in a war with England or the United States." Japan's leaders pledged their allegiance to the spirit of the Tripartite Pact, but agreed to decide independently whether to enter the war launched by Hitler against Stalin. In any case, plans to take advantage of Soviet weakness in the east "will be carried out in such a way as to place no serious obstacles in the path of our basic military preparations for a war with England and America."[28] The July 2 policy decisions, despite their far-reaching and dramatic nature, reflected the views of General Tojo and represented a serious setback for Matsuoka, who had championed an immediate attack against Russia. And just two weeks later Matsuoka found himself out of a job when the entire cabinet was forced to resign by Konoye. Two days later (July 18) Konoye formed a new government with only one change: Admiral Teijiro Toyoda replaced Matsuoka as foreign minister.

Five months later, the United States experienced a devastating intelligence failure when Admiral Isoroku Yamamoto's risky concept of destroying the American Pacific fleet so as to protect Japan's southern advance worked to perfection at Pearl Harbor. In July 1941, the United States scored an intelligence coup because the Magic system was sufficiently developed to intercept, decode, and translate radio messages between Tokyo and such principal Japanese embassies as Vichy, Berlin, and Washington. Within a few days of the July 2 Imperial Conference Washington knew in detail the bases demanded by Japan from the French no later than July 21. The imminence of military action was further suggested by instructions to Japanese merchant ships in the Atlantic to pass through the Panama Canal to the Pacific and by assurances sent to all Japanese consulates that the dropping of Matsuoka did not alter "the principle that tripartite pact forms keystone of Japan's national policy and new cabinet will pursue policy of former cabinet in all other matters."[29]

The response of the administration to the seizure of Indo-China was a textbook example of how Roosevelt so often formulated foreign policy through hastily improvised, uncoordinated, and incoherent actions that represented a compromise between competing governmental factions. At least part of the confusion was attributable to the absence of Hull, who was resting and recuperating from an infection at White Sulphur Springs, West Virginia. Sumner Welles served as acting secretary of state while, by telephone, Hull advised tightening sanctions, using care not to go too far. Roosevelt had already authorized Welles to tell the British ambassador that any Japanese advance would be met by "various embargoes, both economic and financial." At the July 18 cabinet meeting Roosevelt debated the issue with Morgenthau, Stimson, and Ickes, giving "quite a lecture" against imposing a total oil embargo.[30] As an alternative Roosevelt agreed to seize Japanese assets (a step previously taken in regard to Germany, Italy, and the Soviet Union) and to impose a selective embargo on petroleum sales, limiting Japan to amounts it had purchased in the mid-1930s. An export license would be required before petroleum products could be shipped to Japan.

At Hull's instigation, Welles, who was in charge of working out the details of Roosevelt's selective embargo, tried to call Nomura into the State Department on July 21 to warn him that serious consequences would follow an invasion of Indo-China. Temporarily Nomura could not be found because he was driving to Maine to visit a friend. When he finally reached Washington on July 23, the Japanese invasion force had sailed, and Welles informed him that Hull was breaking off further talks. The next day the cabinet approved a plan drafted by Welles, permitting Japan to purchase, through a license system, amounts of low octane gasoline that were not to exceed what Japan had bought in 1935–1936. Payment would come from the release of funds frozen by Roosevelt's contemplated seizure of Japanese assets. So on July 26, by executive order, Roosevelt froze all Japanese assets in the United States. What seemed a logical policy for warning Japan subsequently became lost in confusion. Hardliners, chiefly Assistant Secretary of State Dean Acheson, managed to block the release of frozen funds. They also took advantage of the absence of Welles and Roosevelt at the Newfoundland Conference, and they kept Hull, who was back in Washington but still sick and very busy, in ignorance. What was intended as a limited oil embargo to warn Japan became a total embargo. By the time Roosevelt and Hull became aware that no oil had been sold they concluded it was too late to turn back because a reversal would have been read as a capitulation to Tokyo. The effect of the American embargo was even more pronounced because the British and Dutch also froze Japanese assets. Theoretically the Dutch were willing to sell oil to Japan on a cash-and-carry basis, but deliveries were greatly slowed by the fact that Japan's cash reserves in the United States were immobilized, requiring Japanese tankers to wait for weeks at a time in the harbors of Borneo and Sumatra awaiting funds from home.

The same element of internal confusion that characterized the administration's "limited" oil embargo reoccurred when Prime Minister Konoye requested a face-to-face meeting with President Roosevelt. Nomura first suggested such a summit conference on August 6 when he called on Hull who had returned to his office but was still not fully recovered from his illness. Nomura's mission was to present Japan's reply to a neutralization plan Roosevelt had suggested for Indo-China. Superficially the Konoye government accepted the idea by agreeing not to expand beyond Indo-China and to withdraw from the area, retaining special interests, once the war against China was concluded. Not surprisingly Hull did not find Nomura's arguments acceptable. In passing, Nomura mentioned Konoye's desire to meet with Roosevelt, but Hull gave no encouragement and did not reveal that the president was about to meet secretly with Churchill off the Newfoundland coast. But the idea did not die because Konoye found himself in desperate political straits at home. The implications of the Dutch-American-British oil embargo were becoming all too clear to Japanese military and civilian leaders: within two years Japan's oil reserves would be exhausted. Japan was left with a choice between abandoning the Greater East Asia Co-Prosperity Sphere, fighting for it, or trying again for a diplomatic solution. Already the navy was practicing for the Pearl Harbor attack at Kagoshima Bay on the island of Kyushu, and Japan's war college was about to conduct a gaming exercise. Still unsolved was the problem of designing torpedoes that could be dropped from the air in the shallow waters of Pearl Harbor.

Nomura formally presented the request for a Roosevelt-Konoye meeting during a White House meeting on August 17. Roosevelt had just returned from Newfoundland, and Nomura was called to the White House to receive a warning that Roosevelt had promised Churchill he would deliver. The statement Roosevelt read was not the one favored by Churchill, threatening Japan with hostilities, but a milder warning—which the president called "reference material"—speaking of unspecified steps that would be taken should Japan expand further by force.[31] The harsh effect was further diluted by a second State Department statement read by the president offering to resume the discussions broken off by the seizure of Japanese assets. Roosevelt's initial reaction to the idea of a meeting with Konoye was favorable, and he mentioned Juneau, Alaska, in mid-October as a possibility.

Personal, high-level diplomacy understandably appealed to Roosevelt, for he had just returned from an exhilarating bout of summitry with Churchill. With his immense blend of personal charm and persuasiveness, Roosevelt briefly thought that perhaps he could win over Konoye to the American view and go down in history as a peacemaker extraordinaire. Ambassador Grew passionately encouraged Roosevelt to hold the meeting, arguing that it was a last chance to avert hostilities. He contended that Konoye, with the support of the emperor, would be able to offer "far reaching concessions" that the military leaders would have to accept whether they wanted to or not.[32] At the very least, Japan would repudiate the Tripartite Pact, paving the way for a new era in Japanese-American relations. Hull, then and later, was diametrically opposed to having the president make an exhausting trip to Alaska or possibly Hawaii. Hull's basic instincts, as well as his previous experiences with Konoye, led him to the conclusion that a Roosevelt-Konoye meeting could never succeed. Grew regarded Konoye as the last hope for peace; Hull saw the prime minister as a devious snake who could not be trusted.

The sticking point was whether an advance agreement was essential. Grew held that it was unrealistic to expect Konoye to make specific agreements prior to the meeting since the forces opposed to him would be handed live ammunition they would surely use to subvert any Japanese-American accord. Trust Konoye to overcome the military leaders and deliver peace was Grew's message. Hull feared that Roosevelt was being led to the slaughter of a second Munich Conference producing vague statements that would be stretched out of shape by Japan. "As for me," Hull recalled, "I was thoroughly satisfied that a meeting with Konoye, without an advance agreement, could only result either in another Munich or in nothing at all."[33] The two sides never came close to an advance agreement. On September 6, Konoye told Grew that Japan subscribed "conclusively and wholeheartedly" to Hull's four principles; a Magic intercept a month later contained the admission that there were differences of opinion within the Japanese government about how to apply the principles.[34] Konoye offered to withdraw from China and Indo-China when a peace agreement was signed, while the United States was to end its Pacific military buildup of heavy bombers and its aid to China prior to a settlement. Hull, who could plainly see that Konoye was in danger of being toppled, felt that any agreement on Japan's terms would sacrifice basic American principles and interests and betray China as well. Konoye's anxiety was fully justified since an Imperial Conference held on September 6 set a deadline for Konoye of early October to reach a diplomatic solution. Magic revealed that the Konoye government was pinning its last hopes on a Roosevelt-Konoye meeting.

A glimpse into what Japan was planning in the event a diplomatic solution failed was contained in a message sent by Tokyo to the Consul General in Honolulu on September 24 and decoded by Magic on October 9. The diplomat was instructed to divide Pearl Harbor into five subareas and to report on the number and locations of warships and aircraft carriers. At the time, the significance of the "bomb plot" message was obscured by the fact that similar requests were also addressed to Japanese agents stationed at major American and Canadian ports of the Pacific coast.[35] For all practical purposes Hull and Roosevelt rejected the proposed meeting with Konoye on October 2, the day of Hull's seventieth birthday. Technically the administration did not oppose the meeting in principle and expressed the hope that an advance agreement could be achieved. Two weeks later any prospect of a summit meeting ended with the resignation of Konoye and his replacement as prime minister by General Tojo.

Official Washington had no illusions about the character of the Tojo government or its iron commitment to establishing the Greater East Asia Co-Prosperity Sphere. But Washington had enormous illusions about the strength of Anglo-American defenses in the Pacific and about the ability of Japan to conduct complex military operations. Secretary of War Stimson and General Marshall had become thoroughly enamored of the magical deterrent qualities of air power as represented by the planned deployment of heavy bombers to the Far East. By January 1, 1942, the Army Air Force planned to have seventy B-17 Flying Fortresses available at Manila; a month later they would be joined by thirty-five B-24 Liberators. Stimson went so far as to term the bombers America's "Big Stick," and he felt the presence of the planes would make Japan think twice before launching an attack southward.[36] It was recognized that land-based bombers at the Philippines, for example, were vulnerable to attacks from carrier-based planes, but not from Taiwan, as Japanese aircraft supposedly lacked sufficient range to fly that distance. Adding to American confidence that a deterrent had been established was the decision to station at Manilla a dozen new submarines, which could harass and interdict any Japanese advance. Just as overconfident was Churchill, who dispatched the battleship *Prince of Wales* and the cruiser *Repulse* to the Far East in the mistaken belief that their presence would intimidate Japan. If Japan went to war, Anglo-American planners agreed that Siberia or Southeast Asia were the most likely targets. Hawaii was too far from Japan and too heavily guarded to be a concern. In May 1941, General Marshall had described the island of Oahu as "the strongest fortress in the world." Because the island was defended by modern bombers, "a major attack is considered impracticable."[37] Therefore, the first danger was likely to be from sabotage. What kept American officials awake at night was not fear of a Japanese attack on Hawaii or even the Philippines, but concern that Japan would invade the British and Dutch possessions and bypass American territory entirely.

The advent of the Tojo government, rather than ending negotiations between Hull and Nomura, intensified them. Neither man was at all optimistic that the result would be different this time around. Nomura complained to Tokyo that he was confused and left in the dark, not knowing what was expected of him. Convinced he was a failure, he wished to resign, but was persuaded by Tojo that it was his duty to stay on. To assist Nomura the former ambassador to Germany, Saburu Kurusu, left Tokyo by plane on November 4. Cordell Hull was also in a gloomy mood. At age seventy he was physically tired, mentally worn out from months of circular negotiations, and he was wary of being tricked by devious Japanese diplomacy. Consequently, Hull was dubious that there was any formula that would prove durable. Hull's despondency was also amplified by Magic intercepts of Nomura's instructions and reports that made it clear that a crisis was at hand.

High-level conferences on November 2 and 5 outlined Japan's final diplomatic strategy. Two proposals, labeled A and B, were to be offered, the latter to be used in the event the A proposal was rejected. Nomura was told by the new Foreign Minister Shigenori Togo: "Because of various circumstances, it is absolutely necessary that all arrangements for the signing of this agreement be completed by the 25th of this month. I realize that this is a difficult order, but under the circumstances it is an unavoidable one. Please understand this thoroughly and tackle the problem of saving the Japanese-American relations from falling into a chaotic condition."[38] For the first time a deadline, later extended by four days, was introduced. So, when the cabinet met on November 7, Hull and Roosevelt knew that Nomura had been instructed: "Both in name and spirit this offer of ours is indeed the last."[39] Hull told the assemblage the nation should be on the lookout for Japanese military action at any time. It was stressed that the great danger of attack was against British and Dutch possessions and Roosevelt polled the cabinet as to whether public opinion would support American military action in such an event. Secretary of the Navy Knox and Undersecretary of State Welles were drafted to make speeches for the purpose of alerting the public to the threat posed to American interests.

Roosevelt emphasized to Hull that he must keep the talks with Nomura going at all costs. "Let us make no more of ill will," he said. "Let us do nothing to precipitate a crisis."[40]

Plan A, a revision of Konoye's proposals, was dead in the water when Nomura presented it to Hull on the evening of November 7. Hull, who was already familiar with the proposal courtesy of Magic, concluded that Tokyo was offering nothing that was new. Under the plan Japan agreed to embrace Hull's principle of equality in China, provided the same principle was, in Japan's opinion, applied to all other areas of the globe. Once a peace was signed with China, Japan promised to evacuate China and Indo-China. However, Japan would not withdraw from the Tripartite Pact and would retain troops in North China, Mongolia, and Hainan Island for "a necessary period" of about twenty-five years. Magic intercepts raised serious doubts about the integrity of the proposals, revealing that Japan planned only a sham evacuation from China, and that Japan, in the event an agreement was not reached, intended to "completely destroy British and American power in China. We will take over all enemy concessions and important enemy rights and interests (customs and minerals, etc.) in China."[41]

Roosevelt, like Hull, was cool to the A proposal that Nomura explained to the president at a White House meeting on November 10. When pushed by Nomura to take fast action, Roosevelt demurred in the name of patience. No American counterproposal was offered because Roosevelt and Hull were waiting for the arrival of Kurusu and plan B. A further argument against a counterproposal at this time was that Roosevelt still hoped to keep the talks going (despite Japan's deadline) to gain time. Kurusu's arrival actually slowed the diplomatic process. On November 17 Nomura introduced the new envoy to Roosevelt and Hull, but instead of presenting the B plan (which they realized was unacceptable to the United States), Nomura and Kurusu tried to sell their government on a truce they had devised to return United States–Japanese relations to the status existing in July, prior to America's seizure of Japanese assets. Both Hull and Roosevelt took an immediate dislike to Kurusu who, as ambassador to Germany, had signed the Tripartite Pact and whose unctuous, ever-smiling manner offended them. "I felt from the start he was deceitful" was Hull's impression. Showing his impatience, Hull remarked to the envoys that any agreement that left the Tripartite Pact intact "would cause the President and me to be violently denounced."[42]

Foreign Minister Togo, as revealed by Magic, quickly rejected the ideas of Nomura and Kurusu and instructed them to present proposal B, which they did on November 20. Nomura and Kurusu's judgment on this occasion proved accurate since Hull, becoming more weary and short-tempered than ever, viewed plan B as "utterly unacceptable" and as demanding "virtually a surrender" by the United States and an unconditional one at that. Compressed into five points, the proposal, first, required both sides to halt "any armed advancement," meaning the construction of further fortifications in Southeast Asia, with the exception of Indo-China; second, Japan promised to evacuate Indo-China once a Japanese-Chinese peace treaty was signed and to move its troops immediately from southern Indo-China to the northern part of the country; third, the United States was to assist Japan in acquiring needed goods in the Dutch East Indies; fourth, the United States was to resume trade with Japan, including the supply of "a required quantity of oil"; and, finally, the United States was required "to refrain from such measures and actions as will be prejudicial to the endeavors for the restoration of general peace between Japan and China," meaning that aid to Nationalist China would be terminated. Under Japan's "take-it-or-take-the-consequences" proposal the Tripartite Pact would remain in effect. Japan's only concession—to move troops from southern to northern Indo-China—was meaningless, in Hull's opinion, because they could easily be moved back on short notice. As Hull had earlier told Nomura, there was a good possibility he would be "lynched" by the American people if he agreed to a Far Eastern accommodation with Japan on terms accepting a continued Japanese alliance with Germany.[43] The White House did not disagree.

Official Washington spent the next six days trying to formulate a counterproposal to plan B. Through Magic it was learned that the deadline for an agreement had been extended to November 29. Nomura was told: "After that things are automatically going to happen."[44] However, neither Japanese diplomat knew the details of what was automatically going to happen or where or when hostilities would break out. What emerged from the proposals made by the White House, the State Department, and the Treasury Department was a composite *modus vivendi* or truce to last for three months. Japan would pledge not to expand by force. Furthermore, Japan would withdraw from southern Indo-China and station no more than 25,000 troops in northern Indo-China; in return the United States would resume trade in civilian products including a monthly quota of oil for nonmilitary purposes. No one, including Roosevelt, cared much for the plan or expected great things from it. The president wrote Churchill, "I am not very hopeful and we must be prepared for real trouble, possibly soon."[45] After days of discussion the *modus vivendi* plan was never presented because it had no support or only lukewarm support from China, Britain, Australia, and the Netherlands. Instead, Hull recommended and Roosevelt approved dispatching a "comprehensive basic proposal for a general peaceful settlement." Hull called the document, which restated the principles of the Nine Power Treaty and required Japan's evacuation from China and Indo-China, "an honest effort to keep our conversations going."[46] Roosevelt, in a conversation with Stimson, praised Hull saying he had prepared "a magnificent statement." No one else in the administration was even slightly optimistic since Magic intercepts made it clear that the Tojo government insisted on the acceptance of its plan B and would not consider a *modus vivendi* in any form. When Hull handed the "comprehensive basic proposal" to Nomura and Kurusu on November 26 they spoke disparagingly of the document, and Kurusu predicted the response of his government would be "to throw up its hands."[47] In fact the Tojo government did that and more because at 9:00 A.M. Tokyo time on November 26 the Pearl Harbor strike force sailed from the Kuriles in foggy weather: nine destroyers and a light cruiser led the armada, followed by two heavy cruisers, six heavy aircraft carriers, two battleships, and eight tankers and assorted supply ships. Washington now waited for Japan's reply to Hull's proposal, which finally was presented by Nomura and Kurusu at 2:20 P.M. Washington time on December 7.

In the meantime cabinet officers, military commanders, and the president speculated endlessly, inaccurately, and often amateurishly about Japan's intentions and capabilities. On November 25, for example, the War Council, consisting of Stimson, Knox, Hull, and Roosevelt, joined by the naval and army chiefs Admiral Harold Stark and General George Marshall, discussed, without reaching a conclusion, what to do if Japan attacked without warning. Roosevelt raised the hypothetical question "how we should maneuver them into the position of firing the first shot without allowing too much danger to ourselves."[48] Hull told the group that Japan might launch surprise attacks simultaneously at various points, but he did not elucidate the points he had in mind. Southeast Asia (meaning Singapore, the Dutch East Indies, the Philippines, or Burma) were singled out as the most likely targets because Roosevelt had been notified on November 26 that Japanese troop ships carrying five divisions had been sighted passing to the south of Taiwan—probably en route to Indo-China. Angrily Roosevelt denounced the troop movements as evidence of Japanese duplicity since Tokyo's plan B had promised no further armed advances in the Southeast Asia region. The same day Magic decoded the famous "East Wind Rain" message, stating that the weather forecast on the Tokyo short wave news broadcast would use that phrase if United States–Japanese relations were in danger. On receipt the Japanese Embassy was to destroy all codes and papers, but the message never came. Even had it been received, the message gave no hint of what military action, if any, was intended. The same day (November 27) Hull remarked to Stimson (although he later denied it): "I have washed my hands of it and [the matter] is now in the hands of you and Knox, the Army and Navy."[49] Consequently Stimson drafted a "war warning" to military commanders in the Pacific alerting them that diplomatic negotiations appeared to be at an end. "Japanese future action unpredictable," wrote Stimson, "but hostile action possible at any moment." The warning made it clear that the United States desired that Japan commit the "first overt act" of war; the commanders were "to undertake such reconnaissance and other measures as you deem necessary but these measures should be carried out so as not, repeat not, to alarm civil population or disclose intent."[50] Stimson was later criticized for the ambiguity of his "Do-Don't Message" and for not objecting when Lieutenant General Walter Short, the army commander at Hawaii, merely called a sabotage alert.

The peacetime atmosphere of business as usual that pervaded Hawaii also characterized the last week before the Pearl Harbor attack in Washington. Hornbeck, writing on November 27, downplayed the risk of war and argued that Japan had every intention of avoiding conflict with the United States. "Stated briefly," he concluded, "the undersigned does not believe that this country is now on the immediate verge of 'war' in the Pacific."[51] Roosevelt felt sufficiently confident about the situation that he left Washington for a Thanksgiving respite at Warm Springs after the War Council meeting on November 28, leaving the State Department with the job of composing a message to the emperor of Japan appealing for peace and a second message to be presented to Congress in the event of hostilities. At the urging of Hull, who suffered an apparent attack of nerves in Roosevelt's absence, the president agreed to fly back to Washington on Monday December 1. Hull was concerned because a Magic intercept indicated that Tojo was about to deliver a belligerent speech blaming the United States and Britain for prolonging the China incident and for conspiring "to grasp the hegemony of East Asia."[52] The secretary of state also worried about the meaning of a November 30 Magic intercept alerting the Japanese ambassador to Germany that war might suddenly break out with the United States and Britain. The ambassador was to tell Hitler "that the time of the breaking out of this war may come sooner than anyone dreams."[53] Hull was further worried about a British report that Japan was about to seize Thailand and the Kra Isthmus. But with the president back in town Hull took a day of sick leave and Stimson went to New York for a dental appointment.

On his return Roosevelt had on his desk State Department drafts of messages to the emperor of Japan and Congress and a request from Churchill asking that the United States send Japan a specific warning that the president would go before Congress in the event of further Japanese aggression. Before taking such a step, Roosevelt told the British Ambassador Lord Halifax he would ask the Tojo government for an explanation of its intentions. That proved a pointless exercise because the Japanese reply, presented by Nomura and Kurusu on December 5, struck Hull as "unworthy of a child's intelligence." That was because it claimed the reinforcements sent to Indo-China were for the sole purpose of protecting against the threat of Chinese aggression.[54] In his conversation with the British ambassador, Roosevelt displayed once again his penchant for promising tough action that he might or might not be able to deliver. He spoke of providing "armed support" to assist Britain's defense of Malaya with a long range naval blockade or perhaps air power from the Philippines.[55] But no details were supplied, probably because Roosevelt had just improvised the idea.

Hornbeck had offered odds of five to one that the United States and Japan would not be at war by December 15, and many outward indications suggested that he was correct. From the Japanese Foreign Office came the reassuring announcement that Japan's best known passenger liner would leave on December 2 for Los Angeles and Panama. The impression was thus created that Japan would avoid hostilities at least until the *Tatsuta Mara* returned home. And, although naval intelligence had lost track of Japan's aircraft carriers on November 16, fictitious radio traffic and generous shore leaves granted to sailors at Tokyo and Yokohama seemed to show that the Imperial Navy was still training in home waters. By December 6, as the American civilian government and military establishment entered a normal peacetime weekend, the Pearl Harbor strike force, having increased its speed from thirteen to twenty-six knots, was nearing its launching point.

Saturday, December 6, 1941, at the White House began uneventfully. Steve Early, Roosevelt's press secretary, told reporters they ought to go Christmas shopping because Roosevelt had no scheduled appointments and intended to spend the day on routine paperwork. Actually Roosevelt had two appointments, neither of which pertained to foreign policy. First Roosevelt met with Justice William O. Douglas for an hour at 10:00 A.M. (the subject of their discussion is unknown), and at 11:15 A.M. he received Harold Smith, the director of the budget. During the conference with Smith, Roosevelt was interrupted by a phone call from Navy Secretary Knox, who reported that two large Japanese convoys were sailing toward Thailand and Malaya. Smith remembered Roosevelt saying he would send a letter to the emperor of Japan, and the president remarked, "We might soon be at war with Japan." During the afternoon hours Roosevelt worked on a message to the emperor, basically taking the State Department's November 27 draft and adding a section explaining why the peoples of Southeast Asia regarded Japan's troop movements as similar to sitting on a "keg of dynamite." Having accepted several editorial changes suggested by the State Department, Roosevelt jokingly said to a White House guest, Judge Justine Wise Polier, "Well, Justine, this son of man has just sent his final message to the Son of God."[56] The message was sent to Ambassador Grew but was not decoded, translated, or delivered before the outbreak of hostilities. Also awaiting decoding and translation were two Magic intercepts from the Japanese consul at Honolulu in which he reported the number and types of ships present at Pearl Harbor, and the absence of torpedo nets, barrage balloons, and air patrols. The final sentence, a summary of Pearl Harbor's defenses, contained the incriminating notation: "I imagine that in all probability there is considerable opportunity to take advantage for a surprise attack against these places."[57] Whether the messages would have aroused suspicion or would merely have been filed is unknown, since their contents were not discovered until after the attack.

Throughout the afternoon Magic personnel had been on the lookout for Japan's answer to Hull's proposal of November 26. The so-called "pilot" message, intercepted by Magic at 12:05 P.M., had alerted the Japanese Embassy that an important diplomatic note consisting of fourteen parts was on the way. During dinner Roosevelt was called to his second floor White House study because the first thirteen parts had just been delivered by Navy Lieutenant Lester Schulz. Harry Hopkins, Roosevelt's friend and trouble-shooter, was present when Schulz delivered the message and listened to their reactions—which he later described to the Pearl Harbor investigating committee in 1946. After both Roosevelt and Hopkins had read the message (a lengthy condemnation of America's efforts to encircle Japan and thwart its legitimate aims and aspirations), Roosevelt stated, "This means war." Hopkins agreed and ventured the opinion that it was "too bad we could not strike the first blow and prevent any sort of surprise." Roosevelt's response, remembered Schulz, was, "No, we can't do that. We are a democracy and a peaceful people," and he concluded, "But we have a good record." Conspiracy advocates were disappointed by the rest of Schulz's testimony, in which he said that Roosevelt and Hopkins mentioned only the threat of war in the region of Indo-China and made no mention of Pearl Harbor. Next Roosevelt wanted to call Admiral Stark, but decided not to have him paged when he found he was attending a performance of *The Student Prince* at the National Theater. Schulz went away with the impression that Roosevelt and Hopkins, after reading the thirteen paragraphs, were focusing on Southeast Asia and that their demeanor suggested there was no imminent danger of hostilities between the United States and Japan.[58]

Sunday, December 7, 1941, began normally at the White House. Roosevelt rose at 9:00 A.M. and enjoyed a leisurely breakfast in bed. Secretaries Hull, Knox, and Stimson met at the State Department at 10:30 A.M. to work on a draft message to Congress, and General Marshall went horseback riding. At 10:00 A.M. the fourteenth paragraph was delivered to the White House. It read: "The Japanese Government regrets to have to notify hereby the American Government that in view of the attitude of the American Government it cannot but consider that it is impossible to reach an agreement through further negotiation." Roosevelt's interpretation was that Japan intended to break diplomatic relations. By 10:20 A.M. translators had ready a final message from Tokyo directing Nomura and Kurusu to present the fourteen-part message to Hull "at 1:00 P.M. on the 7th your time." After the Japanese Embassy, at about 11:00 A.M., requested a 1:00 P.M. meeting at the State Department, Hull phoned Roosevelt who asked to be informed of the result. When the Pearl Harbor attack began at 12:55 P.M. Washington time, Roosevelt was entertaining the Chinese ambassador by reading him word for word his message to the emperor of Japan, often pausing for dramatic effect. Shortly before the Chinese ambassador left

Roosevelt's study, Nomura called Hull and requested a postponement of their meeting until 1:45 P.M. Roosevelt and Hopkins were eating lunch served on trays when Knox called at 1:35 P.M. with the news that Pearl Harbor was being attacked by Japanese planes. Roosevelt then began calling cabinet officers. "Harry," Roosevelt said to Stimson. "Come down here at once. The Japs have struck." When asked if the war had broken out in Southeast Asia, Roosevelt responded, "Southeast Asia, hell. Pearl Harbor!"[59]

Hull heard the news from Roosevelt just as Nomura and Kurusu arrived at the State Department to present the fourteen-part message, the contents of which were already well known. For months Hull had endured the strain of talking to Japan's diplomats without accidentally revealing that he knew the contents of their reports and instructions. This time he knew something else they didn't know, namely that Pearl Harbor was under attack. Joseph Ballantine took careful notes of the final Hull-Nomura conversation, which Hull later used in preparing his *Memoirs*. Nomura stated that translation difficulties at the Japanese Embassy had prevented the delivery of the note at 1:00 P.M. and so he was delivering it at 2:20 P.M. instead. Hull skimmed a few pages, which he had previously read via Magic, and spit out an indignant reprimand. Eschewing mountain invective, Hull "put my eye on him," saying to Nomura: "I must say that in all my conversations with you during the last nine months, I have never uttered one word of untruth. This is borne out absolutely by the record. In all my fifty years of public service I have never seen a document that was more crowded with infamous falsehoods and distortions—infamous falsehoods and distortions so huge that I never imagined until today that any Government on this planet was capable of uttering them."[60]

The following day Roosevelt rose magnificently to the occasion by delivering before Congress a short, forceful address calling December 7, 1941 "a date which will live in infamy," and requesting a declaration of war against Japan. Roosevelt rejected the advice of Hull that he read into the record a long and dull recitation of Japan's imperialist transgressions, and he also rejected Stimson's plea that Germany be included in the war declaration. With only one dissenting vote (that of Representative Jeannette Rankin, who had also voted against entering World War I), Congress declared war on Japan less than an hour after Roosevelt's speech. Despite the quantities of information gleaned from Magic, American military and civilian planners had been dead wrong in making two fundamental assumptions: first, they were distracted by Japan's plainly visible expedition against Malaya and therefore assumed that war would only break out in that region, at least 5,000 miles from Hawaii; second, Anglo-American war plans had assumed a defensive war in the Pacific, while the main war effort was concentrated against Hitler's Germany. From the perspective of American war plans, the United States, on December 8, 1941, found itself involved in the wrong war, at the wrong place, at the wrong time, and with the wrong enemy. Hitler, whose armies had stalled before Moscow, had no binding obligation under the vague Tripartite Pact to come to the aid of Japan; Matsuoka's treaty only required Germany to assist Japan in the event the United States attacked Japan. Plausibly Hitler could have remained on the sidelines, since it was Japan that attacked the United States, not the other way around. For reasons that have never been logically explained, Hitler declared war on the United States on December 11, and Italy immediately followed the lead of Berlin. The same day, this time without a dissenting vote, Congress formally ended the interwar period by declaring war on Germany and Italy.

The history of American foreign relations between the world wars is not a pretty picture. Beginning with Woodrow Wilson's headstrong and partisan negotiation of the Versailles Treaty and the Senate's equally headstrong and partisan rejection of that document, American diplomacy toward Europe and the Far East commenced two decades of short-sighted and self-centered policies that were often selfish and sullen. In the belief that World War I had been an aberration, Americans felt the nation could safely and cheaply return to the good old days without binding political and military obligations or such inconveniences as a world court or league of nations. But the term "isolation" remains an imperfect description of America's condition between the wars, since only politically did the United States avoid international engagements, not economically or culturally. Smug moral superiority and a penurious desire to save money were persistent themes of the period. "Uncle Shylock" demanded the repayment of the war debts at the cost of poisoning international relations. Cheapness combined with blind naivete led to the neglect of American armed forces. On the eve of World War II the United States Army had slipped once again to nineteenth among world armies, and the United States Navy, consisting of "treaty" capital ships and aircraft carriers, was no longer the handmaiden of diplomacy. In the sense that America was arrogantly cheap and morally smug, the period was poor in purpose and barren in results.

The interwar period is legendary for providing examples of leaders once hailed as economic miracle workers (Presidents Herbert Hoover, Calvin Coolidge, and Secretary of the Treasury Andrew Mellon were among the best known) who were revealed by the Great Depression to have possessed feet of clay. In foreign affairs likewise a search of the list of presidents and secretaries of state finds many damaged reputations. President Wilson's brilliance as an idealist and wordsmith was largely canceled by his failing health and political judgment and by his visionary schemes for single-handedly revolutionizing international relations. Harding and Coolidge took little interest in foreign affairs. Hoover was preoccupied by the economic collapse that greeted him half a year after taking office. Franklin D.

Roosevelt's foreign policy prior to Pearl Harbor was a curious mixture of courage, caution, and confusion that mixed together inspirational oratorical flashes with such inept fumbles as his mishandling of the London Economic Conference, the Nye Committee, and the Neutrality Acts. The lack of direction was in part a product of Roosevelt's tendency to improvise solutions on the spur of the moment. It was no wonder that many of those who worked with him, such as Henry L. Stimson, were puzzled by Roosevelt's topsy-turvy "happy-go-lucky snap of the moment" administrative style, and his liking for working through such intimates as Sumner Welles and Harry Hopkins, while leaving cabinet members such as Hull in the dark. As a professional politician Roosevelt usually left open an avenue of retreat, and in dealing with congressional isolationists he was more often than not engaged in strategic retreats—as in his signing of the Johnson Act and his ambiguous course following the fiasco of the Quarantine Address. Roosevelt's deviousness and his use of public explanations that were evasive, incomplete, or deliberately misleading were among his least admirable qualities. Fortunately for Roosevelt's historical reputation, the Allies ultimately prevailed in World War II, making less relevant Roosevelt's weakness in fighting isolationism, his slowness in rearming, and his reliance on economic sanctions to restrain a determined and militarily strong opponent.

The reputations of the secretaries of state of the interwar period were as fragile as those of the presidents they served. Robert Lansing, by the time of the armistice, was on Wilson's black list and was practically ignored during the peace negotiations. Bainbridge Colby was a caretaker who articulated virulent anti-communism and well-intentioned Pan-Americanism. The diplomacy of Charles Evans Hughes, hailed by contemporaries for the "Miracle at Washington," appears in hindsight to have been frequently misguided, as does that of Frank B. Kellogg, who actually won the Nobel Peace Prize for the absurd Pact of Paris. Henry L. Stimson's tenure as Hoover's secretary of state was spent in damage control trying to patch together what remained of the political and economic structure left over from World War I. Hoover and Stimson did, however, point the way toward opposing Japanese imperialism, a policy that was inherited and slowly toughened by the New Deal. Cordell Hull was easily the most underrated of the interwar secretaries of state. It is undeniable that he was old fashioned in style, spoke with a lisp and a southern accent, that he was thin-skinned, self-righteous, and frequently bypassed by Roosevelt in favor of his intimates. But Hull's judgment was often surer than others in the State Department and the executive branch. Practically alone Hull saw that an oil embargo would lead to hostilities with Japan and, although he has been criticized for seeking an unreachable comprehensive settlement with Japan, his critics do not make clear what accommodation, short of abject acquiescence in the Greater East Asia Co-Prosperity Sphere, could have been possible. And Hull's nineteenth-century faith in reducing trade barriers in the name of peace and prosperity is an idea that found new life toward the end of the twentieth century.

Amid the gloom and shortsightedness of the interwar period there were a few flashes of light and vision. The bipartisan Good Neighbor Policy launched under Colby and more fully developed by Hoover, Roosevelt, Hull, and Welles proved farsighted commercially and strategically. Moreover, many of the blunders of the period were so obvious they were never repeated. Americans, for example, never returned to the diehard isolationism represented by Hiram Johnson, William E. Borah, and Hamilton Fish, nor did post–World War II America play the Uncle Shylock role and demand the repayment of debts over several generations. The United States also never went back to the days of having one of the world's most decrepit armed forces, while potential adversaries were arming to the teeth. Ironically, the one indispensable "lesson" of the period—assuming that such a thing exists at all—was that aggression must never be appeased. The zealous misapplication of that "lesson" has subsequently lumped together as equals with Hitler and Tojo such lesser and far weaker villains as Kim Il Sung, Ho Chi Minh, Fidel Castro, Saddam Hussein, and Slobodan Milosevic.

NOTES

1. Jonathan G. Utley, *Going to War with Japan, 1937–1941* (Knoxville, 1985), 80.

2. Martin Weil, *A Pretty Good Club: The Founding Fathers of the U.S. Foreign Service* (New York, 1978), 77.

3. Utley, *Going to War with Japan*, 46.

4. Utley, *Going to War with Japan*, 45.

5. Hull to Roosevelt, November 14, 1938, Donald B. Schewe, editor, *Franklin D. Roosevelt and Foreign Affairs* (New York, 1995), Second Series, Vol. 12, 63–64.

6. See Roger Dingman, "Farewell to Friendship: The USS *Astoria*'s Visit to Japan, April 1939," *Diplomatic History*, 10, no. 2 (Spring 1986), 121–39.

7. Herbert Feis, *The Road to Pearl Harbor: The Coming of the War between the United States and Japan* (Princeton, 1950), 41.

8. Robert Dallek, *Franklin D. Roosevelt and American Foreign Policy, 1932–1945* (New York, 1979), 237.

9. Feis, *Road to Pearl Harbor*, 46.

10. Feis, *Road to Pearl Harbor*, 64.

11. Stephen Pelz, *Race to Pearl Harbor* (Cambridge, 1974), 218.

12. Dallek, *Franklin D. Roosevelt and American Foreign Policy*, 239.

13. Dallek, *Franklin D. Roosevelt and American Foreign Policy*, 239–40.

14. Dallek, *Franklin D. Roosevelt and American Foreign Policy*, 240.

15. Feis, *Road to Pearl Harbor*, 82.

16. Feis, *Road to Pearl Harbor*, 98.

17. Feis, *Road to Pearl Harbor*, 101–2.

18. Dallek, *Franklin D. Roosevelt and American Foreign Policy*, 270.

19. Roberta Wohlstetter, *Pearl Harbor: Warning and Decision* (Stanford, 1962), 386.

20. Hull, *Memoirs*, Vol. 2, 987.

21. Hull, *Memoirs*, Vol. 2, 987.

22. Hull, *Memoirs*, Vol. 2, 996.

23. Hull, *Memoirs*, Vol. 2, 995.

24. Hull, *Memoirs*, Vol. 2, 985–86.

25. Feis, *Road to Pearl Harbor*, 199–201.

26. Frederick W. Marks III, *Wind Over Sand: The Diplomacy of Franklin Roosevelt* (Athens, Georgia, 1988), 109.

27. Feis, *Road to Pearl Harbor*, 212–13.

28. Feis, *Road to Pearl Harbor*, 216.

29. Wohlstetter, *Pearl Harbor: Warning and Decision*, 109.

30. Feis, *Road to Pearl Harbor*, 227–29; Dallek, *Franklin D. Roosevelt and American Foreign Policy*, 274.

31. Dallek, *Franklin D. Roosevelt and American Foreign Policy*, 301.

32. Waldo Heinrichs, *Threshold of War: Franklin D. Roosevelt and American Entry into World War II* (New York, 1988), 186.

33. Hull, *Memoirs*, Vol. 2, 1025.

34. Samuel Eliot Morison, *The Rising Sun in the Pacific: 1931–April 1942* (Boston, 1963), 68.

35. Wohlstetter, *Pearl Harbor: Warning and Decision*, 374, 390–91.

36. Heinrichs, *Threshold of War*, 193–94.

37. Wohlstetter, *Pearl Harbor: Warning and Decision*, 69.

38. Hull, *Memoirs*, Vol. 2, 1056–57.

39. Feis, *Road to Pearl Harbor*, 296.

40. Dallek, *Franklin D. Roosevelt and American Foreign Policy*, 305.

41. Feis, *Road to Pearl Harbor*, 295; Hull, *Memoirs*, Vol. 2, 1060.

42. Hull, *Memoirs*, Vol. 2, 1062–64.

43. Hull, *Memoirs*, Vol. 2, 1061–62, 1069–72.

44. Feis, *Road to Pearl Harbor*, 313.

45. Feis, *Road to Pearl Harbor*, 314.

46. Hull, *Memoirs*, Vol. 2, 1083.

47. Hull, *Memoirs*, Vol. 2, 1085.

48. Feis, *Road to Pearl Harbor*, 314–15.

49. Feis, *Road to Pearl Harbor*, 321.

50. Elting Morison, *Turmoil and Tradition: A Study of the Life and Times of Henry L. Stimson* (Boston, 1960), 437.

51. Wohlstetter, *Pearl Harbor: Warning and Decision*, 265.

52. Hull, *Memoirs*, Vol. 2, 1089.

53. Hull, *Memoirs*, Vol. 2, 1092.

54. Hull, *Memoirs*, Vol. 2, 1093.

55. Dallek, *Franklin D. Roosevelt and American Foreign Policy*, 309.

56. Jon Bridgeman, "Saturday, December 6, 1941," in Robert W. Love, Jr., *Pearl Harbor Revisited* (New York, 1995), 147, 157–60.

57. Wohlstetter, *Pearl Harbor: Warning and Decision*, 375–76.

58. Bridgeman, "Saturday, December 6, 1941," 161–63.

59. Bridgeman, "Saturday, December 6, 1941," 166–67; Morrison, *Turmoil and Tradition*, 438.

60. Hull, *Memoirs*, Vol. 2, 1096.

Selected Bibliography

Acheson, Dean. *Morning and Noon*. Boston: Houghton Mifflin, 1965.

Adler, Selig. *The Isolationist Impulse: Its Twentieth Century Reaction*. New York: Abelard-Schuman, 1957.

———. *The Uncertain Giant, 1921–1941: American Foreign Policy Between the Wars*. New York: Macmillan, 1965.

Ambrosius, Lloyd E. *Woodrow Wilson and the American Diplomat Tradition: The Treaty Fight in Perspective*. New York: Cambridge University Press, 1987.

Bacino, Leo J. *Reconstructing Russia: U.S. Policy in Revolutionary Russia, 1917–1922*. Kent, Ohio: Kent State University Press, 1999.

Bailey, Thomas A. *Woodrow Wilson and the Lost Peace*. New York: Macmillan, 1944.

———. *Woodrow Wilson and the Great Betrayal*. New York: Macmillan, 1945.

Barnhart, Michael. *Japan Prepares for Total War*. Ithaca: Cornell University Press, 1987.

Beard, Charles A. *President Roosevelt and the Coming of the War, 1941: A Study in Appearances and Realities*. New Haven: Yale University Press, 1948.

Bennett, Edward M. *Recognition of Russia: An American Foreign Policy Dilemma*. Waltham, Massachusetts: Blaisdell Publishing Company, 1970.

———. *Franklin D. Roosevelt and the Search for Security: American-Soviet Relations, 1933–1939*. Wilmington, Delaware: Scholarly Resources, 1985.

———. *Franklin D. Roosevelt and the Search for Victory: American-Soviet Relations, 1939–1945*. Wilmington, Delaware: Scholarly Resources, 1990.

Bennett, Edward W. *Germany and the Diplomacy of the Financial Crisis, 1931*. Cambridge: Harvard University Press, 1962.

Bishop, Donald G. *The Roosevelt-Litvinov Agreements: The American View*. Syracuse: Syracuse University Press, 1965.

Borg, Dorothy. *The United States and the Far Eastern Crisis of 1933–1938: From the Manchurian Incident through the Initial Stage of the Undeclared Sino-Japanese War*. Cambridge: Harvard University Press, 1964.

Borg, Dorothy and Okamoto, Shumpei, editors. *Pearl Harbor as History: Japanese-American Relations, 1931–1941.* New York: Columbia University Press, 1973.

Browder, Robert P. *The Origins of Soviet-American Diplomacy.* Princeton: Princeton University Press, 1953.

Buckley, Thomas H. *The United States and the Washington Conference, 1921–1922.* Knoxville: University of Tennessee Press, 1970.

Buhite, Russell. *Nelson T. Johnson and American Policy Toward China.* East Lansing: Michigan State University Press, 1968.

Burns, James MacGregor. *Roosevelt: The Lion and the Fox.* New York: Harcourt Brace, 1956.

Butow, Robert J.C. *The John Doe Associates: Backdoor Diplomacy for Peace, 1941.* Stanford: Stanford University Press, 1974.

Castigliola, Frank. *Awkward Dominion: American Political, Economic, and Cultural Relations with Europe, 1919–1933.* Ithaca: Cornell University Press, 1984.

Chatfield, Charles. *For Peace and Justice.* Knoxville: University of Tennessee Press, 1971.

Clavin, Patricia. *The Failure of Economic Diplomacy: Britain, Germany, France and the United States, 1931–1936.* New York: St. Martin's Press, 1997.

Cohen, Warren. *Empire Without Tears: America's Foreign Relations, 1921–1933.* New York: Cambridge University Press, 1987.

Cole, Wayne. *Gerald P. Nye and American Foreign Relations.* Minneapolis: University of Minnesota Press, 1962.

———. *Charles A. Lindbergh and the Battle Against American Intervention in World War II.* New York: Harcourt, Brace, Jovanovich, 1974.

———. *Roosevelt and the Isolationists, 1932–1945.* Lincoln: University of Nebraska Press, 1983.

Compton, James V. *The Swastika and the Eagle: Hitler, the United States and the Origins of World War II.* Boston: Houghton Mifflin, 1967.

Cooper, John Milton. *The Warrior and the Priest.* Cambridge: Belknap Press of Harvard University Press, 1983.

Cronon, E. David. *Josephus Daniels in Mexico.* Madison: University of Wisconsin Press, 1960.

Current, Richard N. *Secretary Stimson: A Study in Statecraft.* New Brunswick: Rutgers University Press, 1954.

Dallak, Robert. *Democrat and Diplomat: The Life of William E. Dodd.* New York: Oxford University Press, 1968.

———. *Franklin D. Roosevelt and American Foreign Policy, 1932–1945.* New York: Oxford University Press, 1979.

De Benedetti, Charles. *Origins of the Modern American Peace Movement.* Millwood, New York: KTO Press, 1978.

De Conde, Alexander. *Herbert Hoover's Latin American Policy.* Stanford: Stanford University Press, 1951.

———. *Half Bitter, Half Sweet: An Excursion into Italian-American History.* New York: Scribner, 1971.

De Santis, Hugh. *The Diplomacy of Silence: The American Foreign Service, the*

Soviet Union, and the Cold War, 1933–1947. Chicago: University of Chicago Press, 1980.

Dingman, Roger. *Power in the Pacific: The Origins of Naval Arms Limitation.* Chicago: University of Chicago Press, 1972.

Divine, Robert A. *The Illusion of Neutrality: Franklin D. Roosevelt and the Struggle over the Arms Embargo.* Chicago: University of Chicago Press, 1962.

———. *The Reluctant Belligerent: American Entry into World War II.* New York: Wiley, 1965.

Doenecke, Justin. *When the Wicked Rise.* Lewisburg, Pennsylvania: Bucknell University Press, 1984.

Dozer, Donald. *Are We Good Neighbors? Three Decades of Inter-American Relations, 1930–1960.* Gainesville: University of Florida Press, 1959.

Ellis, L. Ethan. *Frank B. Kellogg and American Foreign Relations, 1925–1939.* New Brunswick: Rutgers University Press, 1961.

———. *Republican Foreign Policy, 1921–1933.* New Brunswick: Rutgers University Press, 1968.

Faulkner, Harold. *From Versailles to the New Deal: A Chronicle of the Harding-Coolidge-Hoover Era.* New Haven: Yale University Press, 1950.

Feis, Herbert. *The Road to Pearl Harbor: The Coming of the War between the United States and Japan.* Princeton: Princeton University Press, 1950.

Ferrell, Robert H. *Peace in Their Time: The Origins of the Kellogg-Briand Pact.* New Haven: Yale University Press, 1952.

———. *American Diplomacy in the Great Depression: Hoover-Stimson Foreign Policy, 1929–1933.* New Haven: Yale University Press, 1957.

———. *Frank B. Kellogg and Henry L. Stimson,* Vol. 11, *The American Secretaries of State and Their Diplomacy.* New York: Cooper Square Publishers, 1963.

———. *Woodrow Wilson and World War I.* New York: Harper and Row, 1989.

———. *The Presidency of Calvin Coolidge.* Lawrence: University Press of Kansas, 1998.

Filene, Peter C. *Americans and the Soviet Experiment, 1917–1933.* Cambridge: Harvard University Press, 1967.

Fogelsong, David S. *America's Secret War Against Bolshevism: U.S. Intervention in the Russian Civil War, 1917–1920.* Chapel Hill: University of North Carolina Press, 1995.

Freidel, Frank. *Franklin D. Roosevelt: Launching the New Deal.* Boston: Little, Brown, 1973.

Fuess, Claude M. *Calvin Coolidge: The Man from Vermont.* Westport: Greenwood Press, 1976, reprint of 1939 edition.

Gardner, Lloyd C. *Economic Aspects of New Deal Diplomacy.* Madison: University of Wisconsin Press, 1964.

———. *A Covenant with Power: America and World Order from Wilson to Reagan.* New York: Oxford University Press, 1984.

Gelfand, Lawrence E. *The Inquiry: America Preparations for Peace, 1917–1919.* New Haven: Yale University Press, 1963.

Gellman, Irwin F. *Roosevelt and Batista: Good Neighbor Diplomacy in Cuba, 1933–1945.* Albuquerque: University of New Mexico Press, 1973.

———. *Good Neighbor Diplomacy: United States Policies in Latin America, 1933–1945.* Baltimore: Johns Hopkins University Press, 1979.

———. *Secret Affairs: Frankin Roosevelt, Cordell Hull, and Sumner Welles.* Baltimore: Johns Hopkins University Press, 1995.

Glad, Betty. *Charles Evans Hughes and the Illusions of Innocence: A Study of American Diplomacy.* Urbana: University of Illinois Press, 1966.

———. *Key Pittman: The Tragedy of a Senate Insider.* New York: Columbia University Press, 1986.

Goldberg, Harold J., editor. *Intervention, Famine Relief, International Affairs, 1917–1933, Documents of Soviet-American Relations.* Vol. 1. Gulf Breeze, Florida: Academic International Press, 1993.

Grieb, Kenneth J. *The Latin American Policy of Warren G. Harding.* Fort Worth: Texas Christian University Press, 1976.

Harris, Brice. *The United States and the Italo-Ethiopian War.* Stanford: Stanford University Press, 1964.

Hearden, Patrick. *Roosevelt Confronts Hitler: America's Entry into World War II.* De Kalb: Northern Illinois University Press, 1987.

Henrichs, Waldo. *American Ambassador: Joseph C. Grew and the Development of the American Diplomatic Tradition.* Boston: Little, Brown, 1966.

———. *Threshold of War: Franklin D. Roosevelt and American Entry into World War II.* New York: Oxford University Press, 1988.

Hicks, John D. *Republican Ascendancy, 1921–1933.* New York: Harper, 1960.

Hogan, Michael J. *Informal Entente: The Private Structure of Cooperation in Anglo-American Economic Diplomacy, 1918–1929.* Columbia: University of Missouri Press, 1977.

Hoover, Herbert. *The Memoirs of Herbert Hoover.* 3 vols. New York: Macmillan, 1951–1952.

House, Edward M. and Seymour, Charles, editors. *What Really Happened at Paris: The Story of the Peace Conference, 1918–1919.* New York: Charles Scribner's Sons, 1921.

Howard, Esme. *Theatre of Life.* 2 vols. Boston: Little, Brown, 1953–1955.

Hull, Cordell. *The Memoirs of Cordell Hull.* 2 vols. New York: Macmillan, 1948.

Iriye, Akira. *After Imperialism: The Search for a New Order in the Far East, 1921–1931.* Cambridge: Harvard University Press, 1965.

———. *The Origins of the Second World War in Asia and the Pacific.* London: Longman, 1978.

———. *The Globalizing of America, 1913–1945.* New York: Cambridge University Press, 1993.

Jonas, Manfred. *Isolationism in America, 1935–1941.* Ithaca: Cornell University Press, 1966.

———. *The United States and Germany: A Diplomatic History.* Ithaca: Cornell University Press, 1984.

Kamman, William. *A Search for Stability: United States Diplomacy Toward Nicaragua, 1925–1933.* Notre Dame, Indiana: Notre Dame University Press, 1968.

Kennan, George F. *Russia Leaves the War.* Princeton: Princeton University Press, 1956.

———. *The Decision to Intervene.* Princeton: Princeton University Press, 1958.

Kent, Bruce. *The Spoils of War: The Politics, Economics, and Diplomacy of Reparations, 1918–1932.* New York: Oxford University Press, 1989.

Keynes, John Maynard. *The Economic Consequences of the Peace.* New York: Harcourt, Brace and Howe, 1920.

Kimball, Warren F. *The Most Unsordid Act: Lend-Lease, 1939–1941.* Baltimore: Johns Hopkins University Press, 1969.

———. *The Juggler: Franklin Roosevelt as Wartime Statesman.* Princeton: Princeton University Press, 1991.

Knock, Thomas J. *To End All Wars: Woodrow Wilson and the Quest for a New World Order.* New York: Oxford University Press, 1992.

LaFeber, Walter. *Inevitable Revolutions: The United States in Central America.* New York: W.W. Norton, 1993.

———. *The Clash: A History of U.S.-Japan Relations.* New York: W.W. Norton, 1997.

Langer, William L. and Gleason, S. Everett. *The Challenge to Isolation: The World Crisis of 1937–1940.* New York: Harper, 1952.

———. *The Undeclared War, 1940–1941.* New York: Harper, 1953.

Langley, Lester D. *The United States and the Caribbean, 1900–1970.* Athens: University of Georgia, 1980.

Leffler, Melvyn. *The Elusive Quest: America's Pursuit of European Stability and French Security, 1919–1933.* Chapel Hill: University of North Carolina Press, 1979.

Leuchtenburg, William E. *Franklin D. Roosevelt and the New Deal, 1932–1940.* New York: Harper and Row, 1963.

Leutze, James R. *Bargaining for Supremacy: Anglo-American Naval Collaboration, 1937–1941.* Chapel Hill: University of North Carolina Press, 1971.

Libbey, James K. *Alexander Gumberg and Soviet-American Relations, 1917–1933.* Lexington: University of Kentucky Press, 1977.

Lippman, Walter, ed. *The United States in World Affairs: An Account of American Foreign Relations, 1933.* New York: Harper and Brothers, 1934.

Lochner, Louis P. *Herbert Hoover and Germany.* New York: Macmillan, 1960.

Love, Robert W., Jr., editor. *Pearl Harbor Revisited.* New York: St. Martin's Press, 1995.

Maddox, Robert J. *William E. Borah and American Foreign Policy.* Baton Rouge: Louisiana State University Press, 1969.

Maddux, Thomas R. *Years of Estrangement: American Relations with the Soviet Union.* Gainesville: University Presses of Florida, 1980.

Marks, Frederick W., III. *Wind Over Sand: The Diplomacy of Franklin Roosevelt.* Athens: University of Georgia Press, 1988.

McAdoo, William Gibbs. *Crowded Years: The Reminiscences of William G. McAdoo.* Boston: Houghton, Mifflin, 1931.

McCoy, Donald R. *Calvin Coolidge: The Quiet President.* New York: Macmillan, 1967.

McKercher, B.J.C. *The Second Baldwin Government and the United States, 1924–1929: Attitudes and Diplomacy.* New York: Cambridge University Press, 1984.

———. *Transition of Power: Britain's Loss of Global Preeminence to the United States, 1930–1945.* New York: Cambridge University Press, 1999.

Moley, Raymond. *After Seven Years.* New York: Harper and Brothers, 1939.

Morison, Elting. *Turmoil and Tradition: A Study of the Life and Times of Henry L. Stimson.* Boston: Houghton Mifflin, 1960.

Morison, Samuel Eliot. *The Rising Sun in the Pacific: 1931–April 1942*, volume 3, *History of United States Naval Operations in World War II.* Boston: Little, Brown, 1963.

Moulton, Harold G. and Pasvolsky, Leo. *War Debts and World Prosperity.* New York: Century Company for the Brookings Institution, 1932.

Murray, Robert K. *The Harding Era: Warren G. Harding and His Administration.* Minneapolis: University of Minnesota Press, 1969.

Musicant, Ivan. *The Banana Wars: A History of United States Military Intervention in Latin America from the Spanish-American War to the Invasion of Panama.* New York: Macmillan, 1990.

Nevins, Allan. *The New Deal and World Affairs: A Chronicle of International Affairs, 1933–1945.* New Haven: Yale University Press, 1950.

———. *The United States in a Chaotic World: A Chronicle of International Affairs, 1918–1933.* New Haven: Yale University Press, 1950.

O'Connor, Raymond G. *Perilous Equilibrium: The United States and the London Naval Conference of 1930.* Lawrence: University of Kansas Press, 1962.

Offner, Arnold A. *American Appeasement: United States Foreign Policy and Germany, 1933–1938.* Cambridge, Mass.: Belknap Press of Harvard University Press, 1969.

———. *The Origins of the Second World War: American Foreign Policy and World Politics, 1917–1941.* New York: Praeger, 1975.

Parrini, Carl P. *Heir to Empire: United States Economic Diplomacy, 1916–1923.* Pittsburgh: University of Pittsburgh Press, 1969.

Pelz, Stephen. *Race to Pearl Harbor: The Failure of the Second London Naval Conference and the Onset of World War II.* Cambridge: Harvard University Press, 1974.

Phillips, William. *Ventures in Diplomacy.* North Beverly, Massachusetts: privately printed, 1952.

Pike, Frederick B. *FDR's Good Neighbor Policy: Sixty Years of Generally Gentle Chaos.* Austin: University of Texas Press, 1995.

Prange, Gordon. *At Dawn We Slept: The Untold Story of Pearl Harbor.* New York: McGraw-Hill, 1981.

———. *Pearl Harbor: The Verdict of History.* New York: McGraw-Hill, 1986.

Pratt, Julius W. *Cordell Hull, 1933–1944*, volume 13, *The American Secretaries of State and Their Diplomacy.* New York: Cooper Square Publishers, 1964.

Pusey, Merlo J. *Charles Evans Hughes.* 2 vols. New York: Macmillan, 1951.

Rappaport, Armin. *Henry L. Stimson and Japan.* Chicago: University of Chicago Press, 1973.

Reynolds, David. *The Creation of the Anglo-American Alliance, 1937–1941: A Study in Competitive Cooperation.* Chapel Hill: University of North Carolina Press, 1981.

———. *Lord Lothian and Anglo-American Relations, 1939–1940.* Philadelphia: American Philosophical Society, 1983.

Rhodes, Benjamin D. *The Anglo-American Winter War with Russia, 1918–1919: A Diplomatic and Military Tragicomedy.* Westport: Greenwood Press, 1988.

———. *James P. Goodrich: Indiana's "Governor Strangelove": A Republican's Infatuation with Soviet Russia.* Selingsgrove, Pennsylvania: Susquehanna University Press, 1996.

Rock, William R. *Chamberlain and Roosevelt: British Foreign Policy and the United States, 1937–1941.* Columbus: Ohio State University Press, 1988.

Roorda, Eric Paul. *The Dictator Next Door: The Good Neighbor Policy and the Trujillo Regime in the Dominican Republic, 1930–1945.* Durham: Duke University Press, 1998.

Schaller, Michael. *The U.S. Crusade in China.* New York: Columbia University Press, 1979.

Schlesinger, Arthur M., Jr. *The Coming of the New Deal.* Boston: Houghton Mifflin, 1959.

Schmitz, David F. *The United States and Fascist Italy, 1922–1940.* Chapel Hill: University of North Carolina Press, 1988.

Schuker, Stephen A. *The End of French Predominance in Europe: The Financial Crisis of 1924 and the Adoption of the Dawes Plan.* Chapel Hill: University of North Carolina Press, 1976.

———. *American "Reparations" to Germany, 1919–1933: Implications for the Third-World Debt Crisis.* Princeton: International Finance Section, Department of Economics, Princeton University, 1988.

Sherwood, Robert E. *Roosevelt and Hopkins: An Intimate History.* New York: Harper, 1948.

Smith, Daniel M. *The Great Departure: The United States and World War I, 1914–1920.* New York: Wiley, 1965.

———. *Aftermath of War: Bainbridge Colby and Wilsonian Diplomacy, 1920–1921.* Philadelphia: American Philosophical Society, 1970.

Smith, Rixey, and Norman Beasley. *Carter Glass: A Biography.* New York: Longmans, Green and Company, 1939.

Smith, Sara R. *The Manchurian Crisis, 1931–1932: A Tragedy in International Relations.* New York: Columbia University Press, 1948.

Spinelli, Lawrence. *Dry Diplomacy: The United States, Great Britain, and Prohibition.* Wilmington, Delaware: Scholarly Resources, 1988.

Stimson, Henry L. and Bundy, McGeorge. *On Active Service in Peace and War.* New York: Harper, 1948.

Stone, Ralph. *The Irreconcilables: The Fight Against the League of Nations.* Lexington: University of Kentucky Press, 1970.

Sullivan, Mark. *The Great Adventure at Washington: The Story of the Conference.* Garden City: Doubleday, Page and Company, 1922.

Tansill, Charles C. *Back Door to War: The Roosevelt Foreign Policy, 1933–1941.* Chicago: Regnery, 1952.

Taylor, Sandra C. *Advocate of Understanding: Sidney Gulick and the Search for Peace with Japan.* Kent: Kent State University Press, 1984.

Theobald, Robert A. *The Final Secret of Pearl Harbor.* New York: Devin-Adair, 1954.

Thompson, John. *Russia, Bolshevism, and the Versailles Peace.* Princeton: Princeton University Press, 1967.

Thorne, Christopher. *The Limits of Foreign Policy: The West, the League, and the Far Eastern Crisis of 1931–1932.* London: Hamilton, 1972.

Trachtenberg, Marc. *Reparation in World Politics: France and European Economic Diplomacy, 1916–1923.* New York: Columbia University Press, 1980.

Traina, Richard. *American Diplomacy and the Spanish Civil War.* Bloomington: University of Indiana Press, 1968.

Trani, Eugene P. and Wilson, David L. *The Presidency of Warren G. Harding.* Lawrence: University Press of Kansas, 1977.

Unterberger, Betty Miller. *America's Siberian Expedition.* Durham: Duke University Press, 1956.

————. *The United States, Revolutionary Russia, and the Rise of Czechoslovakia.* Chapel Hill: University of North Carolina Press, 1989.

Utley, Jonathan G. *Going to War with Japan, 1937–1941.* Knoxville: University of Tennessee Press, 1985.

Weil, Martin. *A Pretty Good Club: The Founding Fathers of the U.S. Foreign Service.* New York: Norton, 1978.

Weissman, Benjamin. *Herbert Hoover and Famine Relief to the Soviet Union, 1921–1923.* Stanford: Hoover Institution Press, 1974.

Widenor, William C. *Henry Cabot Lodge and the Search for an American Foreign Policy.* Berkeley: University of California Press, 1980.

Wilson, Joan Hoff. *American Business and Foreign Policy, 1920–1933.* Lexington: University of Kentucky Press, 1973.

————. *Ideology and Economics: United States Relations with the Soviet Union, 1918–1933.* Columbia: University of Missouri Press, 1974.

Wilson, Theodore A. *The First Summit: Roosevelt and Churchill at Placentia Bay, 1941.* Lawrence: University Press of Kansas, 1991.

Williams, William A. *The Tragedy of American Diplomacy.* New York: Dell, second revised edition, 1972.

Wohlstetter, Roberta. *Pearl Harbor: Warning and Decision.* Stanford: Stanford University Press, 1962.

Wood, Bryce. *The Making of the Good Neighbor Policy.* New York: Columbia University Press, 1961.

Yoshihashi, Takehiko. *Conspiracy at Mukden: The Rise of the Japanese Military.* New Haven: Yale University Press, 1963.

Index

About the Author

BENJAMIN D. RHODES is Professor of History at the University of Wisconsin-Whitewater. He is the author of *The Anglo-American Winter War with Russia, 1918-1919: A Diplomatic and Military Tragicomedy* (1988), and *James P. Goodrich, Indiana's "Governor Strangelove": A Republican's Infatuation with Soviet Russia* (1996). Author of numerous articles, he has also been a Fulbright lecturer in Finland and the People's Republic of China.